Secrets to Sustainable Solutions

Top Tips from Business, Science, & Non-Profit Experts

In an easy-to-read, real-stories format

LISA BLACKBURN ULLVEN

MBA, BSc in Management Information Systems, PMP®, Lean SSBB®, CHDD, CHDM, ITIL®

Certified Wellness Recovery Action Plan® (WRAP®) Facilitator
Certified Wraparound Coach, Facilitator and Trainer
Certified Recovery Peer Specialist – Family

Published by Richter Publishing LLC www.richterpublishing.com

Book Cover Design: Richter Publishing LLC images from 123RF

Editors: Marisa Beetz, Margarita Martinez, Brianna Miranda

Book Formatting: Monica San Nicolas & Erica Bouza

ISBN: 978-1-945812-89-7 Hardback

DISCLAIMER

This book is designed to provide information on Sustainable Solutions only. This information is provided and sold with the knowledge that the publisher and author do not offer any legal or medical advice. In the case of a need for any such expertise, consult with the appropriate professional. This book does not contain all information available on the subject. This book has not been created to be specific to any individual people or organization's situation or needs. Reasonable efforts have been made to make this book as accurate as possible. However, there may be typographical and or content errors. Therefore, this book should serve only as a general guide. This book contains information that might be dated or erroneous and is intended only to educate and entertain. The author and publisher shall have no liability or responsibility to any person or entity regarding any loss or damage incurred, or alleged to have incurred, directly or indirectly, by the information contained in this book or as a result of anyone acting or failing to act upon the information in this book. You hereby agree never to sue and to hold the author and publisher harmless from any and all claims arising out of the information contained in this book. You hereby agree to be bound by this disclaimer, covenant not to sue and release. You may return this book within the guaranteed time period for a full refund. In the interest of full disclosure, this book may contain affiliate links that might pay the author or publisher a commission upon any purchase from the company. While the author and publisher take no responsibility for any virus or technical issues that could be caused by such links, the business practices of these companies and/or the performance of any product or service, the author or publisher have used the product or service and make a recommendation in good faith based on that experience. All characters appearing in this work have given permission. Some names, places and inconsequential facts were adjusted to protect privacy. Any resemblance to other real persons, living or dead, is purely coincidental. The opinions and stories in this book are the views of the authors and not those of the publisher.

DEDICATION

Dedicated to the little girl with the bluest eyes: When I was young, I always wished I had blue eyes until I met a little girl in elementary school with the bluest eyes I had ever seen. I thought it was so strange that she looked like a little adult. She completed her schoolwork, but she never spoke to anyone. One day, the other children were all talking about how she was in the newspaper. They said their parents read in the news that a family member had taken very inappropriate photos of the little girl and a neighbor had reported it to the police department.

When she came back to school, the little girl was different. She still didn't talk, but now she didn't do her schoolwork either. She appeared to float with the other children from class, to lunch, to recess, and back to class. She just kept floating. The other children talked about her, right in front of her, and almost to her, but her empty blue eyes just stared straight ahead. The children kept saying, "It's so horrible that everyone knows what happened."

I kept thinking to myself, "The adults must be doing something," but I could also hear the adults hopelessly saying, "The system is broken. Nothing we can do."

Little girl with the bluest eyes, I am dedicating this book to you for inspiring me to keep my eyes open to how we can fix the system.

Dedicated to Dr. Munyan at The University of Tampa: In my first college computer class, you told us, "If you want to help people, learn about systems." Then you added, "If you really want to help people, become a liaison to help people work with systems." To thank you, I am dedicating this book to you and the mentors and professors at The University of Tampa. By the way, I kept studying systems per your advice, so thank you to Florida State University, St. Petersburg College, University of Buffalo, University of Florida, Peace4Tarpon, Central Florida Behavioral Health Network, Project Management Institute, and Lean Six Sigma Institute for confirming that systems are just a way of getting things done—and for teaching me that there is always a better way. Thank you, Pete McGarahan and Ivy Meadors. Together, you all inspired me to create this book to illustrate how we can "be the change."

Dedicated to the caseworkers, social workers, after-care workers, guardians ad litem, youth and family advocates, peer support specialists, volunteers, help desk analysts, nurses, doctors, first responders, peace builders, and thousands of others who devote their lives to helping others. I hear so many of you say that your job constantly shows you the bad side of human nature. I look at you and see the incredible good in human nature, and I hope that you will soon look in the mirror and see the same. My aspiration is that this book will help our silos come together because, as you have stated many times, "There are not enough community service workers" to solve these issues. This book is dedicated to you and your vision to help silos come together to create a safer, happier planet.

Dedicated to my second families at Tech Data and Nielsen who showed me that Walt Disney was so right when he said, "It's kind of fun to do the impossible." When people said things like, "It has always been that way; you can't change the system," we continued to make the system better.

Last but not least—thank you to my family and friends for putting up with my schedule and years of work in 24/7 crisis management. That hands-on experience, research, and travel to learn from global experts gave me added insight to share via this book. Thank you for being so amazing and patient.

CONTENTS

FOREWORD

As an academic leader and international consultant, I especially enjoy events where students and community members co-create solutions. Lisa and I met through a Community Health Action Team (CHAT) where individuals and organizations united to design and implement better solutions for health and equity within her Florida community.

In my work with communities experiencing environmental injustice, I know how impactful the right tips and stories can be in the lives of individuals, families and, ultimately, communities. Fortunately, Lisa did the hard part for us as she compiled 20 years of problem-solving and solution design tips into this book.

This book is different because Lisa shares real stories to help the reader relate to and visualize how to apply the tips in their own context. The story-telling format makes it easy to create a shared language to discuss ideas and options with community members. This book provides examples and stories filled with hope and possibilities that you can adapt to develop community-centered solutions for the future.

Dr. Sandra Whitehead
The George Washington University
Sustainable Urban Planning Program Director and Assistant Professor
United States Environmental Protection Agency (U.S. EPA)
Appointed Member, National Environmental Justice Advisory Council

1. ALL HANDS ON DECK—EXPERTS AGREE INTERDEPENDENCE IS KEY

"Life doesn't make sense without interdependence. We need each other, and the sooner we learn that, the better for us all." – **Erik Erikson** (German-American developmental psychologist and psychoanalyst, known for his theory on psychological development of human beings.)

"Be yourself. Everyone else is already taken." – **Oscar Wilde** (Irish poet and popular London playwright.)

People often ask me about the meaning of *best practices*. Webster-Merriam describes best practices as "a standard for widespread adoption" that is "proven by research and experience to produce optimal results." Yet, these treasures are often hidden within business, science and nonprofit structures. Webster describes how these isolated silos can hinder communication and cooperation. With that in mind, the purpose of this book is to reveal 180 Silo Secrets.

1.1 Life's Deck of Cards. What Is in Your Hand?

True Colors® is a program that helps you easily discover what powers are naturally strong within you. (True Colors®, 2019) We all have a primary and a secondary inborn strength. While the program uses colors to describe the four personality types, I find it easier to remember them by using a cards analogy.

(1) **Hearts:** Sensitive, compassionate people who love to help (**Caring Hearts or Helpers**).

(2) **Diamonds:** Stable and responsible people who get things done (**Solid Diamonds or Leaders**).

(3) **Clubs:** Adventurous people who ensure we have fun along the way (**Fun Clubs or Change Agents**).

(4) **Spades:** Sharp thinkers and inventors who like solving problems (**Sharp Spades or Problem Solvers**).

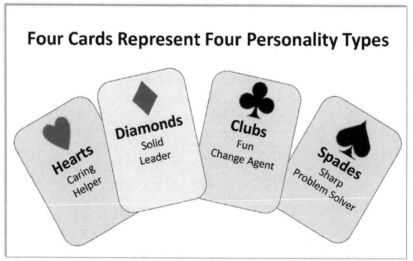

Figure 1.1a Four cards based on the True Colors personality model.

While every story has two sides, every solution has four.

Essentially, the four cards represent the four sides (personality types) that must be included in order to achieve interdependence, which is what top experts concur is needed to solve the world's problems. Think of it as each of us having two superpowers necessary to save the world, but the world needs all four powers to achieve balanced solutions. Together, we are the Fantastic 4 or the Avengers. Since we are all born with cards that are key to solving problems, this makes that game of "Go Fish" that some of us played as children make more sense.

If we're working to solve a challenge, we'll be more successful if we look around at the team we have and ensure we have a full hand of all four sides. We may find that we need to "go fish" for a card that is missing. Most of the cards are easy to spot. The Caring Hearts often wear their heart on their sleeve. The Solid Diamonds are always on time and are constantly crossing off items on that long to-do list. The Fun Clubs are off having fun, so you may need to bring some good doughnuts to encourage them to join in. The Problem Solvers are the smallest group by far, and they are often in the lab, so you may need to fish them out or be creative in bringing the challenge to them versus asking them to emerge. This is essentially what *interdependence* is all about. It is about understanding and valuing each of our differences to ensure diversity of personality in order to have a winning hand. Having a balanced hand will also help ensure overall diversity.

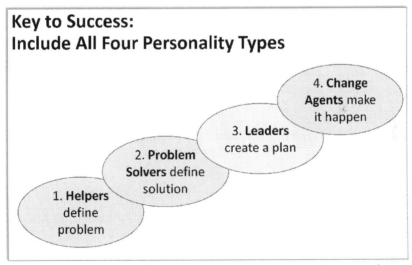

Figure 1.1b Each personality type has a key role in progressing to a solution.

Going back to 460 BC, Hippocrates, known as "the father of Western medicine," observed that people in general seem to primarily have one of four main approaches to life. Ancient Greeks categorized these four main personality types as fire, water, earth, and air. Today, many companies use personality assessments to determine what employees' personality types are. Since there are so many different personality classifications that use the same four personality types, many use a common color scheme of blue, green, gold, and orange to correlate the four classifications. Really, the key is to find a way that is easy for you to remember. When I got excited about the incredible benefits and showed people how you can use personality trait knowledge to have more harmony and less conflict, they liked the concept but wanted a trick to easily remember the personality types. So, I came up with the deck of cards and people seemed to relate.

The chart below, showing the similarity of personality models, was modified and used with permission from Mary Miscisin. (Miscisin, 2019)

Many Personality Models Include the Four Types

Deck of Cards Description	True Colors	Inner Hero	Ancient Greeks	Galen (2000 BC)
Helpers	Blue	Helper	Fire	Phlegmatic
Problem Solvers	Green	Thinker	Water	Choleric
Leaders	Gold	Planner	Earth	Melancholic
Change Agents	Orange	Doer	Air	Sanguine

Figure 1.1c Side-by-side comparison shows similarity of personality models.

The first personality, the Helpers, is the only personality type that puts people first. Naturally, a lot of Helpers gravitate toward careers where they can excel in caring roles like teaching, nursing, or caregiving.

Then you have the other three personality types, which are all outcome-focused. If Taylor Swift and Cyndi Lauper sang a duet about outcome personality types, they'd sing, "The Problem Solvers want to solve, solve, solve, solve, solve; and the responsible leaders want to plan, plan, plan, plan, plan; and the last group, the Change Agents, well, they just wanna have fun ... Oh yeah, the Change Agents just wanna have fun."

Below is an illustration of some well-known names to more easily visualize the value of the four main personality types.

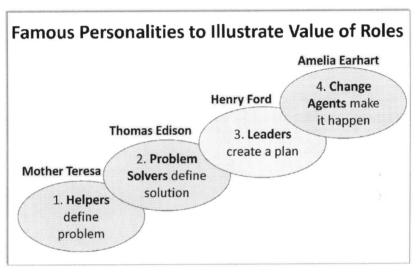

Famous Personalities to Illustrate Value of Roles

Amelia Earhart

Henry Ford

4. Change Agents make it happen

Thomas Edison

3. Leaders create a plan

2. Problem Solvers define solution

Mother Teresa

1. Helpers define problem

Figure 1.1d Above famous people illustrate how each personality is key.

In this next story, I'll use the above-mentioned famous personalities to make it easier to visualize how the four personalities interact.

Pastor Will asked Mother Teresa (**caring Helper**) to come help the young children in a very poor area with no electricity. During the day, the children helped their families on the farm, and Mother Teresa helped to educate the children in the afternoon, but they ran out of daylight fast. She was sad that the children had no light to read or write, but she accepted the darkness as a situation out of her control.

Pastor Will had been bugging Thomas Edison (**sharp Problem Solver**) to come to church. Thomas was doing his 2,307th test on an experiment, but he managed to get to church. Pastor Will asked everyone to pray for the children with no light. Thomas dozed off a little, thinking Pastor Will was speaking in metaphors, and then realized this was a real and serious problem. The moment church ended, Thomas rushed home without speaking to anyone. He could not wait to test his idea for a portable light (a flashlight).

Thomas' acquaintance, Mr. Henry Ford (**solid Leader**), was funding Thomas' experiments and was surprised to find that they were suddenly delayed. Thomas explained he had been a little distracted building a flashlight for the children with no light. Mr. Ford was impressed, but he told Thomas he needed to work on quality and consistency. He explained, "If I produce 100 lights and only 50% work, we'll have 50 screaming kids."

Whew, that inspired Thomas. He worked nonstop for the next seven days and got that flashlight working consistently.

The next week, there was a potluck at church and, of all people, Ms. Amelia Earhart (**fun Change Agent**) was at the event. Mr. Ford and Pastor Will welcomed Amelia and asked how her travels had been. She told them about villages all over the world with no light. Mr. Ford shared the exciting news regarding Thomas' flashlight. They worked out a plan to produce 100 flashlights to be delivered to Pastor Will, as well as other countries. Amelia was thrilled with the plan for her to bring light to villages around the world.

While that seemed like an exciting ending, the good news continued. As Mr. Ford and Pastor Will got to talking, Mr. Ford asked if the parents of the children could use jobs that paid wages. Pastor Will said, "Of course."

The adults started training right away to work on the new flashlight assembly line. Pastor Will thanked Mr. Ford for his kindness. Mr. Ford said, "Certainly, it is a win-win."

Meet the real people behind the story

For the above example, I merged real stories to show the possibilities of bringing the four personalities together, which, of course, is the essence of interdependence.

The pastor and the children with no light, who inspired the above story, are very real. Like Mother Teresa, Pastor Will is overshadowed by kindness, not yet seeing the light. He is very strong-willed; perhaps that's how he got his name. Hopefully, he will open his eyes to the possibilities and soon see the light.

Thomas Edison's actions were inspired by an actual 15-year-old girl. As a high school student in Canada, Ann Makosinski invented a flashlight powered by one hand's body heat. She was at the Google Science Fair, but she and Pastor Will don't typically travel in the same circles. Imagine the possibilities if his people and her people could get together to combine their strengths. (Google Science Fair, 2013)

The character of Mr. Ford in the story was inspired by Ford Motor Company. The company plans to use the motto "Go Further" to market new vehicles around the world and motivate its employees. (Ford Go Further, 2019)

The character of Amelia Earhart was inspired by an amazing young lady named Mariia, whom I met at the River Phoenix Center for Peacebuilding (RPCP). She was there as part of the U.S. Department of State's Community Solutions Program. (IREX, 2019). Mariia wants to build a better world for children, including her own child. She and her little boy chat each night using Skype or FaceTime. They miss each other greatly, but Mariia's son understands his mom is on a very important mission. (Levchenko, 2018) She studies peace-building practices and bravely travels to many countries to work on projects to spread light across the world.

SILO SECRET #1: The True Colors program is described as "a tool that fosters an environment of understanding and collaboration." (True Colors, 2019) Many companies use this program to help people get along by understanding and valuing each of the four different personalities. Families have commented that knowing each person's True Colors helps them get along better.

REFLECT:

Think of a home or work project that was very successful.

Were all four cards represented? (Caring Heart, Solid Diamond, Fun Club, and Sharp Spade)

_____

_____

What was your natural role on the project?

_____

_____

Note: People often bring a primary and secondary role to solutions.

"The task that remains is to cope with our interdependence—to see ourselves reflected in every other human being and to respect and honor our differences." – **Melba Pattillo Beals** (American journalist and college educator, among students who were the first to integrate Little Rock Central High School.) (Pattillo-Beals, 2019)

1.2 The Perfect Storm to Interdependence

For years, there seemed to be a major focus on moving people from dependence to independence. We've all heard the proverb "If you give a man a fish, he has food for a day; if you teach a man to fish, he has food for a lifetime." Today, experts in every sector (science, farming, international politics, and technology) are in agreement that the problems that the world is facing are more integrated than ever. For this reason, experts agree the key is to move toward interdependence, where all hands will be on deck.

Interdependence is tricky because it involves coming to the realization that we rely on each other for survival. Below is a simplified illustration of something that I realized a while back. I thought everyone loved the excitement of designing solutions. Wow, creating your future—how cool is that? But as it turned out, my experience was just like the percentages show; 70% of society enjoys implementing and getting it done. (Kruger, 2018) Most people are fine with someone else defining the "it" part. Each role has a super strength to add to the table. The challenging part is getting the super strengths to talk and work through the flow. Below is the perfect storm to interdependence without all the sound effects.

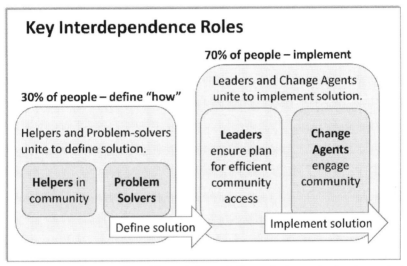

Figure 1.2a Helpers and Problems Solvers define solution to be implemented.

One of my former bosses, Mr. Bob Smith (yes, that's his real name), used to run things through what he called a "logic test." Thinking of it that way, it's logical that the first two personalities are the least common. You only need so many people to come up with the light bulb design. However, once it is designed, you need more people to produce, market, distribute, train, and use the light bulb. The challenge is that the world has become more complicated and Problem Solvers can no longer just sit in a lab and design tangible solutions. Today, many solutions involve resolving community, country, and global challenges that require being in the same room, or at least on the same conference call, and putting minds together, thereby relying on each other to truly reach solutions.

Chart of Personality Types and Percentages

Personality	Percentage of Population	True Color Description	Famous Personalities
Helper	15%	Blue (sensitive)	Mother Teresa Martin Luther King Jr.
Leader	35%	Gold (obedient)	Henry Ford Mr. Rogers
Change Agent	35%	Orange (action oriented)	Amelia Earhart John F. Kennedy
Problem Solver	15%	Green (inventive)	Thomas Edison Eleanor Roosevelt

Figure 1.2b Above percentages based on True Colors personality statistics.

The above general population percentages illustrate how the smaller group of Helpers and Problem Solvers, representing 30% of the population, need to get together in order for the 70% majority of the population, Leaders and Change Agents, to implement the solutions. (Kruger, 2018) With the global population, the Helpers and Problem Solvers represent 38% of the population. (True Colors, 2019)

Back in the day, when we had small villages, there was a natural mix of True Colors as well as different skills. Today, silos often attract the same colors. For example, teachers tend to be Helpers and Leaders, with only about 5% being Problem Solvers. This means that they have to go out of their way to include Problem Solvers to help solve problems in education. Those who are Change Agents, a mere 3% of the teacher silo, hop on a plane to Finland to see why the country's education system is rated so high, but then, being adventurous, they sometimes decide to stay in Finland or come back telling stories of relaxing, barefoot classrooms that vary too far from what we expect of a proper school environment. It's sort of like when we tell our boss that surveys show that employees who take a nap during the day are more productive. The boss read that survey too, but none of us are sleeping on the job yet. Lastly, Problem Solvers are independent thinkers, so we have to go out of our way to get them to the discussion table. Imagine if we invited one or two Problem Solvers to the table to share their perspective on how we might be able to improve our systems. (Kruger, 2018)

SILO SECRET #2: Experts agree that *interdependence* is the key to solving our global and community problems. Part of interdependence is moving through the phases of forming a team, which include the "storm" before the "norm." The four different views represent a healthy, natural opposition of views that add up to a holistic, sustainable plan for the team to eventually excel. The five stages of team development, named by psychologist Bruce Tuckman, include forming, storming, norming, performing, and adjourning. (Tuckman, 1965)

REFLECT:

Think of an unresolved situation or news topic. Was one of the four views missed or overlooked?

_____

_____

*"We have much to do together. Let us do it in wisdom and love and joy. Let us make this the human experience." – **Gary Zukav*** (American spiritual teacher who challenges us to see the depth of our potential in the world and act on that awareness. Author of four *New York Times* best sellers.)

1.3 Meet Famous People Onboard from All Over the World

People all over the world are ready to cruise forward in building a better world via *interdependence*.

At the most basic level, all people share the earth's limited resources and are interdependent when it comes to the quality of the air and water that we need to live. Some of you may have heard Liza Minnelli sing "Money Makes the World Go 'Round." (Ebb & Kand, 1972) We are especially connected now with our global economy. From Buddhists to economists, all agree that interdependence is key.

Below are comments from some of the most powerful people in the world who are onboard! (BrainyQuote, 2019)

Interdependence is valued across the world.

- *"...the central organizing principle of this twenty-first century is interdependence." – **Australia** (Kevin Rudd, former prime minister)*
- *"...new level of interdependence among us." – **Brazil** (Eduardo Paes, politician)*
- *"...highly interdependent economically." – **China** (Xi Jinping, president)*
- *"...growing interdependence with the rest of the world." – **Japan** (Toshihiko Fukui, economist and central banker)*
- *"Global interdependence today..." – **India** (Atal Bihari Vajpayee, prime minister)*
- *"The fundamental law of human beings is interdependence." – **S. Africa** (Desmond Tutu, Anglican cleric and theologian)*
- *"interdependence defines the new world we live in." – **United Kingdom** (Tony Blair, British politician who served as prime minister)*
- *"...our global strength all point to an American declaration of interdependence." – **United States** (Cory Booker, junior United States senator)*

Figure 1.3a Sample of comments from influential leaders across the world.

AUSTRALIA – Prime Minister:

- *"What we have seen in financial markets should bring home to us all that **the central organizing principle of this twenty-first century is interdependence**. For the century just past, interdependence may have been one option among many. For the century that is to come, there is no longer an alternative." – **Kevin Rudd** (Two time prime minister of Australia; addressed United Nations in 2008.)*

BRAZIL – Politician:

- *"**Globalization has produced a new level of interdependence among us.** The economy and multinational supply chains do not abide by political boundaries. A computer ordered in Brazil is designed in California and assembled in several other countries. Economic* *integration was the first strong evidence of this new era." – **Eduardo Paes** (Brazilian politician; former mayor.)*

CHINA – President:

- *"As economic globalization gathers momentum, China and the United States **have become highly interdependent economically**. Such economic relations would not enjoy sustained, rapid growth if they were not based on mutual benefit or if they failed to deliver great benefits to the United States." – **Xi Jinping*** (Top of list on *Forbes*' "The World's Most Powerful People"; chairman of the Central Military Commission of the People's Republic of China since 2013; president of China.)

INDIA – Prime Minister:

- *"**Global interdependence today** means that economic disasters in developing countries could create a backlash on developed countries." – **Atal Bihari Vajpayee*** (Tenth prime minister of India.)

JAPAN – Buddhist Philosopher:

- *"The idea of **interdependence is central to Buddhism**, which holds that all things come into being through the mutual interactions of various causes and conditions." – **Daisaku Ikeda*** (President of Soka Gakkai, Japan's largest new religious movement, as well as a philosopher, an educator, and a peace advocate.)

JAPAN – Economist/Governor:

- *"In this context, the current recovery in the Japanese economy is taking place in tandem with the **growing interdependence with the rest of the world**, particularly with the other East Asian economies." – **Toshihiko Fukui*** (Japanese economist and central banker; twenty-ninth governor of the Bank of Japan, and a director of the Bank for International Settlements.)

SOUTH AFRICA – Cleric and Theologian:

- *"The **fundamental law of human beings is interdependence**. A person is a person through other persons." – **Desmond Tutu*** (South African Anglican cleric and theologian known for his work as an anti-apartheid and human rights activist.)

UNITED KINGDOM – Environmentalist:

- *"...the **core values that underpin sustainable development—interdependence**, empathy, equity, personal responsibility, and intergenerational justice—are the only foundation upon which any viable vision of a better world can possibly be constructed." – **Jonathon Porritt*** (Environmentalist and Chair of Sustainable Development Commission. Commander of the Order of the British Empire.)

UNITED KINGDOM - Politician:

- *"I have long believed this **interdependence defines the new world we live in**." – **Tony Blair*** (British politician who served as prime minister of the United Kingdom from 1997 to 2007.)

UNITED KINGDOM – President of International Think Tank Policy Network:

- *"Instead of saying that globalization is a fact, that it's inevitable, we've also got to demonstrate that while the **growing interdependence of the world economy** is indeed a fact, it's not uncontrollable." – **Peter Mandelson*** (British Labour politician, president of the international think tank Policy Network, and chairman of strategic advisory firm Global Counsel.)

UNITED STATES – Senator:

- *"In America, we have a Declaration of Independence, but our history, our advancements, our global **strength all point to an American declaration of interdependence**." – **Cory Booker*** (Currently junior

United States senator from New Jersey; first African American U.S. senator from New Jersey.)

UNITED STATES OF AMERICA:

While it is great that top leaders across the world agree with the importance of interdependence, let's travel across one country to get views from different lines of work, ranging from actors and artists to energy authorities and talk show hosts. As it turns out, they are equally excited about the importance of creating an interdependence movement.

Here are some views of people across the United States who are onboard with interdependence.

ACTOR:

- *"Interdependence is a fact; it's not an opinion." – Peter Coyote* (American actor, author, director.)

ARTIST:

- *"Collective wisdom is about our capacity to recognize interdependence and to make decisions demonstrating that we have a stake in each other, that we can indeed care for each other and the physical planet we share." – Alan Briskin* (PhD, consultant, artist, researcher, cofounder of the Collective Wisdom Initiative. Won Book of the Year for *Daily Miracles*.)

AUTHOR:

- *"The best relationship is one that does not foster too much independence nor too much dependence, but exists in the **healthy interdependence zone**." – Karen Salmansohn* (Best-selling self-help author.)

ECONOMIST:

- *"The indigenous understanding has its basis of spirituality in a recognition of the interconnectedness and **interdependence of all living things**, a holistic and balanced view of the world. All things are bound together. All things connect ..."* – **Rebecca Adamson** (round-breaking indigenous economist, recognized by PBS as one of the Most Influential Women in America.)

ENERGY (AUTHORITY ON WORLD ENERGY):

- *"**In a world of increasing interdependence**, energy security will depend much on how countries manage their relations with one another. That is why energy security will be one of the main challenges of foreign policy in the years ahead. Oil and gas have always been political commodities."* – **Daniel Yergin** (Pulitzer Prize winner; authority on energy, international politics, and economics. Awarded Lifetime Achievement Award from India and U.S. Department of Energy Security medal.)

FILM ACTRESS:

- *"I believe that dialogue is the key to breaking through our tendency to separate and isolate. **Dialogue changes isolation and loneliness into connection and interdependence.** This, I believe, is the essence of Buddhism."* – **Vinessa Shaw** (Film actress and model; initial role in Disney's *Hocus Pocus* film.)

HISTORIAN and COLLEGE PRESIDENT:

- *"From literature and the arts we gain imagination and empathy, a second sight on our **common humanity**. From history we draw courage against all hope, understanding that things were once different, and can be different again. From science we learn humility and persistence, knowing that **a sudden insight can re-frame the universe**."* – **Drew Gilpin Faust** (Historian and first woman to serve as president of Harvard University.)

INTERNET PIONEER:

- *"Big Data allows us to see patterns we have never seen before. This will clearly show us **interdependence and connections that will lead to a new way of looking at everything.** It will let us see the 'real-time' cause and effect of our actions. What we buy, eat, donate, and throw away will be visual in a real-time map to see the ripple effect of our actions. That could only lead to more conscious behavior." – **Tiffany Shlain** (Internet pioneer, author, and Emmy-nominated filmmaker with over 80 awards and distinctions for her films and work. Uses film to activate global conversations.)*

LAWYER and FIRST LADY:

- *"What I know for sure is that all the sacrifice and challenges we face are worth it if we're creating a better future for our kids. I just think **if the adults are always thinking about the world we want to leave for our kids, we're going to make the right choices every single time.**" – **Michelle Obama** (Lawyer and university administrator who served as the First Lady of the United States.)*

PHILANTHROPIST:

- *"Trees are extraordinary revelations of the spirit in nature. And, given the multitude of ways that trees and their products benefit and enrich human culture, they are an especially appropriate symbol of the **interdependence of spirit and nature.**" – **Steven Clark Rockefeller** (Fourth-generation member of the Rockefeller family, former dean of Middlebury College, and philanthropist.)*

PHYSICIST, SYSTEMS – AUSTRIAN-BORN, but America gets to take the credit ☺:

- *"The new paradigm may be called a holistic world view, seeing the world as an integrated whole rather than a dissociated collection of parts. It may also be called an ecological view, if the term 'ecological' is used in a much broader and deeper sense than usual. Deep* *ecological awareness recognized the fundamental **interdependence of all phenomena** and the fact that, as individuals and societies we are all embedded in (and ultimately dependent on) the cycle process of nature."* – **Fritjof Capra** (Austrian-born American physicist, systems theorist, and deep ecologist. Founding director of the Center for Ecoliteracy in Berkeley, California, and faculty of Schumacher College.)

RADIO HOST/ MINISTRY:

- *"I have an interesting perspective on depending on others. I think it gives people a chance to serve. **And I'm not so much big on independence as I am on interdependence**. I'm not talking about codependence; I'm talking about giving people the opportunity to practice love with its sleeves rolled up."* – **Joni Eareckson Tada** (Evangelical Christian, author, radio host, and founder of Joni and Friends, an organization accelerating Christian ministry in the disability community.)

SYSTEMS SCIENTIST:

- *"**The further human society drifts away from nature, the less we understand interdependence**."* – **Peter Senge** (American systems scientist; lecturer at the MIT Sloan School of Management, co-faculty at the New England Complex Systems Institute, founder of the Society for Organizational Learning.)

You may be wondering if less affluent or less famous people are onboard. To answer that question, I interviewed 135 families from one of the poorest, highest crime areas. Rather than ask them for their top quote, I asked if they wanted to do community service activities, and 98% exclaimed, "Yes!" Over 80% wanted the entire family to help out. While this group of people relies on others for basics like food, they want us to rely on them to help improve our world. As for those in the middle, over 62 million already volunteer. (U.S. Census, 2018) We too want to make a difference.

There are millions of people wanting to build a better world. One example is The Art of Living Foundation's event, where millions of people across multiple countries, including the U.S., unite in celebration of International Peace Day with a vision for global peace and interdependence. (Shankar, 2019) Over 10 years, the Rotary Foundation has trained over 1,000 fellows in peace activities. (Rotary, 2019)

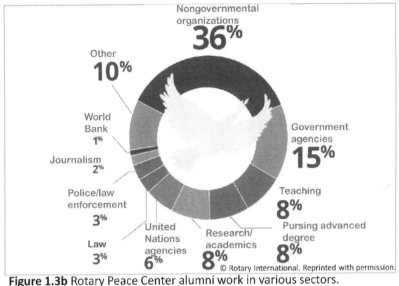

Figure 1.3b Rotary Peace Center alumni work in various sectors.

SILO SECRET #3: There is a wide consensus on the critical importance of interdependence. In addition to the above comments, this book also contains interdependence quotes and actions from people across various other countries.

REFLECT:

Did you find one of the quotes about interdependence particularly interesting or inspirational?

_____

_____

Chapter 1 Summary: *Experts agree that interdependence is the key to solving world challenges. For holistic and sustainable solutions, we need to value and combine all four personality strengths. At a high level, each and every one of us gravitates toward either people-focused or outcome-focused solutions. Combining our strengths, we are able to formulate the best outcomes for people. We each have two of the four superpowers required to save the world. With interdependence, we realize and recognize the importance of finding, valuing, and combining our opposite strengths.*

2. VISION—FULL DREAM AHEAD

*"It's kind of fun to do the impossible." – **Walt Disney*** (co-founded Walt Disney Productions, one of the best-known motion-picture production companies in the world.)

*"We came on different ships, but we are all in the same boat." – **Keith Brown*** (Speaker known as 'Mr. I'm Possible' and winner of the Presidential Lifetime Achievement Award.) (Brown, 2019) (King, 1968)

2.1 All in the Same Boat

From prison to Paris, we are all in the same boat.

First stop: prison. Recently, I had a chance to go to jail. Not a sentence you hear every day! The program is called the Juvenile Justice Citizens' Academy. (JJCA, 2019) As part of the 10-week program to learn the justice system from a kid's point of view, you get an email each week giving you directions to the next stop on the justice journey, telling you where to go and how to prepare. The email instructions get progressively scarier each week. At first, they simply recommend bringing a sweater in case you get a little chilly. Next, they instruct you to lock all jewelry and belongings in your trunk prior to arrival. By the last stop, they advise you to travel in a group, stay close together, wear running shoes, and sign a waiver basically stating that you actually asked to go to jail and assume all liability.

One of the earlier emails directed us to go to a church (of all places) to learn about a program called Children in Need of Services—CINS (pronounced like sins), which I found slightly ironic and memorable. They also have a program called Families in Need of Services (FINS). (CINS and FINS, 2019) Apparently, these two stops are quite effective in helping families turn things around and get back on track to prevent the next steps. Sadly, they referred to these two stops as the "best-kept secrets."

The next week, we got an email to head to a Juvenile Assessment Center (JAC). JAC is the central location where police bring young offenders and truants for processing, assessment, and intervention. Just as we arrived, a police car pulled up with a boy about 14 years old. One person asked why his handcuffs were in the front versus the back. The officer explained that officers are required to put the youth in handcuffs, but they have the option to put the handcuffs on in front versus in back if a child is not perceived to be of any threat.

In this case, the boy's mother didn't know how to handle him anymore, so she called the police. The officer stated that this is a top reason why prison rates are going up. Parents are not sure how to handle teens, so they think the legal system will help. Typically, they change their mind the next day but that is a day too late. I don't consider myself a big hugger, but I have never felt such a need to hug someone in my life. The young boy's eyes looked like Puss in Boots on *Shrek* when his dark-eyed pupils got really big and everyone says, "Aww."

The officer said, "There is not a day that goes by that we do not leave here without a broken heart."

Well, on to the next stop.

So, this was it. The real deal. We were in a room with about 17 young people who had been arrested. Green-eyed Puss in Boots was still going through check-in. The guys in this room were not so huggable. My instinctive thought was to quickly befriend the strongest and fittest person in the room. The corrections officer at the front of the line was the only one who had the slightest idea how to handle a bad situation, so I hung out with him. He told me that he oversaw 80 young men in jail. I asked, "Is a 1-officer-to-80-kid ratio enough to handle conflicts or even any fights that break out?" I'll never forget his response.

He said, "In jail, they have a safe place to eat, sleep, and play, so they are good." He then lowered his head in disappointment, stating, "Then they go out in the real world and don't have a safe place to eat, sleep, and play, so they end up back in jail."

Second stop: Paris. Well, I promised I'd take you to Paris, the city of love, lights, and romance, or perhaps the city that will take your literal breath away. With the air quality worsening, BBC is reporting that the mayor of Paris is stepping up the "war on diesel." (Leggett, 2018) The mayor is working hard to restore Paris' famed beauty. For now, though, he is helping get the city back to the basics, with an emphasis on clean air.

Whether in prison or Paris, people all seem to have similar needs:

A safe place to:

✓ Eat

✓ Sleep

✓ Be

SILO SECRET #4: Maslow's Hierarchy of Needs is still relevant. Most of us have a common mission to have a safe place to eat, sleep, and be. In *Psychology Today*, Dr. Neel Burton discusses how Maslow's Pyramid, from 1943, reflects those same basic needs. More and more studies are showing the critical importance of socially connecting with others. Once we have those basics, we seek to build up our ego. And, if time permits, we then seek out creativity and development. Below is Dr. Burton's illustration of Maslow's Pyramid. (Burton, 2015) (Maslow, 1954)

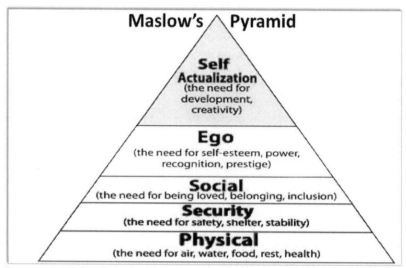

Figure 2.1 Maslow's Pyramid provided by Dr. Neel Burton, *Psychology Today*.

According to the World Health Organization (WHO), developing and developed countries, including China, the U.S., and England, have challenges ensuring both safe air and safe water. 91% of the world population lives in places where pollution levels exceed WHO safe air quality limits. (World Health News, 2019) We are all in the same boat.

REFLECT:

The consensus seems to be that we need a safe place to eat, sleep, and be. Rate your environment:

_____ Safe food to eat (easy access to healthy food; i.e., lettuce that is free of pesticides and E. coli)

_____ Safe place to sleep (no worries about finances, health, work or crime; get right to sleep)

_____ Safe place to be (air is free of pollution; feel safe walking to park, store, school, or work)

If you could change one thing to be happier, what would it be?

_____

_____

If you could solve any world problem, which one would you want to solve?

_____

_____

"Twenty years from now you will be more disappointed by the things that you didn't do than by the ones you did do. So throw off the bowlines. Sail away from the safe harbor. Catch the trade winds in your sails. Explore. Dream. Discover." – **Mark Twain** (Author of *The Adventures of Tom Sawyer* and *The Adventures of Huckleberry Finn.*)

2.2 The Best in the Universe

Imagine we discover another planet and its inhabitants then come to visit Earth. A comedian said, "Rather than imagine green not-so-attractive aliens, let's imagine these visitors are quite attractive"—so let's imagine away. Are we proud to have these quite captivating aliens visit our home planet? With them only visiting for a couple days, they ask to see "the happiest place on Earth."

Well, I guess we're taking our good-looking visitors to Disney World, a place that has the official tagline of "The Happiest Place on Earth." That is a pretty bold statement, setting the bar quite high, but millions of people come each year to Disneyland, Disney World, and Euro Disney. Living in Florida, I had the opportunity to get to know multiple people who have had the pleasure of being part of the Disney cast.

So let's go behind the scenes of the Florida Disney World location to learn some of the steps they take to fulfill their promise of providing you with "The Happiest Place on Earth."

Safe air: Realizing that they are in Florida and, on top of that, in the middle of swamps, Disney wants to ensure guests are free of itchy bug bites. Plus, there's the West Nile virus to worry about, so the organization takes added precautions when it comes to mosquitoes. In addition to having pest control throughout the park, Disney has chickens—yes, chickens—strategically located around the perimeter. According to my buddy Joe, they have a schedule to test the birds to ensure that they are free of the virus. If any chicken shows a sign of illness, Disney will take added precautions in that area of the park to ensure the guests are free of those tiny, potentially deadly little guests. They even take care of the chickens, so relax and enjoy your stay in the wonderful world of Disney. (Plays, 2018)

Another key to Disney's safe air relates to planning and transportation. Visitors staying at hotels can pretty much get a free bus ride every 15 minutes to and from key destinations. Inviting guests to simply hop on a bus takes carpooling to a new level. Each bus keeps an estimated 40-plus cars off the roads. Orlando and surrounding areas (Kissimmee and Sanford) often earn the Environmental Protection Agency's top rating of 'green' on the AQI (Air Quality Index), showing that it is possible to ensure a green environment while still making plenty of green at the bank.

Safe water: One time, I was at Disney, and they stopped the water ride that I was about to board. It wasn't a scary flume or anything, just a relaxing little boat ride, but they stopped it to do a safety inspection. I asked some of my Disney cast friends about this, curious to know what could possibly be risky about this boat ride. They said, "Oh, someone must have dropped something in the water," and explained that they monitor the water for safety. If there is any foreign object in the water, it triggers an alarm and the employee on duty shuts the ride down for an urgent inspection to ensure the health and safety of all. For example, if someone drops a plastic bottle into the water, they don't want to risk it getting caught in equipment and presenting any danger or inconvenience to guests or employees.

Beauty of the land: Disney has various behind the scenes and even "underground and/or backstage" functions to ensure that all guests' activities are magical and run like clockwork. Front stage as well as backstage cast members share a common mindset that is part of the employee orientation training. A key goal is to ensure a consistent service experience for all Disney guests. In addition to being there to take that perfect group photo, each employee seems to naturally ensure that the smallest piece of litter is immediately picked up and placed in the proper trash receptacle. To illustrate, an amazing speaker named Char LaBounty worked "behind the scenes," overseeing Disney's Worldwide IT Business Services organization. While she is now a Public Speaker and Consultant, she still applies her Disney service mindset to her everyday life.

Population comfort: Disney is not exempt from challenges with growing populations. No matter what state the economy is in, thousands eagerly wait each day for their kingdom doors to open. The "underground" casts are hard at work designing ways to best manage the flow. Cast member John explained that Disney works hard to manage expectations for wait-time in lines to get to attractions, carefully measuring and announcing a "25-minute wait time" or "15-minute wait time." That way guests can decide if they would prefer to come back later. They even created a Fast Pass that everyone talks about as guests feel like they won the lottery, getting to jump to the head of the line.

John went on to share how Disney has designed twists and turns to manage the flow of people waiting in line. It provides a sense of hope when people can see the finish line as they go back and forth. When there is not a line, some people put their hands on the bars, push themselves up, and leap forward like children. Some even climb under or hop over the bars, feeling a sense of satisfaction as they race back and forth through the empty rows of metal separation bars. It makes them feel like they hit the jackpot as they move fast to catch up with the line that they now perceive as "short."

Proactive steps: In addition to the proactive steps Disney takes to ensure rides and equipment are safe, Disney has cast members strategically located throughout the park for their visitors' comfort and safety. Before the advent of selfies, employees were always there to take photos of families and guests so they had a tangible memory of their great experience. For at least the last 25 years, the same photographer has been in front of Cinderella's castle to take your photo. On that note, you may not remember the photographer because Disney goes out of its way to have all cast members fit right in. Rather than remember the cast member's deep blue eye shadow or spiked hair, the cast blends in to help with the overall mission to ensure that you have an incredible memory of your visit to "The Happiest Place on Earth."

Welcome everyone: When you walk through Disney, you'll likely hear a variety of accents and languages. They naturally embrace and value diversity. Disney's "It's a Small World" attraction strives to recognize and welcome all countries with small but significant details like including signs in multiple languages. Even if you do not speak the other languages, it is kind of a reminder for us all that we are part of this very connected "small, small world." Disney cruises continue this same harmonious spirit. Staff and guests that are from countries with strong conflict manage to dine and participate in fun activities together aboard their cruise ships.

Lasting impression: People have told me stories of things that Disney employees have done which they will always remember. One of my favorite stories involves a friend's daughter. Only three years old, Jenn loved getting autographs from her favorite characters. Because of her young age, she only had three autographs so far (Winnie the Pooh, Goofy, and Minnie Mouse), but she cherished her shiny blue autograph book and carried her gigantic autograph pen everywhere. My friend and Jenn went on some rides and somehow lost track of the autograph book. They looked everywhere but could not find it. Jenn's mom reported it to the Disney Lost and Found. That afternoon, Mickey Mouse personally delivered Jenn an autograph book signed by each and every character at Disney. Jenn was so excited. It was the highlight of her trip and years later, she still tells that story.

SILO SECRET #5: If we take time to care for our *air, water,* and *land*, both in safety and beauty, we can be similar to Disney and put steps in place to build a safer, happier planet.

SILO SECRET #6: As we face the challenges of a *growing population*, we can look at ways to better manage the flow of people for the convenience of both local people and tourists. As an example, BBC news featured five beautiful locations that are facing serious issues due to an influx of tourists. One such place is Maya Bay, where 77% of coral is at risk from boat anchors. (Baker, 2018) Maya Bay looks very much like a Disney water resort. Maybe we could utilize similar steps to protect the real resorts.

SILO SECRET #7: All *countries can exist in harmony*. This is true of Disney World as well as Disney cruises. Staff and guests from countries that are at odds off the ship are able to dine, mingle, and participate in activities together.

SILO SECRET #8: *Make a lasting impression* and people will come back. It surely worked for Jenn.

REFLECT:

Is there something that Disney is doing that could possibly be a model to improve our world?

_____

_____

"With a clear vision, you know where you are going and you make progress because you are guided by the map of your mind and the compass of your heart." – **Ivette K. Caballero** (Writer, speaker, personal development coach.) (Caballero, 2019)

2.3 Double Vision Can Lead to a Collision

Right out of high school, I headed to Southeastern Academy to get certified in the travel industry. Of the many career options that they told us about, one airline stood out. Instructors said Optimal Airlines was by far the hardest to get into, describing their tough interview process where you had to first make it into a pile of the top 5,000 applications, with only 500 selected to participate in group interviews of 50 people each. The airline then interviewed and selected five candidates to hire. Many applicants heard frightening stories of how their pilots had to fly with one engine, simulating an engine failure, emphasizing their high standards. They were known as the best and having a career with that airline was my dream.

Our instructor, Mr. MacCarthur, was tough. He had been in the travel industry for 40 years and reminded you that it was a tough business and you had to work hard. If you were caught even slouching in his class, he made a point to make sure you didn't do it again. One day, he went around the room, asking each student to share their dream job when they graduated from the academy. Each person answered somewhat generically like "I want to be in tourism" or "I want to work at a travel agency." When he got to me, I was a little nervous. I succinctly stated, "I want to be a central reservation control agent for Optimal Airlines at their central headquarters in Tampa, Florida." I expected he would yell, "Did you hear anything I said? Did you hear they pick five out of 5,000 people? Who do you think you are?" He paused, and paced the room in what appeared to be deep thought. I tried to prepare for his negative response, and then he looked at me and said confidently, "And that you will be."

Knowing I had to figure out how to get my résumé into that pile of 500, I made a pact to myself that, to stand out, I would get a 100% in the hardest class, Computer Reservations. From what I was told, this was an impossible task, so I studied intensely and asked questions any time I was unsure.

After school, I was swimming in the pool. Mr. MacCarthur walked by and shockingly asked, "What are you doing? Why are you in the pool?" *Seriously, bud, can a girl get a break?* I thought to myself. He said, "You are supposed to be in the group interview for Optimal Airlines. They are in the conference room; go now!"

I rushed to my dorm room, put on my one and only business suit, plopped my wet hair up into a bun, and off to the conference room I went. I managed to slip in just in time, wet hair and all. They went around the room asking every person the same exact question: "Why do you want to work for Optimal Airlines?" It was clear that 49 applicants were going to say "I love people" or something very similar, so I thought, *Forget that, I have to stand out.*

I agreed that we were all there because we enjoyed people, but I said my own reason was because "I love computers!" Well, they all took note, probably noting "wet head likes computers—go figure." But it did the trick; they selected me for round two.

Round two was at their headquarters in Tampa, Florida. They selected 10 of us to go through the final interview process. The academy recruiter suggested that we carpool as it was a long drive up there. One of the candidates, Jill, was clearly from a wealthy family. Actually, most of the students there seemed to be from very wealthy families. Anyway, Jill had a supercharged Camaro with custom wheels, a custom paint job, and even a custom computer chip that made it extra loud and fast. *Coolest carpool ever,* I thought.

Due to the message alert light not working on my dorm telephone, I'd learned last minute about the interview date and hadn't gotten much sleep the night before, so they were fine with me sleeping in the car. They already had a driver and two navigators, so what could possibly go wrong? Well, things went very wrong. I woke up and saw signs for Disney World. Somehow, the navigator had the wrong address.

We were over two hours from Tampa. We had already been told that being early was critical and that they'd select and notify new hires before they left, so we felt there was no chance we would be considered. Nevertheless, we got the correct address and headed to Tampa. It was torrential rain pretty much the entire way there.

Finally, we arrived. We, of course, had no umbrellas. Dressed in suits and business heels, we ran through the parking lot toward the building. It was raining so hard, we could barely see in front of us, but I could see there was a large puddle coming up. I yelled, "Jump!" and did my best to leap over the large pond, making a splash upon landing as I hit the outer edge.

Just as I landed, I realized there were three men in black suits, white shirts, and black umbrellas standing right before me. Richard, the director, looked totally disgusted and said, "Explain what happened."

Standing in the pouring rain, feeling like my dream had just gone down the drain, I knew there was no good answer. Of all the possible answers, I said, "Sir, we were so excited to get here; we walked here." Not sure how that worked, but he made some kind of a grunting noise, pointed to the meeting room, and said, "Meet us there in 20 minutes." Jill, Sarah, Mary, and I took turns putting our soaked selves under the restroom hand dryer.

We headed to the waiting room, and they called us in, one by one, for what we felt was just a going-through-the-motions interview as we were three hours late. Trying to stay positive, I convinced myself and the team to make the best of it and treat this like a practice interview. "Let's be ourselves and do our best," I urged.

After the long interview, we hopped into the car to travel back to the academy. Jill let me drive her hotrod. That would have been awesome, except that the umbrella trio saw and heard us leave with her supercharged, super-loud car. Richard extended his head to look closely at who was driving the car and again had that disgusted look. By that point, we just had to laugh. It was definitely one of those laugh-so-you-don't-cry moments, so we chuckled about our answers to the questions from the interview. The funny question I got was, "Do you have different hairstyles?" Keep in mind, these people had only seen me with my hair soaking wet. I replied, "Yes. My hairstylist does different styles with my hair."

To my surprise, and I mean *surprise*, they called me to say I had the job. Unfortunately, my Camaro crew didn't get any offers, but they did get other job offers, so it worked out well for all of us.

So, I was now officially in my dream job. I absolutely loved it. After three months, I was promoted to the VIP desk where I worked with travel agents. They saw that I liked variety, so they gave me all kinds of unique opportunities. Things were going fantastic. People used to come to me all the time and say how much they admired my life. It was like living like a queen on minimum wage. I was soaring in every way.

Soon, however, there was turbulence in the air. My boss, Mr. Stan, had charts on his wall showing how profits were slowly but surely spiraling down. He warned that our core competency was being the best intrastate airline carrier, but we now had a few influential board members taking us outside of our core area to be an interstate versus intrastate airline. Many thought it was just one additional airline route and didn't see the big deal. Some figured they would just wait it out, thinking the new route would fail and be canceled. In addition to allowing that unclear vision to ripple throughout the organization, this philosophy of letting us fail contradicted our strong values of high quality, professionalism, and service excellence.

It was like a virus had spread through our once vibrant, happy team. Reservation agents were divided like two rival high school sports teams. Experienced agents who had been with the airline for years felt we were going against our business model and therefore doomed for failure. There was actually a high demand for the new route, but travel agents were leery as they could sense the lack of faith that our long-term employees had. Therefore, they booked very cautiously, fearing their customers would be left in the dust. By trying to give the new route a chance, we lost money, flying with planes half filled. Those of us who followed the vision kept booking passengers to fill the planes, while the others, sure the plan would fail, convinced travel agents to cancel reservations.

Even from the airline's central control office, the debates were increasing. Financially-focused reservation agents argued that every time we flew with less than 80% of the plane full, we lost money, putting the entire company at risk. Newer reservation control agents argued that if we keep canceling, no one would trust us so we would never fill the flights. Eventually, we went bankrupt as our number-one airline took a nosedive. For weeks, several of us got together for lunch and dinner. We didn't want the dream to end. We were the best, but even the best can fail when they are heading in two opposing directions. Thus, our dream took a crash landing.

SILO SECRET #9: With a clear mission, all understand and buy into a plan. Double vision divides the team. While it seems obvious, I worked with two companies who were soaring with sales but took a nosedive because part of the team was packing for Alaska and the other part was packing for California. Both were great places to go, but it is not possible to prepare for or be in both places at the same time.

SILO SECRET #10: The risk of doing nothing is dangerous. In school, then work, then college, I remember people were always talking about a bell curve. I can't say I understood the importance back then, but I get it now. When you have a *normal (normalized) bell curve*, there is unity in our society. Sure, we still want to compete with the Joneses, but it is mainly on silly things like who has a better lawn. But now, we are forming a non-normalized curve, which is very bad in statistics, serving as an alert that immediate attention is required. If you have two groups headed in opposite directions, both ultimately lose.

REFLECT:

Think of a positive team accomplishment. Was everyone clear on the vision?

_____

_____

Think of a personal vision you want to achieve. Are the people in your life aligned with your vision?

_____

_____

*"A clear vision, backed by definite plans, gives you a tremendous feeling of confidence and personal power." – **Brian Tracy** (Canadian-American motivational speaker and author of over 70 books.)*

2.4 A Clear Path Can Lead to Fortune

Now for a success story. Years after my time at Optimal Airlines, I worked for Tech Data. At a company meeting, leadership said our vision was to "be the number one distributor." I asked around for what people thought that meant. One thought it meant "be number one in sales," selling products at a low price, if necessary, to increase sales. Another person thought it meant "be number one in profits," ensuring high profit margins even if it meant less sales. Still another person thought it meant "be number one in quality," meaning quality over quantity, so if you had to slow sales to get it perfect, you did.

Not wanting a repeat of my double-vision-leads-to-collision experience, I asked leadership to clarify so that when we made our daily decisions, we were aligned and working toward a common vision to be number one in any area. Leadership thanked me for my question. At the next meeting, they made it clear that we wanted to "be the number one choice for our customers," explaining that our customers had two buttons to choose from on their phone. Our competitor, number one at the time, was the first button on our customer's speed dial. We were the second button.

Leadership explained that our mission was to create such a great experience that our customers were inspired to reach a little further to press the second button. We wanted customers to call us. It was that simple. That clarification helped us all know, at all times, what our mindset was for doing our job. We all worked together to ensure a great experience, and we ended up in several magazine articles for our success. It was awesome because it was a very united family with a united vision. Even when our price was a little higher, customers would say, "We're fine paying a little more to call you because you have such great customer support and technical support." Our clear path eventually led to us being featured in *Fortune* magazine as one of the fastest-growing companies. Hence the title, "A Clear Path Can Lead to *Fortune*."

Communities can have beautiful visions too

One small town has an event called "Friday Night Done Right," where all are invited to a party with safe, healthy choices including video games, card games, board games, sports, and more. As Debby, an event coordinator told me about their "one red light town," she explained that most previously felt the only thing to do in their small town was drink and smoke. This event brought everyone together to share positive choices. One man brought his entire family and said, "This is the first time we experienced joy."

This town, like others, has challenges. A big one was that it was once part of the opioid crisis, making it to the top of the drug overdose list. Caring about their community members, the townspeople investigated further and found that a key issue related to people accidentally mixing medications. Debby advised me that the drug that people were overdosing on is commonly prescribed as a pain killer for things like a broken leg. She added that people did not realize that mixing this seemingly harmless but potent pain medication with a glass of wine at dinner had the power to relax the heart to the point that it stops. Well, this little town made thousands of postcards and put them all over town to educate all ages. Something else happened in the process. People realized that they are connected to a community who truly cares. (Sweem, 2019)

SILO SECRET #11: In addition to creating a clear vision, a purposeful vision will more likely appeal to all four personality types, captivating both the people-focused and the outcome-focused view. Einstein spoke of how exciting goals inspire the mind to work toward a solution even as a person sleeps. We did just that at Tech Data. People would often say, "Last night, I had a great idea to improve a process."

SILO SECRET #12: The brain does not register the word "not," so when you state visions and goals, present the goal in a positive state so the mind can visualize what you want it to do. (Carter, 2017)

Example:

Less effective goal: Reduce percentage of children without access to healthy meals.

More effective goal: Increase percentage of children with access to healthy meals.

SILO SECRET #13: Another benefit of phrasing goals in a positive fashion is that it translates easily to charts. If all goals are stated positively, you can see at a glance if things are going well versus having to read under each chart and figure out if a percentage is good or bad.

REFLECT:

Do not imagine a pink elephant. Do not look down. Stop. Pause for a second here.

Did you visualize a pink elephant? Did you think about your eyes looking down? _____

If your brain is like most, it could not help but visualize the pink elephant and your eyes likely looked or were tempted to look down because your mind didn't register the "not" word. As mentioned, stating the positive goal also helps inspire people to visualize what you want to achieve. For example, instead of saying "do not do drugs," state "make positive choices" or some phrase where people visualize themselves making the right choices. Better yet, invite them to "Friday Night Done Right."

Imagine how you might think or act differently if people rephrased some of the common phrases below.

Common phrases:	Instead of common phrase, what if people said:
Have a nice day.	Don't have a bad day.
Drive safely.	Don't crash. Don't drive recklessly.
Be careful. Watch your step.	Don't trip. Don't fall.

While we have a lot of common phrases stated positively like those above, we have an opportunity to use the same positive language in other areas of our lives. Rather than say "Don't text and drive," we could say something like "Be safe, save your text for later." One time I was in a hurry and my daughter could have said, "Don't speed," but instead she said, "It is more important to me to have you arrive than it is to have you arrive on time." Her choice of words was a little lengthy, but it was positive and quite effective. Now I remind myself using positive self-talk, "Drive safely."

Chapter 2 Summary: *Whether you look at how the brain works (not registering the word "not") or Einstein's view that the brain loves to work on solving exciting problems, our best hope is to create a united vision where we are all onboard with the bigger picture mission. For now, we can keep it simple—safe air, water, and land. We need a new phrase, "United we stand [period]." Even the slightest division leads to collision.*

3. A NEW VIEW—POSSIBILITIES TO PURSUE

*"As you grow older, you will discover that you have two hands, one for helping yourself, the other for helping others." – **Audrey Hepburn** (British film and fashion icon; despite cancer, she worked as UNICEF Goodwill ambassador, helping Somalia, Kenya, the U.K., Switzerland, France, and the United States.)*

*"I believe that if you show people the problems, and you show them the solutions, they will be moved to act." – **Bill Gates** (Principal founder of Microsoft Corporation, investor, author, philanthropist, and humanitarian. He co-founded the Gates Foundation to improve global health.)*

3.1 Our Mission If We Choose

Philanthropists and funding organizations often say that we need to "get out of our silos" and collaborate. A big challenge is that the nonprofit agencies tasked with solving the world's issues are barely able to meet 30% of the current demand. I've seen the overwhelmed looks of despair in their eyes as people at those organizations realize, "There are not enough of us." Having spent much of my career implementing integrated solutions for business and nonprofit organizations, I know there are silo secrets that we can share to help nonprofit organizations help us. Quinn, a local city planner, stated that part of our challenge is that "our silos have the same goal, but don't speak the same lingo." Below is an illustrative chart showing the growing number of problems.

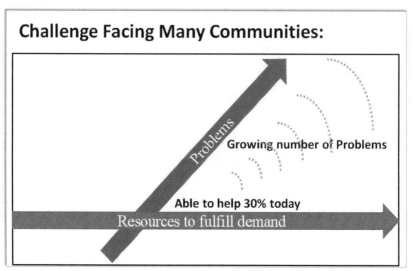

Figure 3.1a Above is high-level illustration of supply and demand issue.

Working with community service providers across multiple cities, I've observed that 30% seems to be the not-so-magic percentage of community members that providers are able to serve. Dave Ramsey, a well-known financial advisor, explains that 78% of people live from paycheck to paycheck. (CareerBuilder, 2017) The Juvenile Justice Citizens' Academy warns that nearly 70% of people in jail are there because they cannot afford bail, leaving 30% there for the right or wrong reason, depending on how you look at it. (Torgovnick May, 2018) "About 70 percent of the people who need mental-health treatment in this state can't get it," says Donna Wyche, manager of mental-health and homeless issues for Orange County. (Kunerth & Santich, 2019)

About seven years ago, I joined Peace4Tarpon (formally known as Peace4Communities and recognized for being the first trauma-informed community). (Peace4Tarpon, 2019) Since my career was in integrated systems design and development, several people said, "Peace4Tarpon has great ideas for the community but they could use a model." At first, I was flattered—sure, I am good-looking—but enough to be a model? Just kidding. I knew they meant they could use my background in systems and strategy to look at ways to magnify the great connections they were making in the community.

Responding to their request, I enthusiastically presented a design to make it easy for any child or adult to tap a button to find out where to go for help. When I presented the idea at the city hall meeting, everyone unanimously agreed, and the city manager approved funding on the spot for us to get a computer at our local community recreation center to host the application. Wow, things were moving quickly. Yes, you're ahead of me. It was too good to be true.

We had a planning meeting with a room full of top leaders who supported the community, schools, children, and families. I asked the question, "If I get every child who needs help to ask for help, can you handle it?" There was dead silence, and the looks on their faces clearly showed that the answer was no.

That day, it hit me that ignorance is bliss ... until reality hits. For me, the reality was painful, and that represented the moment that I had to figure out a way to help people see that there were answers outside their silo that could help us meet a critical supply and demand cycle—the demands of children and families in need. That project was like a dream come true, but I put it on hold to step back and figure out how I could first help them handle the demand. Otherwise, it was like a life preserver equipment store having a grand opening, but only having supplies for 30% of the customers.

While there are incredibly successful programs in place, many of those programs face that same barrier of not being able to fill demand. An amazing program that has figured out a way to help at-risk youth achieve college graduation rates greater than the national average has a wait-list to train mentors. In this case, they actually have a positive supply of volunteers lined up wanting to help, but they lack the capacity to teach them. While they have a solution model that exceeds expectations, they could use a business tool like *just-in-time inventory* (McKinney, 2019). The result is they are unable to fulfill the demand even though they have people eagerly lining up and ready to help. A strategic online or in-person training program to develop volunteers could enable them to maximize their extraordinary program.

Another innovative youth program was formed by combining the strengths of two diverse silo views. When the River Phoenix Center for Peacebuilding and the Gainesville Police Department united on community solutions, juvenile arrests dropped 53% from 2014 to 2018, yet the 30% number still applies. (RPCP, 2019) One police officer spoke enthusiastically about the program, but dismally shared that only 30% of youth were able to participate due to limited resources. With input from the business silo, they could magnify their amazing results, providing a repeatable model for other cities eager to follow their lead.

State governments, faith-based organizations, businesses, schools, and colleges are making a concerted effort to unify strengths. More and more, they are discovering that when they combine community and business best practices, they get remarkable results. The challenge is "we don't know what we don't know." Many times, the obstacle is simply that we are missing some knowledge that exists within silos in our own communities. My goal is to illustrate the challenge along with the solution. While the diagram below represents a fraction of the opportunities, the illustration reflects how we can combine the best methods used by community service organizations with the best methods used by businesses to achieve the best results for communities.

Figure 3.1b Interdependence enables business to community best practices.

As reflected in Figure 3.1b, community service organizations could leverage the above methods used by businesses to define more repeatable, sustainable solutions by utilizing tools like root-cause analysis. Likewise, businesses could leverage new information from science and nonprofit providers to help improve employee health, productivity, and attendance. Many times, organizations are unaware of information readily available in the silo next door. By combining best practices, we can get the best of both worlds.

Not that we need another challenge to add to this integrated puzzle, but a key challenge as described by my local chief of police is that the internet and social media can perpetuate issues. A person can press a couple buttons and cause thousands of problems. Knowing that computers can magnify greatness or sadness, people in information technology are very aware of risk mitigation strategies. Most seek to optimize value-added items like high-quality products and services and minimize not-so-great items like errors or items with a negative impact. By working together, we can combine business and community organization strengths to reach optimal solutions.

Imagine if we could tap some of the top tools used by the business silos to help community service providers use repeatable solution techniques to magnify their greatness. They could enhance their knowledge of tools like economies of scale and ways to minimize administrative costs, allowing them to reallocate staff to more client-focused, value-added activities. In the business world, they would say we are only fulfilling 30% of the market demand. They'd get a task force, or whatever departments necessary, to increase our market share by defining an action plan and milestone goals aimed to meet 100% of the demand.

Over the past year, I have personally seen incredibly strong people have tears in their eyes as they say, "There are not enough of us." Our mission, if we choose, is to help our own communities. All ages and all denominations are welcome. The Florida Dream Center is growing the Adopt-a-Block program where they go out every Saturday, rain or shine, to say, "Hey, how can we help?" (Lasasso & Cleveland, 2019) At recent Saturday events, they have had over 10 different denominations all working together. All faiths and all ages are joining in.

Later, we will discuss a new way of thinking. We'll share success stories and tips to handle overwhelming demands on staff and volunteers.

SILO SECRET #14: While many communities are facing serious challenges in meeting supply and demand, there are pockets with organizations eager and willing to share best practices to help. In many cases, these pocket areas are already uniting two silos to achieve more efficient, effective solutions.

One example of a pocket making a difference is Jacksonville, Florida. They initiated a pilot program called Project Saves Lives that united two silos and reduced repeat opioid overdoses by 70% in just one year. Dr. Pomm, the creator of the program, stated "Our model right now is the only model I know of in the country." (Denison, 2018)

SILO SECRET #15: There are several evidence-based practices being implemented statewide. With the Wraparound model to help community members use strengths to meet their goals, they have proven that with full engagement (high fidelity), the program has great results. Yet, when they have partial utilization (low fidelity), the statistics actually show that conditions get worse for families and communities. (Radlauer-Doerfler & Thomas, 2015) In chapter 10, we'll highlight business models for statewide implementation that we can leverage to ensure high fidelity.

SILO SECRET #16: There are some communities where businesses are sharing their skills versus donating money. By sharing business tips and tools such as the Lean approach covered later in this chapter, the benefits of the skill donations often help the bottom line more than the monetary donations.

REFLECT:

Einstein liked to prompt thinking via questions. In the spirit of Einstein, would it be possible for us to increase one of the percentage of community service requests fulfilled from 30% to 31%?

_____

_____

"Amazing things happen when you share your hopes and dreams, and you may end up helping more people than you can ever imagine." – Christian Bucks (At the age of 8, he introduced the concept of Buddy Benches to his school in America, offering a solution for lonely children to find companions.)

3.2 Unlimited Resources, Starting with Grandmas

Not enough of us – bad case of *kufungisisa* across the world

Chances are you or someone you know has got a bad case of *kufungisisa*. The World Health Organization estimates that, globally, more than 300 million people have this condition. While nonprofit organizations are striving to raise awareness, the World Health Organization advises that across the globe, *kufungisisa* takes a life every 40 seconds, even though it is treatable. It impacts every race, every sex, every country, and even every socioeconomic status. Young, healthy people who we think have the world ahead of them die every day of this tragic, yet treatable, epidemic. Dr. Darlene Williams says that it takes the life of a veteran every 15 minutes. Be aware that if you know anyone between the ages of 15 to 29 years old, *kufungisisa* is a leading cause of death for this age group. Even famous people who "have it all" (good health, good looks, money, and mansions) are not immune.

So what exactly is *kufungisisa*, you might ask? In Africa, it means "think too much." It is known in many countries as depression. Some call it mental illness. A lot of people don't like those words. A university in Florida explained that they have the mental health treatment office in an area that is intentionally away from the main activities because students say that they do not want to be seen asking for help. Prince Harry of England has a different view. While many are trying to get rid of the stigma surrounding mental illness, Prince Harry talks about a need for "mental fitness."

Doctors across the world agree that *kufungisisa* can be treated, and the deaths can be avoided. So what is stopping us? How is it possible that so many die unnecessarily? If you get down to it, experts concur that the answer is often related to supply and demand. Community service providers are increasingly saying that there are simply "not enough of us to go around" to treat those with the condition. As noted earlier, there is also the challenge that it is difficult to navigate the system to get help.

Time for a New View – Unlimited Resources to Help, Starting with Grandmas

The statistics are overwhelming, causing many to feel like there is no end in sight. One day, Dr. Chibanda, a doctor in Africa, received a call from the mother of one of his patients. She explained that she could not afford the $15 to travel to his office to save her daughter's life. This was the turning point where Dr. Chibanda decided something had to change.

Realizing that traditional methods could not meet the needs of 90% of the people in his country, he brainstormed with friends, family, and colleagues to arrive at a new solution. It dawned on him that there is a resource that we have all been overlooking. He said, "One of the most reliable resources we have in Africa is grandmothers." This inspired him to create a "Friendship Bench" program, which trains grandmothers in evidence-based talk therapy from a friendship bench. He empowered the grandmas with listening skills and advanced skills in behavior activation. Last but not least, he ensured the grandmas had support themselves via a cell phone.

Limitless Possibilities – from Zimbabwe to the U.S.A.

The bottom line is these grandmas are embracing this opportunity—and wait until you hear their results! In 2006, Dr. Chibanda started his first group of grandmothers. Today, there are hundreds of grandmothers working in more than 70 communities. In 2016 alone, more than 30,000 people received treatment on a Friendship Bench from a grandmother in a community in Zimbabwe. This amazing solution has now been published in the *Journal of the American Medical Association*. These grandmas are a legend in their own time.

In Dr. Chibanda's inspirational Ted Talk, which I encourage you to watch, he shares how the "results show that six months after receiving treatment from a grandmother, people were still symptom-free: no depression; suicidal ideation completely reduced." Since "grandmothers were more effective at treating depression than doctors," Dr. Chibanda is expanding the program. To illustrate his point of unlimited resources, he explains that there are more than 600 million people currently aged above 65 in the world. By the year 2050, there will be 1.5 billion people aged 65 and above. His eyes light up as he invites us to, "Imagine if we could create a global network of grandmothers in every major city in the world, who are trained in evidence-based talk therapy ..."

This astounding solution is spreading through the nation, as well as other countries. In my community, we have psychiatrists, social workers, and lots of grandmas from the Kinship Care organization raising their hands to hop on a bench. All kinds of grandmas are signing up, and I can tell you, grandmas are persistent, calling and asking, "When will the benches be ready?" They are eager to help. Two college students, too young to be grandmas but wanting to help, offered to use their architectural skills to help us with the design of the benches. The idea is inspiring people to think outside the bench.

All Ages Can Play – Kids are Setting up Buddy Benches

When then 8-year-old Christian Bucks learned that he and his family may be moving to a new country, his mind was filled with questions. Christian thought he was moving to Germany, so his mom showed him brochures about the possible new schools he might attend. Concerned that he would be the new kid with no friends, he was intrigued by a "Buddy Bench" that one of the schools in Germany showed in their brochure.

Even though Christian didn't move to Germany, he presented the idea to his principal, Matthew Miller, and they installed a Buddy Bench at his current school. Their project was covered by the local newspaper and then went viral. Now, Christian continually accepts invitations to travel to other schools to support their Buddy Benches. There are an estimated 2,000 schools with benches across the United States along with about a dozen other countries. Christian said, "I didn't like to see kids lonely at recess when everyone is just playing with their friends." One 2004 study in London found 80% of kids between eight and 10 years old described being lonely at some point at school. (Berguno, 2004) These benches are a simple way to help kids connect and make new friends. Buddy Benches are popping up on school playgrounds around the world.

Yellow is for Hello – College Students Can Participate Too! (Fiorella, 2016)

Another incredible program involves yellow benches. Sam Fiorella created "Yellow Is For Hello" friendship benches for college students in memory of his son, Lucas. Following Lucas' death, many students came forward and said that Lucas was always there to provide a friendly hello for those who needed it. By promoting peer-to-peer conversations, there is less of a mental health stigma so more students ask for help when needed. A study by Sensei Marketing showed that nearly 30 schools in Canada have adopted the Yellow Is For Hello campaign and there was an 18% increase in the number of students asking for mental health services.

Strategic Community Service Programs Can Provide Significant Help
Statistics show that a strategic volunteer program enables volunteers to be four to six times more valuable to an organization. Such a program helps volunteers feel better too, as they feel like they are able to contribute more value to a great cause. All the types of benches are an excellent model that is inviting and repeatable. Participants on both ends experience tremendous value.

SILO SECRET #17: Many world problems come down to supply and demand, but there are millions who want to be part of the solution and just need an avenue, or maybe just a simple bench, to help.

SILO SECRET #18: Rather than feel overwhelmed when demand is greater than supply, have a seat, sit on a bench, and figure out where you may be able to get some relief with your heavy load. Just like conversations, the bench works both ways. Some days, you can offer a listening ear. Other days, you may be the one in need of a listening ear.

SILO SECRET #19: The above programs demonstrate that all ages, 10-year-old kids, 20-year-old college students, and 80-year-old grandmas, can help. Grandmas (Friendship Benches), college peer-to-peer support (Yellow is for Hello Benches), and elementary kids (Buddy Benches) are just the beginning of possibilities of how we can connect to solve problems together. Looking at this from Prince Harry's point of view, people can jog to the bench to get physically fit and then chat to get mentally fit.

SILO SECRET #20: Strategically designed volunteer programs can empower volunteers to add four to six times more value. In Chapter 4, we'll cover the 5 Steps to Success model as a method that can be utilized to strategically engage volunteers to align and grow with an organization's goals.

SILO SECRET #21: In surveying families as well as organizations, nearly all expressed a desire to contribute to the betterment of our community. An example of the endless possibilities happened when a few dads built an area for kids to grow vegetables at a pre-kindergarten school. While it was not quite a bench, the kids and dads sat together playing in the dirt, making sustainable soil. The school was thrilled as the number of male mentors went up. Parents were thrilled because the kids loved to eat the vegetables that they grew. Attendance is also way up and teachers aren't sure if it is because kids love coming to school now or the dirt helped boost their immune systems. (Knight, Gilbert, & Blakeslee, 2017)

REFLECT:

Was there ever a time in your life when it would have been nice to just sit and have someone listen?

_____

_____

Do you sometimes feel like your demand is greater than your supply? (at work or at home)

_____

_____

"Economics—supply and demand—that is it."– **Don Novello** (Excerpt from Father Guido Sarducci's "Five-Minute University" on all you need to remember from college economics.) (Played character of Father Guido Sarducci on *Saturday Night Live*, writer, film director, producer, actor, singer, and comedian.) (NBC, 2007)

3.3 A New Formula for Supply and Demand

Chugging down an extra-strength headache aspirin and antacid pills during our brief elevator introduction, Jim was a great example of an overwhelmed business person faced with the need to do more with less. Forcing out a zealous laugh, he said, "I love my job. So what do you do?" Keeping the conversation light, I smiled and said, "I make good numbers go up and bad numbers go down." Jim replied, "I've got the job for you!" He then added, "All jokes aside, I can't sleep at night knowing that people's lives depend on me to produce medical supplies and I'm sinking fast." I asked him if he had heard about a streamlining tool called Lean. As Jim exited the opening elevator door, he looked down at his belly and jokingly said, "Do I look like I know about lean?"

Since I had another client in the building, I was in the shared café later in the day and heard a hearty voice loudly say, "Hey, Lean Lady." It turned out to be Elevator Jim. He said, "I spoke to my son and he urged me to learn more about Lean." As he offered to buy my coffee, I assured him that I would give him $1.93 worth of insight with a money-back guarantee. Being in the same building, our paths crossed often so we started the "Lean Latte Lessons" tradition where we met at least once a week over coffee. Below is a highlight of our Lean Latte Lessons along with how Jim applied Lean to turn things around in less than six weeks.

Traditional View:

With a traditional view of supply and demand, the assumption is the demand is all on your shoulders. The thought is that you need to do it yourself, sink or swim. The view is often that the only way to solve the Supply and Demand challenge is to increase supply. The challenge is demand is often rapidly growing due to factors such as an increase in quantity, complexity, time to solve, and turnover as people sometimes head out the door when the going gets tough.

A New, Lean View:

The new view is to look at ways to reduce waste. Lean management is a continuous improvement approach where everyone is invited to identify small incremental changes to make things easier, faster, or better. You can use the eight-character word "downtime" like a checklist as you think of ways to improve the efficiency and quality of a process. (GoLeanSixSigma.com, 2019)

Checklist	8 areas of waste	Description
D	Defects	Need resources to correct
O	Overproduction	Produce too much of a product
W	Waiting	Need to wait on prior step
N	Non-utilized talent	Employees not engaged effectively
T	Transportation	Transport when not needed
I	Inventory	Inventory or information is sitting idle
M	Motion	Unnecessary motion due to setup, etc.
E	Extra processing	Performing unneeded activity

Above table illustrates eight areas to include in a check-list when working to reduce waste.

As I shared with Jim how Lean is a mindset to streamline activities and minimize waste, he chuckled as he recalled studying videos from his college days. He explained to his son how they played movies of people working, but when they played the movie in fast motion, it was comical to watch as people ran in circles or back and forth to get things done. Jim's son teased, "So, Dad, when you go into the room three times looking for the glasses that are on your head, it may look inefficient on the video."

Creating a better future with Lean:

Jim and his son were having fun using a piece of string to map out the production path to see where steps could be saved. They mapped out a current state diagram and then proposed small incremental changes to make the future state a little better. Just like the scientific model suggests, they tested their hypothesis. When it worked well, that became the new current state with the opportunity to continue to grow better using that same mindset to:

- Prevent problems (educate to eliminate or reduce problems)

- Simplify (reduce the complexity of requests along with the time to solve the request)

- Optimize the workflow (find ways to improve efficiency by streamlining the flow of work)

- Find ways to improve lives (look for ways to make life and work easier and more enjoyable)

- Increase satisfaction for staff, clients, and vendors (partner to find better, easier methods for all)

The proof is in the numbers:

One commonly overlooked area is non-utilized talent. With Jim's son Jim Jr. being an accountant, we tapped his talent to help us monitor and measure before and after results. Running the numbers, he showed that they had 80,000 hours of work and only 40,000 hours of resources to get it done. Jim instinctively said, "No way I can double my staff," but that was the traditional thinking. Below are the three steps Jim took to get on track with a new Lean way of thinking, along with the results.

(1) **Classify your to-do pile into small, medium, and large.** In this situation, here is what we found.

- 1,000 small issues with average of 30 minutes to solve = Demand of 30,000 minutes

- 500 medium issues with average of 80 minutes to solve = Demand of 40,000 minutes

- 50 large issues with average of 200 minutes to solve = Demand of 10,000 minutes

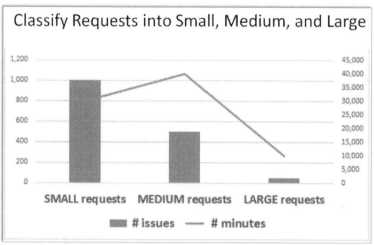

Figure 3.3a Classifying requests is often a great first step to devising a strategy.

(2) Don't sweat the small stuff. Give others some tips to help you with the small requests.

- We created funny, inviting booklets to show how to fix the top five small requests.

- By following the easy steps, people solved 50% of small requests completely on their own.

- By doing the first few steps, people helped cut the average resolution time to 15 minutes.

- This effort cut the time spent on small requests from 30,000 minutes to just 7,500 minutes.

- The result was that overall demand went from 80,000 minutes to 57,500 minutes!

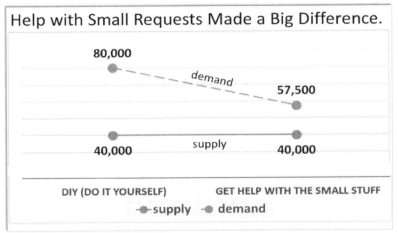

Figure 3.3b Getting help with small requests reduced the demand.

(3) Invite a few helpers to further grow skills to help with medium tasks.

Some helpers were interested in growing their skills to step up their game to help with medium-sized tasks. With their help, all requests were fulfilled. Demand equaled supply. We did it!

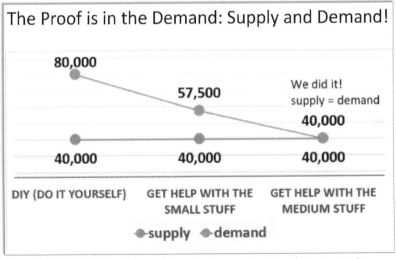

Figure 3.3c With help with medium-sized requests, Supply now met Demand.

A New View on Supply and Demand Partnerships

The new way of viewing supply and demand focuses on continual improvement and partnering with your community, employees, or volunteers to prevent or solve issues or requests together. Just three minutes of basic troubleshooting steps on a 30-minute problem saves 10% of your time. Preventing problems or minimizing the time it takes to solve a problem then reduces the demand on you. Both Jim and his son mentored local college students. They invited the local Lean Six Sigma college students to tour their organization and make observations on even more ways to streamline operations.

Two-For-One Special

Nearly everyone likes a two-for-one special. When you have a lot of issues, it is a great time to look for opportunities to solve more than one issue at the same time. Jim Jr. was impressed when one of his computer support employees stopped by another department to help with a computer question and ended up solving two requests while there. They ended up making these field visits a part of their process. The visits often prevented more complex issues from developing.

Another benefit of the proactive support visits was that they provided an opportunity to share quick productivity tips on ways to better use Microsoft Excel, Word, and PowerPoint. Customers loved the convenient training tailored to what they needed to know. Lastly, it often turned 10 or so unplanned inbound support calls into a single planned visit. Helping with goals created a spirit of collaboration.

SILO SECRET #22: Even if you empower people to help for eight hours on a two-week (80-hour) project, it equates to a 10% productivity gain. Helpers can include volunteers, interns, or employees helping in another area to assist with the organizational goals and/or grow their own skills.

SILO SECRET #23: Lean provides a list of eight areas of waste that can be improved to save resources. Saved time can be reallocated to value-added activities to further contribute to existing or new goals. With Lean, everyone is invited to be a part of positive change. While this model started out being used in the business world, it is a natural fit to engage communities in improving their part of the world. Many hospitals are already onboard, improving quality and service delivery via these tools.

REFLECT:

Do you have someone who would like to help you (a child, an intern, a mentoree, a trainee at work)? Try it. (Ex: They get experience or a mentor, and you may get an extra 30 minutes a week in your schedule.)

"Never get so busy making a living that you forget to make a life." – **Dolly Parton** (American singer, songwriter, multi-instrumentalist, record producer, actress, author, businesswoman, and philanthropist. Known primarily for her work in country music.)

3.4 Five Is Less Than Four. Tell Me More.

"No way! That four-day workweek thing will never work here." Since I tend to implement things before they become popular, these were generally the words I heard when I initially mentioned the idea of a four-day workweek. So, I learned a much easier way to propose these type of programs, and it worked every time. Looking at it from the view of the four personalities or even the simple two values (people-focused vs. outcome-focused), most tend to associate a four-day workweek with the warm and fuzzy *people-focused* benefits. Decision makers with an *outcome focus* often resist this type of program. Even though four days multiplied by 10 hours is still 40 hours, the employee is getting paid for taking a day off, right? It definitely sounds like the employee wins at the expense of the employer. So, let's look closer and see if that is true.

Knowing that I had to get buy-in and approval from a finance (outcome-focused) view, I changed the wording of this program to "Rapid Response

Program" and provided evidence of how we would increase ROI (return on investment) by delivering faster and enabling more revenue via this program. I didn't ask for approval to implement a four-day workweek. Instead, I asked the chief financial officer, "If we have an idea that will enable us to get 30% more output with the same resources, would you consider that idea?" For my clients who got wind of the idea and said, "No way," I asked them, "If we have an idea that will enable you to get guaranteed 24-hour turnaround, even when you submit projects on Friday night, would you consider that program?" This helped them open their minds to consider the tremendous employer and client benefits.

With this ultimately benefiting our clients, I let them decide, asking, "How many days would be a fair amount of time for us to demonstrate the benefits in order for you to approve or disapprove the program?" Lynn, our main client, like most, answered, "A couple months seems fair." Technically, I just got approval to implement this radical program for a couple months. Now, I just had to get approval to keep it going. That was easy because the new status quo generated substantial benefits. This approach also helped because it created a spirit of working together to work out any improvement areas as it was viewed as a pilot program. The clients quickly became supporters as they experienced the new benefits.

After getting buy-in from the leaders and clients, I reminded the employees, "This is a great benefit to all of you, even those who choose to work five days versus four days, but we have to work together to make sure we communicate and ensure this program works smoothly."

You are likely asking, "How in the world does this help those who stay on a five-day schedule?" and "Doesn't four days mean four days for everyone?" Actually, my experience is just like the studies show—about 25% of employees will prefer to work five days, and that is great! Those employees will enhance continuity and communications to help the flow and transition of work from one day to another. They also love it when it is 5 p.m. on Friday and they get to go home and let scheduled staff handle last-minute weekend projects.

According to a global survey of nearly 3,000 employees across eight countries conducted by the Workforce Institute at Kronos Incorporated, 71% of employees say work interferes with their personal life. (The Workforce Institute at Kronos Incorporated and Future Workplace, 2018) This is an opportunity for that service profit chain to do wonders (improve employee satisfaction, which improves customer satisfaction and ultimately improves profits) (Heskett, W. Earl Sasser, & Schlesinger, The Service Profit Chain, 1997).

Below is an example of how Joe can have bingo and weekends with the kids, Mary can go on her weekend excursions, and Lynn and Lou can volunteer. They will also brag about how your progressive company gives them flexibility to volunteer in the community, etc. Some complimented how we helped the environment (less fuel, less traffic). Traditionally, we just list "OOO" (out of office) for time off, but I went ahead and listed examples of how the schedule helps employees improve their work-life balance.

Team Member:	Monday	Tuesday	Wednesday	Thursday	Friday	Saturday	Sunday	Work Hours
Joe	10	10	bingo	10	10	time with kids		40
Mary	jet lag	10	10	10	10	weekend travel		40
Lou	8		8	8	8	coach	8	40
Lynn	7	10	7	10	volunteer	6		40
Mike		10	10		10	10		40

Team Totals:	Monday	Tuesday	Wednesday	Thursday	Friday	Saturday	Sunday	Total Hours
Hours scheduled	25	40	35	38	38	16	8	200
Hours needed	25	40	35	38	38	14	10	200

While the employees are bragging about their benefits, finance and leadership are thrilled with the results. Below is an illustration of how schedules can help balance low and high workload projections.

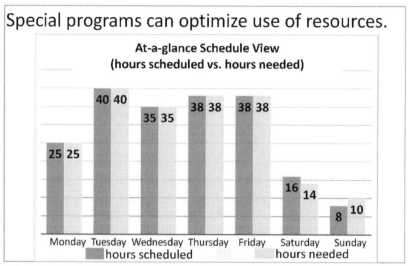

Figure 3.4a Four-day work programs can be used to balance resources.

Below are some tips on how to get started on creating a new schedule.

1. Manage expectations that individuals will not get all their schedule preferences.

2. Have each employee give you their preferences on the schedule. (e.g., five day vs. four day; flexible schedule; any time of day they would really like to be off work).

3. Create a spreadsheet to plan out "needed hours" based on workload.

4. Work to fill in hours based on employee preferences to best meet employer needs.

5. Create modules or blocks of work to easily label and pass work between shifts.

6. Put quality controls in place to ensure quality checks along the way.

7. Publicize wins. In our case, we earned new business by being able to quickly turn around requests. Our marketing team actually publicized the wins for us!

At first, it can be like a strategic puzzle figuring out the right schedule to optimize business demands with personal preferences. You'll soon learn the hard-to-fill times. For me, it was typically weekends, so when we hired people, we posted for weekend hours. Sometimes, we agreed to give a little perk to the person who ended up working Super Bowl weekend, for example.

As people get better at working on modules, you can evolve to have more flexible schedules where you post a schedule online and give people the opportunity to coordinate together if they want to swap a shift. The supervisor can still approve it, but it saves time. An example of the type of thing that would happen every now and then would be something like, "Hey, congratulations on your son graduating this week. Do you need to swap a shift?" The employees would agree to trade a four-hour block, assuming the supervisor approved. This created a high level of satisfaction for employees as well as their families.

SILO SECRET #24: When you have a special program to introduce that sounds like an incredible benefit for employees (e.g., flexible schedule, four-day workweek, work from home) be sure to put on your employer *outcome-focused* hat and speak that language when you present the idea to finance and leadership. When you talk with employees, inspire them with the incredible *people-focused* benefits, but also remind them of the need to achieve the organizational benefits to ensure ongoing success.

REFLECT:

Is there an area of your life where more flexibility would improve your life?

Chapter 3 Summary: *In many areas, demand exceeds supply. Businesses have been doing the "do more for less" thing for years, so they have decades of practice. Really, it is about time available and time required. If you can help educate people to prevent issues, that is a great way to reduce demand. If you have grandmas, college students, and kids all willing to help, you have increased your supply, and you are building hope by creating a path for people to build a better world.*

4. BRINGING OUT THE BEST IN YOU— GRAVITATING TO GREATNESS

"You must expect great things of yourself before you can do them." – **Michael Jordan** (Considered one of the best basketball players, Olympic athlete, businessperson, and actor.)

"The universe is so well balanced that the mere fact that you have a problem also serves as a sign that there is a solution." – **Steve Maraboli** (Behavioral scientist and author of *Life, The Truth, and Being Free.*)

4.1 Raging to Raving Customers

Right out of college, I got a job at one of the fastest-growing computer distribution companies. Looking back, I was very lucky to graduate in an employee market. While in college, I also worked part-time at a Big 3 accounting firm. With that on my résumé, I got to choose from the best of companies, and I chose Tech Data. I wanted to do every part of the system development life cycle, and they were happy to let me do it all— plus free T-shirts, free cruises, black-tie holiday parties, and fun parties for all the silos.

Even though I worked in the big development tower, the for-profit tower, I made friends with the nonprofit tower. They had fun beach parties, pool parties, billiard parties, ping pong parties, Seinfeld-marathon parties; if anyone could find an excuse to party, it was them. They worked in positions that supported the sales and development tower. They were part of departments such as administration, purchasing, credit, customer returns, and vendor returns. I thought we were all living the good life, but I learned that although they loved their nightlife, they didn't always feel the same way about their day life.

I eventually realized that they were great at parties because they needed an escape from their day job. I asked them, "Why is it that you view your job as bad when people would love a chance to work for our company?"

My friend Joanie said, "Well, for one, I get yelled at all the time; customers yell at me every day." I could not imagine. She said, "Customers don't care that it is not my fault; they yell anyway." Hearing my friends jump in about how hard their job was due to these screaming customers, I wanted to help. My friends all said, "No, that is just the way it is; our job stinks; customers will always yell at us."

Finally, I convinced one of my friends to let me try to help her out. So we took a small step. We selected a common scenario where customer voices were loud, causing her to have to remove her telephone headset.

In talking through the challenge, we realized that when the company started, most of the people were all in one room. It was kind of like a village where people could walk over and easily talk to a coworker to speed up processing on an urgent order or ensure clear communication. Hey, you could pretty much hear all the conversations, so communication was simple, sometimes too loud, sometimes a little annoying, but everyone was kept up-to-date. The employees and the customers all knew what to expect, and if there was a gap, people could easily work together to fix the gap or explain and manage expectations.

But now, we were rapidly growing. Vice presidents (VPs) used to say things like "34% compound annual growth." For us, that meant you were busier every day. VPs also talked about "price declines due to globalization" and "we must work on 3% margins," which meant "do more with less." Small tasks grew to such large volumes that the steps quickly evolved into small departments in different rooms and, in some cases, different buildings. This quickly resulted in communication gaps— like telling a customer three days to get a computer when the new turnaround time was now five to seven days. Basically, what we had was a failure to communicate. So, we got a few people together and agreed we needed to make sure we delivered on promises. In the short-term, we agreed to tell customers the way it was now. We set expectations to say it would take up to seven days for a customer to get a computer. Yelling was greatly reduced simply by setting *clear expectations*.

My friend updated me. "Customers don't yell anymore, but they are not exactly thrilled to wait seven days." Joanie said they still complain a little, and she repeated the same phrase as she had earlier, saying, "That is just the way it is." It took some convincing, but she agreed to try some basic tips and see if we could improve things a little more. Our goal was to find a way to cut a half day off the process, a small improvement. Joanie called a couple friends from other departments to map out the timeline.

Current cycle time:
SALES enters order → CREDIT approves → PACKING of order
Day 1   Days 2-3   Day 4-5

→SHIPPING of order →CUSTOMER moans
   Day 6   Day 7

I asked questions like whether credit and packing could happen at the same time, and they responded, "No." When I asked why, they responded, "It has always been that way—can't change it." As they realized that they had already made a small change, and had gotten pretty good results, going from angry customers to mildly annoyed customers, they were a little more open to change. What minor change could we try next? It was like the scientific model where you test your theory. If it doesn't work, scratch that experiment. Worst case, we could just go back to the way it once was—seven days.

I had a friend in the credit department, so I asked her. She said, "Ugh, we are slammed with screens of orders to approve, and then we get calls to check a particular order and that slows us down more! I am exhausted. I don't want to talk about work." I got assigned to help the department with a system improvement, so the timing was great. We automated a lot of the credit steps, so if a customer had a great credit line, for example, the order was sent right to packing.

That was a computer program change that helped—but I was still working to help my friends see how they could make their lives easier at work and ultimately go home happier campers. So I asked, "What percentage of customers get their credit approved?" It was high, something like 98%. So, I asked if it would make sense to do packing and credit at the same time, especially for high-priority orders next in line. While the initial answer was, "No, it has always been this way," one person said, "Why not try one order?" It only takes one person to try out an idea.

They started naturally brainstorming on improvement options. Someone asked, "Why do we put the computers on the shelf and then someone else has to pull them off?" and "Why not place orders in a staging area to help speed things up by getting the products closer to the door?" So we decided to try that too. They were creating a *culture of continual improvement*.

Even when they talked to a customer who did not like the process or wait time, it was different because they said things like, "Thank you for your input; we are growing fast, so your input is helping us improve." Then, we would tweak another process, test it out and implement, and document a new method once we proved it worked well. By doing credit and packing in parallel, we cut the cycle time from seven days to five days and kept improving.

New cycle time:
SALES enters order → CREDIT approves → PACKING of order
Day 1   Days 2-3   Days 2-3

→SHIPPING of order →CUSTOMER happier
  Day 4   Day 5

Customers and employees were much happier. More importantly, employees had the confidence and skills to continue to improve service and efficiency.

SILO SECRET #25: Only 15% of people are natural Problem Solvers, but the other 85% can easily learn and enjoy the reward of improving the way things are done. This is based on True Colors' personality population statistics.

SILO SECRET #26: With the Lean model, the engagement of all employees to identify and implement improvements is often referred to as a culture of continual learning and improvement.

SILO SECRET #27: When ideas make life easier and more pleasant for employees, the employees tend to be happier, resulting in them providing better service. This then creates more satisfied customers and ultimately results in higher ROI. This is called the *service-profit chain*. (Heskett, Jones, Loveman, Jr., & Schlesinger, 2008)

SILO SECRET #28: In the situation just described, we managed expectations and were candid with clients on continual improvement goals, inviting them to participate. With clients, we found that they liked the fact that we were listening to them and working to improve the situation.

SILO SECRET #29: Parallel processing is a strategy often used with computers, but this method works with manual processes too. Like a buffet line that is set up to go faster by providing access from both sides, we can look at activities that can happen in parallel. We can also look at activity prerequisites to see how we can arrange activities to happen sooner if a person is available to work on that activity. This relates to the Lean *wait time reduction* to speed up the process. (Principles to improve access, 2016)

REFLECT:

Try to think of a task that you may be able to streamline to make your life easier or better.

_____

_____

*"Growth is never by mere chance; it is the result of forces working together." – **James Cash Penney*** (Founder of J.C. Penney stores, which survived the Great Depression by providing good value for customers.)

4.2 Helpless to World-Class in 90 Days

This is an I-can't-believe-I-didn't-get-fired story. While working on a systems development team, I volunteered to do the American Cancer Society's Relay for Life, but I got an email back saying, "You are the only volunteer, so our department will not have a team, and you will not be able to volunteer." To this day, I can't believe I did this, but I sent an email to our brand new CIO (Chief Information Officer) with the subject line, "Permission to jump ship, sir." I asked if I could volunteer on another team for another department.

From what I heard, this prompted the CIO to ask his assistant, "Who is this Lisa lady?" The assistant replied, "Lisa is the person you call when you have a problem that no one can solve; somehow, you just carbon copy Lisa and the problem gets solved." I was basically doing interdependence way before it became cool. Most of the time, I just figured out who was missing from the problem-solving table and then inspired that person to join in on the fun.

Back to the "jump ship" email. I knew that, being a brand-new CIO of the largest department, the CIO would likely want his department to have a team. It was a big deal. Even the president stopped by these events. He told his assistant, "We need a team, fast." At that time, we were working on a major software upgrade, and I was working massive hours like everyone else, so I didn't want a time-consuming role like captain. I just wanted to be on a team to help a good cause.

You may have guessed it; I was voted captain. The CIO asked me how much money I needed. I said $250. He opened up his wallet with a bulging stack of money and pulled out $300. Note to self: when someone asks how much money you need, give them a bigger number than what is in your head. ☺ Anyway, I told the team we would be up all night, running for 24 hours around a track, so we should have a theme where it made sense that we looked messy and wild. They came up with "Code Warriors." We had a blast, got tents, tiki torches, a military net, and the CIO's wife went out and got us all squirt guns—after all, we were warriors.

They had competitions for creative food, best campsite, best team spirit, and most distance covered— we won all four plaques. We may or may not have kept the other teams up all night too. People from other companies came over, offering me jobs in front of the CIO. I had to laugh as my boss' boss was standing there watching me get job offers. He said, "You have done this before." I said, "Put me in the right spot, and I'll do this for you." Keep in mind, at the time I was basically in a cave doing systems integration development. It was a high-paying job where they didn't want you to leave the cave, and I wanted sunlight.

The next week, a manager named Sue pulled me out of the cave and said they were promoting me to be in charge of all the company's problems— 25,000 requests per month and growing. This included requests for new employees, new customers, technical issues, network issues, printer issues, training, support questions, and more. Oh boy. The phrase "be careful what you ask for, you may get it" definitely came to mind. For over 25 years, my job has been solving problems, but to this day, that was the biggest and most rewarding challenge. The things we learned are so relevant to challenges we are having in our community that I will share how we took this supply and demand issue and soared to be world-class.

While some think it is impossible to "grow out of business," we were on that high-risk path. The help desk call volume kept going up, and the volume of irritated customers and employees was also going up because the team did not have the resources to answer the phone, let alone solve their problems. Being that I was very new to it all, Sue updated me that there was a Help Desk Institute (HDI) Conference in California. I checked it out and saw that the best of the best were appearing at an HDI excellence panel. I said to the team, "I am off to California to learn from the experts." On the plane ride there, I had spreadsheets out and did the math. It was physically impossible for us to solve the backlog of problems or even keep up with the current problems.

Literally, the only physically possible solution was to engage our customers and peer support to solve our problems together. My plan was to integrate departments, which involved cross-training. This involved integrating two large groups that stayed in their own silos, except for company meetings when they mostly still mingled within their same silo group. The technical team often labeled the people-focused support team members as "warm and fuzzy." Similarly, the support team often labeled the high-tech people as "cold, numbers people." My plan was to marry these two groups.

So I arrived at the big conference in California. I listened to every word and took careful notes. After the discussion and presentation, I went up to ask a question directly to the panel. People who were the best of the best in customer service were at this table. They had won awards for being leaders and trendsetters in service. The table included leaders from top organizations like Boeing, Disney, and Taco Bell. While my big-picture plan was to engage all departments, I didn't want to be laughed out of the room, so I just showed the most basic plan to integrate two departments. Below is an illustration of how the problems were growing, but the funding was the same, along with proposed solution to integrate departments.

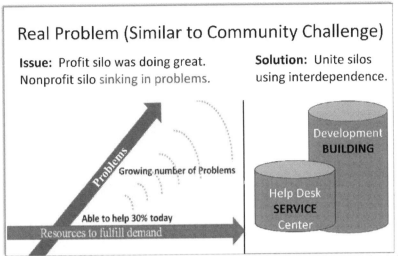

Figure 4.2a The growing problems (left) was addressed by uniting silos (right).

I showed one leader on the HDI excellence panel my plan to integrate the warm and fuzzy people with the tech people. To make it very easy to read, I had the plan on one page. He looked at my plan, and you could see him thinking. Then he said aloud, "This has never been done before. No one has ever integrated these departments." That sounded like a "no," but then he pulled another excellence panel winner into the conversation, and he said, "If you are able to make this happen, you will solve the top problem in our industry." The other gentleman said, "Actually, it would solve the top two or three problems in our industry."

Peter, the gentleman I'd approached, said, "If you can make this happen, I want you to come back and teach everyone at the conference how to do it."

I said, "This is my only option, so I will make it happen."

I went back to Tech Data and told everyone that they wanted us to come back and share our story to help others unite departments to more efficiently and effectively solve problems. I didn't mention any skepticism. Instead, I said it with confidence because I knew we could do it if we believed we could do it.

Well, we gave a whole new meaning to "storming" to form a team. At that time, the tech team made about four times the salary of the customer service team members, so the tech team managers actually confronted me and said, "You can't do this. You are one of us," emphasizing the clear division between the two silos.

I said, "Are you concerned about job security?"

They agreed and said, "Well, yeah, we earn a great paycheck for our certifications, and now you are cross-training others to do that kind of work."

I asked one more question. "If I do not figure out a way to solve this problem, do we as a company—and all of our jobs—go away?"

It was then that you could see it hit them like a ton of bricks that we were truly all in the same boat. We relied on them as much as they relied on us. If the nonprofit support people couldn't bail out the water in the boat, we would sink with them. Most understood that the nonprofit silo relied on the for-profit silo for their paychecks and to keep the company going, but most kind of assumed that the nonprofit support side would just take whatever we threw over the wall. However, the back of the boat was sinking fast.

We worked on a strategy together. We split up the work into easy, medium, and hard categories and trained entry-level employees to knock out as many of the easy tasks as possible. We had experienced staff focus on taking one or two common activities and figuring out ways to streamline and save time. For example, Joe set up new warehouse employees, which was one of the more complex and time-consuming tasks. I said, "Joe, check to see if you log in and out of the same application more than one time." Then, I asked him to figure out a puzzle where he only logged into the application one time versus 20 times throughout the day. We constantly looked at ways to cut out non-value-added steps.

It was hard for the team to visualize their success, so we put four-foot bar chart posters along the outside help desk walls to show that the numbers were improving each week. Unfortunately, it also showed that the volume of calls was going up. The better our reputation got for solving problems, the more people called us. But our turnaround per problem kept getting faster.

Things were looking great. The turnaround time was down to a three-week average, then a two-week average, then one week. Then it was down to days, and we finally got to a three-day turnaround. I said, "If we keep this up, we will be able to guarantee all requests in 24 hours. That would be worthy of a party, and we'll invite the president!" Well, we did it, and we had a really uplifting party where we invited the president of our company. The HDI conference asked me to come and present to share our story as trendsetters in the industry. People came from other countries to study our results, but interestingly, they mainly came to study how we had such high employee retention. Turns out, the employees loved the feeling of climbing to be world-class.

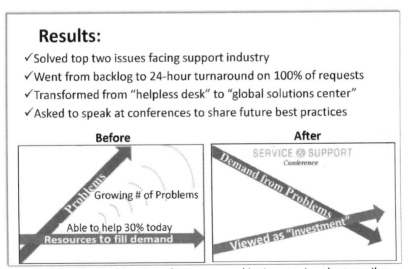

Figure 4.2b The problem trend was reversed by integrating the two silos.

SILO SECRET #30: With crises related to supply and demand, there are several options to achieve balance. Most assume they need to increase the supply to handle the demand (e.g., need more money, more jail cells, more foster parents, more mentors), but a lot of the options discussed above to reduce the time required also work great.

SILO SECRET #31: Cross-training non-technical staff to handle the easier tasks gives experienced subject-matter experts more time to design better and faster ways to resolve requests. In our situation, the experts came up with self-help and self-healing solutions along with proactive alerts to address a situation before it turned into an urgent request.

SILO SECRET #32: Hospitals are seeing the value of uniting high-tech and low-tech silos. Dr. Christine Cauffield, CEO of LSF Health Systems, stated "Hospital systems are not accustomed to credentialing a non-clinical individual. But with return visits to the ER now down considerably at the pilot site, the outlook among hospital personnel is changing." She added, "Peers serve as a critical component to an interdisciplinary treatment team." (Enos, 2019)

SILO SECRET #33: The best way to solve a problem is to prevent it; the next best way is to solve it. If solving is not immediately possible, the next best solution is to simplify or diffuse the issue until you are able to solve it.

REFLECT:

Think of a task that you currently perform. Is there a way you could do that task just one second faster?

_____

_____

"You only live once, but if you do it right, once is enough." – **Mae West** (American actress and entertainer whose entertainment career spanned seven decades.)

4.3 Five Steps to Success

At Tech Data, we had an odd challenge where globalization caused sales and demands on staff to rapidly increase, but tight margins left us continually having to figure out how to do more with less. While hiring new staff to help was often not feasible, we did have access to college interns. Even though these graduates were top of their class, most managers found it too time-consuming to invest time and energy into training them. Managers were especially frustrated that just as they got them trained, it was time for the interns to move on, so they didn't feel it was a good return on their investment.

Perhaps out of desperation, I offered to do the intern training within my department. We identified modular tasks that we could quickly train the interns to do, giving them a sense of value and providing us with much-needed help. As full-time staff started realizing how it gave them some relief, they were more willing to teach the interns additional modular tasks. The interns also took on the role of clearly documenting the steps.

Eager to grow, the interns wanted to take on more advanced tasks. We had to be very strategic and thorough in designing steps to ensure high quality and high quantity, especially with thousands of requests being handled each week. Things went so well with training that managers from other departments started plucking staff just a month or two into training. We then agreed to essentially turn my department into a career development center where we grew exceptional employees for the other departments. We designed a strategic plan where employees went through a one-year skill development program, which we called the "5 Steps to Success."

In addition to growing key soft skills and technical skills, the five steps helped individuals identify their passion and define their ideal career path. Managers often commented that employees that went through our skill development program performed better. We realized that one success factor was that the trainees gained an appreciation for how all parts contribute to a solution. For instance, those who thought computer hardware support was more important gained an appreciation for those who programmed the software. By performing a portion of each role, they saw how every role, and even each personality type, added value. By going through the 5 Steps to Success, they also discovered their passion along the way. Below are the 5 Steps to Success that we used for skill development.

Figure 4.3a New hires and trainees progress through 5 skill development steps.

1. **Easy-to-learn orientation tasks:** At the first level, new hires started with easy-to-learn orientation tasks to get started. We identified low-risk tasks that enabled them to contribute right away. They were productive and helping within the first day or two, which also grew their confidence. This step helped to welcome both new hires and customers.

2. **Internal administrative tasks**: At the second level, the trainees were given back-office or behind-the-scenes tasks. These internal tasks provided a way to learn without pressure. It was low risk because it involved internal administrative tasks such as handling emails, electronically submitted requests, or paperwork that didn't involve working directly with waiting clients.

3. **External client-facing tasks:** Trainees went to this third level once they had the confidence to perform tasks with clients waiting. They had performed similar tasks at level two, but the main difference was that now they were interacting with clients. We still phased the trainees in by starting with easier tasks and then moved them to handle more advanced tasks once they were comfortable.

4. **Communications Coordinator (connect solutions):** With the importance of crisp, clear communications, we created this level-four role where employees facilitated collaboration between the employees performing internal tasks (level two) and client-facing tasks (level three). In this role, they learned to facilitate solutions. They could start by taking ownership of a known problem with defined steps. Those with an interest in this role had the opportunity to go on to lead more complex interaction to coordinate solutions and resolve outages.

5. **"Make it Better" Job Rotation:** At level five, trainees essentially did a job shadow or job rotation with another department where they collaborated to define and lead one continual improvement idea from start to finish. As they rotated through more departments, they gained more insight into how all the departments worked together. Those who chose to continue in this role evolved to have the skills to lead more integrated, interdependent solutions.

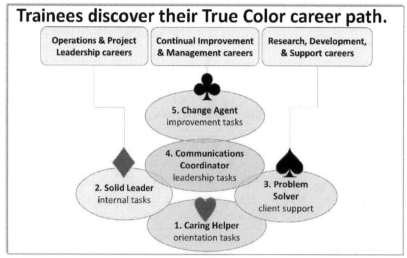

Figure 4.3b With 5 Steps to Success, trainees discover their ideal career.

While initially, we considered the steps to be progressive career steps, we found that some people earned promotions to level five, but then expressed a desire to return to level two or three or even asked about a career at level one. As we talked more with people about their career interests, we saw how this clearly related to the four personality types discussed in chapter 1. For those who were very people-focused, it made sense that they were more interested in level one or level three, which were very client-focused. Level one is often like the greeter at a store. It is a high volume of short-length tasks where you interact with many people. Those who enjoyed client support as well as problem-solving found that they enjoyed level three. Some preferred problem-solving but also enjoyed adventure, so they fit quite well into the exciting level-five role where they explored to find new solutions. Some were naturals at taking on the responsibility of ensuring crisp communications to facilitate solutions, making the level four communications coordinator role a great fit that often led to management. Having trainees learn the types of tasks they enjoyed helped us plan their career paths.

Note: The fifth step to excellence was essentially cross-training employees to work toward interdependence, where they relied on each other's skills and experience to improve their part of the company.

SILO SECRET #34: With the 5 Steps to Success, the company benefits by having a central place to develop employees with knowledge of key organizational goals and practices. This facilitates collaboration and interdependence between department silos to work out solutions.

SILO SECRET #35: When I spoke at conferences, people from all industries asked for help on how to get started in implementing the 5 Steps to Success. Like everything, you just start with step one. Find simple tasks that you can cross-train someone to do in a day or two. This frees up time to focus on step-two tasks once you are ready.

SILO SECRET #36: Hiring and succession planning becomes easier because you are always developing employees to be ready for the next step. Employees naturally support and mentor other employees to be ready to backfill their position when they get promoted. Often, we would have triple promotions because it was almost like a baseball game where everyone moves to the next base at the same time. All were in position and ready. This makes filling open positions easier as well because nearly 100% of the hiring can be for the first level and potential employees can easily see the career growth opportunities.

SILO SECRET #37: Handling spikes in work is easier because you have people trained and ready to help with overflow work and they are happy to help as it aligns with their career development goals.

SILO SECRET #38: Attracting new employees was easy. They often volunteered to shadow our team to see if the job was a good fit for them. Some said, "No way, José," and that was good for both of us as we didn't waste time in the interview process. The majority enjoyed the job shadowing because they came onboard knowing exactly what it would be like and knowing it was the right fit.

SILO SECRET #39: These simple steps apply to every area. I'm incredibly excited about the opportunity to implement this program for the upcoming Peer Support Movement and Community Service positions.

SILO SECRET #40: When we initially started the program for our Help Desk in the business world, many referred to the help desk as the "Helpless Desk." People urged, "We need to change the name so people do not call us that anymore." I told them, "We will earn a new name" and we did. We went on to earn the name of Global Solutions Center as we grew our solution rate from 3% to 93%.

SILO SECRET #41: Sharing these steps with community service workers is an incredible opportunity to help community service staff as well as children and families. Many have heard of the national crisis with Case Manager Turnover (Child Welfare Worker Turnover, 2019), but there is also a well-known formula that relates to the impact on children. Currently, a child's chance of being reunified with his or her own family or placed with an adoptive family drops from 74% to 17% if a case manager leaves and the child's case has to transition. It drops to a mere 5% success rate if an additional transfer happens. (Stewart, 2016) I use the word "currently" because we have the power to make this sad formula a thing of the past. Uniting children and families warrants the highest standard.

Imagine the impact of applying this program to offer career paths to case managers and peer support specialists along with community service volunteers and employees. That vision has served as a major inspiration for me to write this book.

REFLECT:

Was there a particular type of role in the 5 Steps to Success that stood out to you?

_____

_____

*"If you want to experience joy in your life, you have to be able to step outside yourself and become part of a cause that is much larger than you; one that brings a greater good to a greater community." – **Srikumar Rao*** (Creator of The Rao Institute Creativity and Personal Mastery course.)

4.4 Four Steps to Interdependence

Rocking in the corner of his room, nine-year-old Sam covered his eyes and tried to tune out the flashing red and blue lights and sirens as the emergency staff stormed into his home for the 30th time this year. This time, they were here for his sister, so he knew the rule: stay out of the way. As Sam rocked, he heard a soft knock on his door and looked up to see an out-of-place lady wearing jeans and a shirt with a sunshine kind of logo. Still in the doorway, she said, "Hello, I was hoping I could ask you a question. This may sound kind of funny, but my job is to find out what will make your life better.'" Caught a little off guard, Sam hopelessly muttered, "Bring my grandpa back."

Intrigued as the soft-spoken lady introduced herself as Vicky and gently sat down in the doorway, Sam looked up with a confused look on his face. He said, "We already got lots of social workers." Vicky smiled and explained, "I am not a social worker. I ride along in police cars to talk to people to help them come up with a plan to make things a little better." Sam replied, "We have this long list of places we need to go. They tell us to go to court, go to therapy, go to anger management, and take pills, but the sirens keep coming to our house." Vicky smiled and said, "This is different. With this plan, you are in charge." With a grin, Sam responded, "For real? I'm in charge?" Vicky answered, "Yes. This plan is from your view. You mentioned wanting your grandpa back. Can you tell me about your grandpa and how things were when he was here?"

It was almost like Sam went into a dream as he shared, "Everything was great when Grandpa was here. He got a check every month to buy groceries and he was a great cook. I helped him make cherry pie. He paid for the food. Dad paid the rent and took Grandpa to the doctors. Mom took care of me and my sister. My best friend, Tommy, came over every day after school to play. His big brother is smart so he helped us with our homework when we got stuck. I got gold stars at school. Grandpa put my award on the fridge."

Sam's body language shifted as he then muttered in frustration, "Everything changed when Grandpa went away. My mom and dad fight over money now. Lots of times we don't have any food. My sister has epilepsy and now she has seizures all the time. Dad gets mad when he can't fix the car so he throws things. People call me Siren Sam because the ambulances, police, and fire trucks are at my house all the time. My best friend is not allowed to come over anymore because I am trouble. I turned into a bad kid."

Vicky assured him, "You are still a good kid. What makes you think you are bad?" Sam said, "I messed up. Trying to be a good kid, I picked up apples from the tree next door and got reported to the police. Earlier that day, I stole a poster to do a school project. I couldn't ask my mom for school supplies. Dad and Mom yell all the time that they can't pay the rent." Sam added, "The worst part is that Grandpa wants to come back. He went to New York to help a friend and got into an accident. He is okay now but we can't afford to fly him back and his airline ticket is no good anymore."

Sam's mom and dad interrupted with good news, "Sis is going to be okay. We just ran out of medicine." Vicky said, "That is wonderful news that your daughter is okay." She added, "Sam was just telling me about how he misses his grandpa." Sam's mom agreed, "Yes, we all want him back but he is kind of stuck in the snow." Vicky acknowledged, "Sounds like a rough situation," and mentioned that her job is to help guide kids and families to achieve solutions that they define. Vicky summarized, "In this case, the solution may be to bring Grandpa back. We may just need to get a few people together to make that happen. Does that sound like something you want to do?" Sort of in disbelief, they replied, "Yes."

Vicky pulled out a tiny notepad and said, "These are all problems that can be fixed by bringing the right people together." She jotted down "Bring

Grandpa back" as the need to focus on. Then she invited Sam and his family to help her identify their strengths. She took the notes below.

- Need: Pay airfare and arrange transportation for Grandpa to get back home.

- Strengths: Great support system with mom, dad, sister, and social workers wanting to help.

- Strengths: Grandpa has an income. (Note: income is being used to pay for hotel in New York).

With Vicky guiding them, the family jotted down who could help with this goal. They defined tasks along with who would do what and when they would do it. Mom agreed to call Grandpa and he was thrilled! Since Vicky knew of a senior transportation service, Dad offered to call them to see if they could help in transporting Grandpa to and from the airport. The case manager talked with the 211 crisis center about ways to help fund the airline ticket which Grandpa insisted on paying back, so it was essentially a small loan.

Before, the family was spinning, trying to juggle nearly 30 appointments a month from counseling and therapy to anger management and court dates. Now, they had a facilitator to help ensure they had a plan that was feasible with just four meetings a month to ensure all were on track. Things went so well that Sam and his family wanted to continue to use the process on their own. Empowerment is part of the goal, so Vicky was happy to help transition things. She let them rotate leading the meetings. Sam always had them laughing with his artistic drawings of solutions.

Once Grandpa was back at home, he and Sam brought some strawberries to their neighbor to apologize for Sam taking the apples. The entire family went to a fun training at the recreation center to learn ways to "save for a rainy day" as Grandpa put it. They still bickered a little, but the sirens faded away as they realized they were taking control of their lives and learning ways to make things a little easier and a little better. Like all families, they would have ups and downs, but they went to a training called Protective Factors (Protective Factors Framework, 2013) and realized they were quite resilient after all. Soon, Tommy was coming over to play again. Together, the family bounced back, one need at a time.

This story is a small but significant example of interdependence at a community level. Vicky is essentially facilitating interdependence via a best practice called Wraparound. The initial interdependence was simply having a non-police member travel with the police. This practice is initiated by mental health professionals to add that additional insight to help achieve real solutions. Facilitators like Vicky look at things from the view of a project coordinator, helping to pull in all the different skills and mindsets needed to come up with better solutions. In the end, communities and families win as screaming sirens are replaced with peaceful talking and laughter.

Steps to interdependence

Interdependence can happen in business as well as the community. In business, I have intentionally given people the freedom to improve any part of their world. It could be their carpool to work, their schedule, their work-life balance, or a technical issue. When people's lives are easier, it frees up their mind to think and improve. This creates a culture of boundary-less continual learning and improvement. The same was true for Sam and his family. They were simply empowered to be positive change leaders. Below are the steps to interdependence.

Step 1: Step outside your silo to meet with an individual from another department or silo.

Step 2: Agree on one thing to collaborate on to identify a way to make it better in some way.

Step 3: Share each other's knowledge and skills and invite others to design a better way.

Step 4: Test, validate, and refine to finalize and document recommendations to share with others.

In the nonprofit world, grant sponsors and philanthropists are often looking for holistic solutions that engage different ways of thinking for a comprehensive, sustainable solution. Below is a sample of a logic diagram used to engage coaches, young people, families, and communities for a healthier, safer community for all members. The chart can be a great tool, almost like a checklist, to ensure you've thought through the different views for a holistic, interdependent solution. The body of the chart below is a sample from a grant to grow life and job skills. The structure of the chart (Maslow's needs in left column), along with the input to impact columns on the top, can be used as a template.

Logic Model Format for Holistic Solutions

	INPUTS	ACTIVITIES	OUTPUTS	OUTCOMES	IMPACT
Physical Needs	Coaches, youth, and caregivers	Collaborate on solutions	Food, housing, and transportation	Presentation skills	> Self-sufficiency < Society costs
Safety Needs	Coaches, youth, and families	Learn how to avoid risks	Safety tips and personal budget	Awareness and stability	> Safety and stability < Drugs and homelessness
Social Needs	Coaches, youth, and volunteers	Partner to solve common goals	Team Accomplish-ments	People, career and life skills	> Social connections > Friends and positive role models
Confidence	Coaches, youth, and organizations	Solve real-life problems	Success stories for interviews	Top 30 job and survival skills	> Graduaton rates > Workforce ready
Self-actualization	Youth and community	Explore careers and discover	Lifelong learner and contributor	Experience reward of giving	> Community benefits > Mentors repeat

Figure 4.4 Template can be used to ensure consideration of Maslow's needs.

SILO SECRET #42: The Wraparound approach facilitates interdependence in communities, starting at the child level, bringing people together to apply their strengths to fulfill defined needs.

SILO SECRET #43: An area where both business and nonprofit silos are uniting in a good way relates to SMART goals. Together, they agree on SMART goals (specific, measurable, attainable, realistic, and timely). Some people use the words achievable and relevant. (Doran, Miller, & Cunningham, 1981)

SILO SECRET #44: The four steps to interdependence are about engaging the right silos for the given goal. Solutions can involve two or more people, departments, organizations, communities, counties, or countries. It is about relying on each other to get to more sustainable solutions.

REFLECT:

Can you see how using the Wraparound approach benefits communities as well as children?

_____

_____

Chapter 4 Summary: Models like the 5 Steps to Success in skill development help employees and volunteers gravitate to greatness by finding their passion. The four steps to interdependence help create a culture of learning and sharing across silos, creating better solutions for everyone. We have all heard the phrase "two heads are better than one." That is a simple way of saying interdependence is better than independence.

5. COMMUNITIES PAVING THE WAY

"The way to change the world is through individual responsibility and taking local action in your own community." – **Jeff Bridges** (Actor, producer, and singer; earned Academy Award for Best Actor.)

"Rather than dwell in despair, I invite you to take actions that genuinely contribute to the creation of a better world and amplify the stories of success, breakthrough, and possibility." – **Stephen Dinan** (CEO and president of The Shift Network.)

5.1 VIP Falling—Call in the HAT team

When I was younger, my family was driving in a snowstorm with a friend. Our car slid on the ice, and we ended up suspended over a cliff because a traffic engineer had put up a guardrail at the particular section of the mountain cliff that we collided into. I remember wondering how many people had gone off the edge of that mountain before the guardrail was put up. How many deaths did it take to inspire someone to put up a guardrail? Then I looked to the left and right of the guardrail at the wide-open space with nothing stopping any car from flying off the edge into oblivion.

I suspect that an engineer calculated that this spot of the road was likely to form ice and had a curve to it, earning its title of "the danger zone." Next, I suspect that a team of engineers calculated the likely path an out-of-control car would slide given icy road conditions, thereby putting up that sole guardrail that kept my family and I suspended safely over a cliff, like two skinny fingers of a silver hand cupping us until the ambulance arrived. It wasn't like in the movies where it seems precarious, squeaking, and unstable—where everyone is in fear that the slightest movement will cause the vehicle to come loose and fall. Instead, we were somehow securely held by this thin rail, suspended at the end of the cliff overlooking what could have been a horrifying end to our lives.

I've read articles about infants, children, and adults losing their lives because of a system failure. Reading the articles is hard because I can see that no one realizes that they can get an engineer to stop, or at least reduce, the cycle of people flying off life's cliffs. We can't stop everyone from going off that edge, but we can learn and continually add safety features to prevent deaths or at least mitigate the risks. While that team of engineers was likely not called a HAT (High Availability Team), it likely performed similar steps to a HAT team. I'd like to thank that engineer for that skinny rail on that winding mountain road in Georgia because if it were not for him or her, I would not be here today to tell you about the value of HAT teams.

For 25+ years, my jobs included enterprise-wide system design and problem-solving. Eventually, I was promoted to the Global HAT Severity 1 Crisis resolution team. Most considered being recruited to the HAT team an honor, but it was kind of like being selected to be a Navy SEAL. The pressure was intense. Over 40 countries could call us anytime, day or night. If they had an issue that put a VIP or client at risk, our job was to diffuse the situation and come up with a permanent solution.

Our progress was emailed to the entire company, and we didn't sleep until we had a solution. It was exciting to be in the hot seat, working with people all over the world to solve or prevent a crisis. We laughed that our initial job was to get the company in the news (developing innovative solutions), but our job on the problem-solving HAT crisis team was to keep the company out of the news. As I write it, it doesn't sound so glamorous, but it was actually kind of rewarding. Everyone knew our role to "save VIP clients." Things were looking great from my silo (top pay, home on the water, hot red convertible).

Then, I got a rude awakening when I decided to apply my skills in the community more than the traditional walkathons and activities. As I investigated further, I was stunned to see the number of formerly declared crisis issues in the U.S. It was most concerning that items were being added to the crisis to-do list but not being resolved, checked off, and removed from the list. I went to nonprofit leadership meetings and heard conversations in the lunch lines about community service employees and faith-based organizations having families sleep under their desks until they could find a bed for them. Stories of children running into horrifying situations were common.

I kept saying to myself, "Why isn't someone calling the HAT team?" The most chilling moment was learning that there was no HAT team and worse yet, that it was a totally new and foreign concept to most. The silos would have to open their minds to believe in the possibility of designing solutions to minimize the chances of children and families spinning out of control and heading directly into danger. I get it. Even now, I see those guardrails and think, "Wow, hard to believe that skinny thing saved my family." Likewise, people likely look at me and say, "Seriously? Standardized descriptions and severity levels can save lives?" The answer is yes. I actually found one attorney general in Missouri who came to this realization and initiated a team to focus on standards to save lives.

To illustrate, some nonprofit organizations have thousands of at-risk families. Clear severity levels can ensure crisp communication in life-threatening circumstances. A severity 1 indicates a person's life is currently in danger and people must act now. A severity 2 indicates a person has an imminent threat of danger. Since many nonprofit organizations have hundreds of clients who are in what most would describe as a severity 2, the term "at risk" is well-known. By having a clear differentiation for when a person's life is in danger, the term severity 1 can be used to facilitate urgent action without spending precious minutes trying to prioritize.

I have seen front-page fatal news reports that are essentially due to a situation being treated as a severity 2 versus a severity 1. In my role on the HAT team, I saw a huge difference when we used this international best practice to have standardized severity level descriptions. When I called a person at 3 a.m. with a severity 1 situation, there was no questioning to determine priority. Together, we jumped in to ensure a solution. Afterwards, we shared that solution to prevent or minimize future occurrences.

Since HAT teams work across the world, finding the best resources to help solve problems, I researched and found that other countries are in the same boat as the United States. However, if you look closely, there is often one lone city here, and another lone country there, that has found a better way. Yet, all the other cities and countries are often so busy that they may not realize there are some incredible evidence-based solutions with proven success.

Mainly, the challenge is we have mastered organized crime, and those committing crimes are leveraging technology and best practices to do worst practices. Yet, *organized kind* is falling behind. We need to at least level the playing field and give the good guys some modern tools and practices that are accepted around the world as being the best tools for managing projects (Project Management Institute principles); solving problems (ITIL and Problem Management practices); optimizing workflow (Lean); maximizing quality and consistency (Six Sigma); and designing best solutions (Agile and Systems Development Life Cycle). In looking at it from a quadrant view as shown below, organized kind would pave a new path by combining the best of both worlds (high efficiency and high value). With best practices in efficiency, local community service agencies could maximize the impact of their high-valued purpose or mission, paving a new path of organized kind.

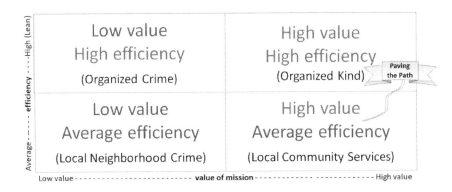

Imagine if we share best practice solutions more efficiently. To illustrate, Walmart advertises that it can wire money from 200 countries. Yet, one out of 20 people are victims of one email scam where they are asked to wire money to a criminal and it's generally accepted that nothing can be done about the scam because the crime originated in another country. However, if we offered to give a global corporation a 10% commission on money retrieved, I bet they would figure out a way to post 'smile for the camera' signs at locations where money is transferred and at least minimize such crimes. Virtual bounty hunters may soon be a lucrative career.

Since I have rolled out solutions to 40 countries, I know this is very possible. Working closely with many nonprofit organizations over the past seven years, I have found that more and more people are seeing that solutions are just a matter of sharing secrets between two silos. The great news is most people can continue to hang out in their silo doing the great things they are already doing. It just takes a few people here and there to step out and then return home with some tips and tools to share. Many seem to think they have to learn to fluently speak each other's language. That definitely helps, but it is kind of like when my best friend in high school went to Spain. Knowing a few key phrases like "Donde está el baño?" (Where is the bathroom?), and "Donde están los chicos guapos?" (Where are the good-looking boys?) got her through her summer trip just fine.

One secret that I learned was that setting up a career development program within an organization facilitates people learning the language of the other silos. They can then be liaisons or ambassadors to add extra support by being able to naturally look at issues from more than one view.

My experience in the nonprofit world is that many nonprofit organizations are better than anyone at measuring problem frequency and impact. However, as Einstein points out, the key is to truly understanding the root cause. The HAT team dug deep into the root cause of a severity 1 call. They would then work on solutions for that particular set of circumstances. The solutions could be shared to help prevent and mitigate other bad situations by addressing the root cause. It was a lot like firefighters, but the emphasis was on understanding the causes in order to focus on prevention. Eventually, you spent more and more time on preventing the fires versus reacting to the fires. As we'll discuss in section 8.4, sometimes we have to react and urgently put out the fire, but as Benjamin Franklin used to say, "An ounce of prevention is worth a pound of cure."

SILO SECRET #45: The concept of a HAT team can be applied to any problem. We never had any idea what type of call we would get, and the issues covered a wide range of emergencies from broken air-conditioner issues and overheating computers to data corruption or an employee resource gap. However, the problem-solving approach was almost the same every time.

SILO SECRET #46: Standardization of severity levels is an international best practice used by businesses. These best practices could make a dramatic difference for community and nonprofit goals.

SILO SECRET #47: With clearly defined severity levels, a crisis team could be in place, where all know the rules and roles for handling various severity levels.

REFLECT:

If you could assign a HAT team to resolve a problem in your community, what issue would you select?

_____

_____

*"...What happens to the earth happens to the children of the earth. Humankind has not woven the web of life; we are but one thread. Whatever we do to the web, we do to ourselves." – **Rebecca Adamson*** (Ground-breaking indigenous economist, recognized by PBS as one of the Most Influential Women in America.)

5.2 Code Red Alert: Partly Sunny with a Chance of Air Mask

Jim was up north in the snow and Laurie was what Jim described as "living the good life in Florida." As they chatted on the telephone, Jim laughed and said, "What is the point of watching the weather? It's always cold, with a chance of snow." Any other day, Laurie would have chuckled and said, "Yeah, I am living the good life—hot, with a high chance of muggy," but this day was like no other. Laurie was experiencing a double crisis. The air conditioning in her house and car had gone out at the same time. How could this happen? She explained to Jim that it was so bad that a police officer pitied her and escorted her back to her house.

"What? Seriously, what happened?" Jim said in shock.

Laurie exclaimed that she was driving to work, sweating profusely, when a police officer pulled her over to tell her she was going a little over the speed limit. Jim refrained from asking what she meant by "a little" over the speed limit as he could hear the frustration in her voice. Laurie, still without air conditioning, took a deep, gasping breath and said, "Being in a heated state of mind, I did something that I have never done; I actually forgot my purse and cell phone at my house, so I literally had no identification on me." When the police officer said, "Ma'am, do you realize I could take you to jail?" Laurie desperately replied, "Is there air conditioning at the jail?" Luckily, Laurie was able to remortgage her house to get a new air conditioner for her house and car, and it all worked out.

The reason for sharing this story is, I agreed with Jim: what is the point of watching the weather when you know it is "hot with a chance of muggy" or "cold with a chance of snow"? But then a coworker-turned-friend named Anne Marie called me from Arizona. We had traveled together to London on business, so I mentioned that I had seen a sad article about how a school in London was giving masks to children to protect them from air pollution. (BBC London, 2017) While I was feeling concerned for our mutual friends and associates in London, she was unusually silent. She didn't say anything, making me feel like she didn't care, and then she broke down crying. She explained that her four-year-old, Matthew, was on the high-risk danger list because he has asthma and as a child, his lungs and heart are very small.

Anne Marie said little Matthew started getting bullied at school because the other children saw him wearing the same air mask that the children in London were wearing. She explained that the pre-kindergarten teacher let her drop Matthew off early so he could wear the mask from the car to the classroom and then take it off before the other children arrived. She described how Matthew was upset and lonely, but now two other children, Julie and Jeffrey, were arriving early too. With their three little masks, they became known as The Three Musketeers.

Anne Marie said she watches the news like a hawk and looks forward to a new phone app that would enable her to get EPA air quality alerts more proactively. She shared how several private companies were working on apps to help people who travel know when it is safe to go outside when they visit a new city or country. She tried to end the conversation in a positive way, jokingly saying, "Your weather report is 'hot and muggy.' My weather report is 'sunny with a chance of air mask.'"

Having traveled to Phoenix and London, I could not help but wonder if we should have worn a mask. At the time, it never occurred to me to check the air quality index. I was a travel agent for years, so I naturally checked the weather, but never even thought to update my clients on the air quality level. What about the other places that I visited?

The good news is that many cities have improved air quality significantly over the past decade. The better news is that these cities are showing that we really can have safe and clean air if we put our minds to it. Yet, some cities have spikes where the air is labeled "unhealthy for all." Do 100% of the people in these cities own a mask to put on during code red, or worse, code purple alerts? Even Anne Marie told me, "I guess it is like the airplane instructions where you should put your own mask on first and then help your children, but I am so worried about Matthew that I forget all about my own mask."

The air plot thickens (NOAA, 2019)

As I sat reflecting, one of my friends, Theresa, texted me that her high school reunion was canceled due to fires. I texted back, "Aren't the fires way west of where you are going?" Being an ecology student, she forwarded me a satellite map of time lapse data, showing how the wildfire smoke expanded throughout and even beyond the United States. She explained that the dots on the map below showed where the fires in British Columbia, California and Ontario were located. Yet, the big blob in the satellite photo showed how the smoke covered most of the United States. The toxic pollutants adhered to Merriam-Webster's definition of a gas as air pollutants tend to "expand indefinitely," causing air alerts across the nation.

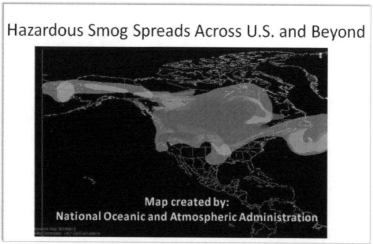

Figure 5.2a Above map shows how far smog or other pollutants can spread.

On a positive note, Theresa then texted me with exciting news that she had been selected to do an internship on a big project to improve the air. She got so excited that she actually stopped texting for a moment and called to tell me more. We joke that she has the fastest thumbs in the west, but her thumb texting could not keep up with her enthusiasm to be part of this project to improve the air across the world.

Former anthropologist Margaret Mead summarized it well when she stated, *"The atmosphere is the key symbol of global interdependence."* In the world of measurement, we often use traffic light colors where green means "good" to go, yellow means "caution," and red means "stop." The air map below shows that pretty much half of the earth is flaring red, telling us to please stop. Reiterating the millions of deaths, the corresponding article emphasizes a critically important fact: "It doesn't have to be that way." (Zeller, Mironski, & Price, 2019)

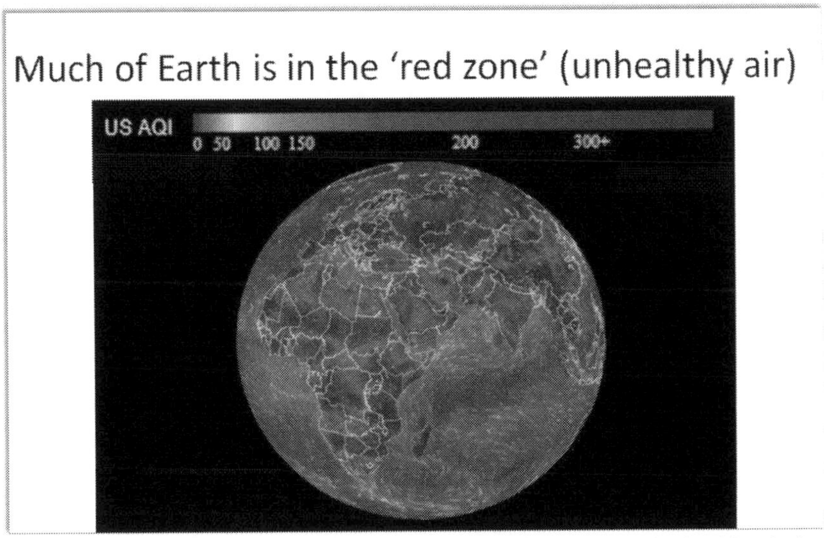

Figure 5.2b IQAir shows AirVisual Earth view of PM2.5 – PM10 with wind.

The American Society for Quality seeks to "empower people, communities, and organizations of the world to achieve excellence through quality" so who better to help us improve our air? (The Global Voice of Quality, 2019) Lucky for us, their experts across 130 countries are likely familiar with DMAIC (define, measure, analyze, implement, control), a globally recognized best practice that may just be the perfect fit. To see for yourself, below is a highlight of the five phases of this Lean Six Sigma methodology.

1. **DEFINE: The sky is the limit—what is important to you?**
   Together, as consumers of Earth's precious air supply, we must define our expectations and air requirements. In some parts of the world, air masks are becoming somewhat of a status symbol, affordable only to the affluent. Envisioning an air mask with shiny gold trim, I have to wonder if, in our haste to go outside, we may have jumped ahead, missing the meaning of this vital step.

   This tool is often considered as critical to use when lives are at risk. Typically, PM2.5 is the most damaging form of air pollution. It contributes to heart disease, strokes, lung cancer, respiratory infections, and other diseases. While the black and white print doesn't do it justice, the air maps show we have plenty of flaming red unhealthy air across the world.

What is important to you? With this first phase, we "define" that. We set the standard. We decide if running through red lights is okay, knowing the penalty. While the earlier story happened to take place in Phoenix, this issue affects all of us.

2. **MEASURE: Just how big is the air issue?** With this step, we quantify the problem. Astronauts warn that they can see the pollution in Los Angeles from outer space. They describe the thin layer protecting the earth as looking like a thin, delicate cloud and hope that we realize how critical it is to protect that thin wall that protects us all.

The international chart below shows that many countries have had 100% of the population exposed to unhealthy pollution levels. (World Development Indicators, 2017) AirVisual Earth shows real-time air quality data along with actual photos. (IQ Air: AirVisual Earth, 2019)

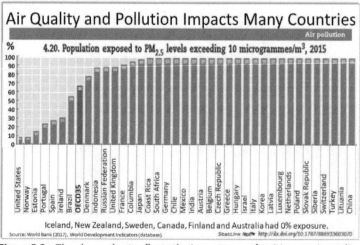

Figure 5.2c The above chart reflects the importance of uniting on air quality.

Cities are gathering real-time readings on particulate matter air pollution less than 2.5 microns in diameter (PM2.5). It is great news that people all over the world are gathering the key data needed. (Air Quality Real-time Map, 2019)

3. **ANALYZE: Let's dig a little deeper.** Let's identify the causes to get to solutions. With nearly half of our world's land covered in red, I had to dig deeper to find out what it would take to get us to stop speeding through these hazardous air red lights. It seems that where there is a will, there is a way!

   - China was able to "control air pollution" during the 2008 Olympic Games, resulting in a **41.6% decrease** in the average number of outpatient visits for asthma. (Sierra-Vargas & Teran, 2012).

   - Mexico City focused on lead and particles like dust, soot, and chemicals, resulting in a **90% drop** in the presence of lead in the air and a **70% drop** in suspended particles. (Kanti, 2017)

In Delhi, dust contributes 33% to 56% of the most harmful pollutants in the atmosphere. Polash Mukherjee, a researcher with the Delhi-based Centre for Science and Environment, shared how much of this could be addressed by adding pavement and planting vegetation along dividers and road shoulders to capture dust so it does not blow down the road. So a few bushes or even temporary planters at construction sites can help us get out of the red. (Safi, 2017)

Let's check out some trends. Back in 2000, we were all talking about Y2K when we should have been talking about PM2.5. Below is a U.S. trend map showing the number of days that reached unhealthy air quality levels. The first bar shows a 10-year average along with the number of unhealthy air days in 2015 and 2016. The good news is almost every city shows a lower number in 2016 than the 10-year average. Comparing the last two bars is an easy way to see if the unhealthy air trend went up or down.

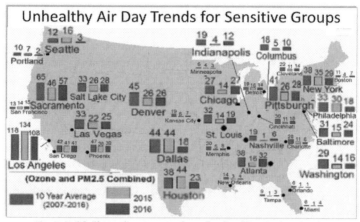

Figure 5.2d Chart showing number of unhealthy air days by city.

With 35 cities posting the above data daily, it is an opportunity to analyze the data to identify what factors may be making things better as well as what factors may be making things worse. With so many factors, sometimes it makes it easier by having a wider sample of data. We can also group data by region or common feature, like being close to water, to do further analysis.

4. **IMPROVE: The proof is in the numbers.** This is where we implement and verify solutions. Imagine if a business had 10 out of 35 sites showing consistent improvement in sales or consistent reduction in administrative costs. The business would likely look at those sites to identify factors that contributed to its success and then implement that shared knowledge at other sites. We can do the same with community statistics. We can analyze and talk to cities to learn what they are doing to make things better and then share their experience with other cities.

Below is an illustration showing how 10 cities consistently improved air quality based on the above 2016 study comparing 10 years of data.

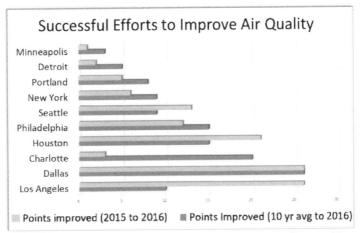

Figure 5.2e 10 Cities showed consistent improvement in air quality over 10 years.

5. **CONTROL: Keep up the good air!** This is where we maintain the solutions. About 15 cities improved when compared to the 10-year average, but worsened in 2016. While most only declined one to three points, three cities (Chicago, Sacramento, and Atlanta) had air pollution worsen by over 11 to 16 points. Studying changes in those cities for that time frame can help us isolate root problems and develop real solutions.

SILO SECRET #48: DMAIC (define, measure, analyze, implement, control) represents the five phases of the Lean Six Sigma problem-solving methodology. Six Sigma is all about reducing defects. While there will not be a quiz on this, Six Sigma sets a very high bar for the level of performance at 3.4 defects per million opportunities (3.4 DPMO). (Six Sigma Performance, 2019)

SILO SECRET #49: The good news is steps are in place to reduce pollution, and many cities have seen a decline. However, pollution levels are creeping back up in some cities. There is a great opportunity for cities to learn from each other. What did cities do to make the numbers go down? What situations made the numbers go up? These are all part of problem-solving best practices to monitor, find root causes, and diffuse and eliminate failure points.

SILO SECRET #50: New apps (phone applications) are being created so people will be able to know if pollution levels are too high to go outside (measuring ozone and PM2.5).

SILO SECRET #51: The EPA Air Now site has detailed instructions on how to minimize exposure to air pollution. They publish air quality statistics along with recommended steps to take during Air Action Alerts like "limiting energy usage, setting air conditioners to higher temperatures, carpooling, refueling after dusk, limiting travel, and avoiding gas-powered lawn equipment." To watch for Air Quality Action Days in your area, check airnow.gov. The EPA site includes transportation and household tips. (AirNow EPA Tips, 2019)

Transportation tips:

- Drive less: carpool, use public transportation, bike, or walk when possible.

- Inflate tires to the recommended pressure.

- Combine errands to reduce "cold starts" of your car and avoid extended engine idling.

- Keep car, boat, and other engines properly tuned, and avoid engines that smoke.

- Follow gasoline refueling instructions for efficient vapor recovery.

- When refueling, be careful not to spill fuel and always tighten your gas cap securely.

Household tips:

- Use environmentally-safe paints and cleaning products whenever possible.

- Use low-VOC paint and cleaning products, and seal and store them so they can't evaporate.

- Properly seal cleaners, paints, and other chemicals to prevent evaporation into the air.

- Conserve electricity. Turn off lights you are not using.

- Consider setting your thermostat a little higher in the summer and lower in winter.

- Participate in local energy conservation programs.

- Look for the ENERGY STAR label when buying home or office equipment.

- Consider using gas logs instead of wood. Burn only dry, seasoned wood.

- Check EPA design specifications. (ENERGY STAR, Burn Wise, and EPA for Citizen Action)

- Research online lawn and garden tips (including composting steps).

SILO SECRET #52: The EPA site also provides Action Day Tips for days when your air is unhealthy. They have a list of what to do when the ozone and particle pollution are expected to be high. (AirNow EPA Tips, 2019)

Days when ozone is expected to be high:

- Conserve electricity and set your air conditioner at a higher temperature.

- Choose a cleaner commute—share a ride to work or use public transportation. Bicycle or walk to errands when possible.

- Refuel cars and trucks after dusk.

- Combine errands and reduce trips.

- Limit engine idling.

- Use household, workshop, and garden chemicals in ways that keep evaporation to a minimum, or try to delay using them when poor air quality is forecast.

Days when particle pollution is expected to be high:

- Reduce or eliminate fireplace and woodstove use.

- Avoid using gas-powered lawn and garden equipment.

- Avoid burning leaves, trash, and other materials.

SILO SECRET #53: Smoke from fires can be very damaging to our health. Sometimes a fire smells great, reminding of us of campfires and the great outdoors, but the EPA warns of dangers and provides instructions on how we can be safer if smoke is hovering over us. Below are some tips from the EPA on what to do when fire smoke poses a threat. (Fire Smoke FAQ, 2019)

Days when fire smoke is expected to be a possible threat:

- Pay attention to local air quality reports during a fire or check airnow.gov.

- Take precautions to protect those at risk due to lung disease, respiratory system issues, heart disease, and diabetes.

- Take precautions to protect children, teenagers, and pregnant women.

- Work out a plan with your health provider on what to do in a fire including instructions on when to leave the area, prescriptions, how much medicine to have on hand, and action plan.

- Have a several-day supply of nonperishable foods that do not require cooking. Avoid frying and broiling as it can add to indoor pollution levels.

- Consider buying an air cleaner to help reduce particle levels indoors. (Air Cleaning Devices, 2019)

- Have a supply of N-95 or P-100 masks on hand and learn proper use. Paper "dust" masks, surgical masks, scarves, or bandanas (wet or dry) may look cool but they will not protect you. (Air Mask Demo, 2019)

- If it looks or smells smoky outside, it's likely best to avoid outdoor activities to reduce exposure.

- If you are advised to stay indoors, take steps to keep indoor air as clean as possible like keeping the filter clean to prevent bringing additional smoke inside.

- If you don't have an air conditioner, staying inside with the windows closed may be dangerous in extremely hot weather so seek alternative shelter.

- Don't vacuum because it stirs up particles inside your home.

REFLECT:

Since some cities have gone from high pollutants to almost no pollutants, do you think it is possible we can learn and apply those best practices to ensure all cities eventually have safe air?

_____

_____

Would you rather work to ensure safe air or have a new app tell you if it is safe to go outside?

_____

_____

"The wind that destroyed Greensburg is also the wind that would make us energy sustainable." – **Mayor Bob Dixson** (Recognized nationally for putting people first in achieving real solutions to dire dilemmas.)

5.3 Devastated into Greatness

What do a small farm town (Rock Port, Missouri), a community half destroyed by a tornado (Greensburg, Kansas), an island (Kodiak Island, Alaska), a small quaint town (Burlington, Vermont), and a ski resort city (Aspen, Colorado) have in common? From the outside view, they represent quite a variety of cities. The one thing they very much have in common is that these communities are leading the way in renewable energy. They are joining other cities around the world to show the possibilities. (Sierra Club, 2019)

One of these five towns, Greensburg, is described by one survivor as "the town that refused to disappear." On May 4, 2007, at 9:00 p.m., a tornado whirled at up to 205 miles per hour through the town. The unforgiving tornado leveled and devastated the entire town. While it lasted just over an hour, the tornado completely destroyed 961 homes and caused major damage to 216 businesses and homes. Over 7,600 volunteers put in over 50,000 hours to try to help. (Tornado Facts and Photos, 2007)

In the morning light, it was clear to see that nearly all homes and possessions were gone. The EF5 tornado leveled at least 95% of the city. The feelings of intense emptiness seemed to rush in as people realized the memories swiped away in an instant included small but irreplaceable things like childhood photos, Sarah's little soccer trophy on the seemingly sturdy brick fireplace, and that silly knickknack that had so much sentimental value. All had vanished along with their homes. The townspeople were left with virtually no possessions. Having nothing, they relied on and found strength in each other.

Mayor Bob Dixson and his citizens could have given up and headed to a new town. That would have been the easier path, but instead, they came together and turned this devastation into greatness. As they will tell you proudly, they turned that weakness into a strength that made them one of the top five leaders in the nation in renewable energy.

By leaping forward with a shared sustainable energy vision, the five cities provide a virtual support system for each other. Together, they also demonstrate how a city can move forward at its own pace and maintain its unique culture and style. To illustrate, Vermont's largest city, Burlington, had a sustainable energy mission to move away from their reliance on coal. The city of Burlington has been using 100% renewable electricity since 2014. It bought a hydropower facility and now uses a combination of energy from burning wood chips, wind, solar, landfill methane, and hydropower. The city estimates it will save $20 million over the next two decades.

Alaska's Kodiak Island was already ahead of the curve in using hydropower, but the government chose to also purchase wind turbines to stop burning 2.8 million gallons of diesel each year. This move was great for the green environment movement with the added benefit of saving $7 million per year in diesel costs. At the time, wind turbines didn't exactly come with a user manual on how to create steady voltage from variable wind power. Darron Scott, CEO of Kodiak Electric Association, described the transformation of Kodiak Island by simply stating, "It was uncharted territory." Amazingly, their electric utility company achieved its renewable energy goals six years ahead of schedule! (Guevara-Stone, 2015)

Okay, time to go skiing in Aspen. This winter ski destination is one of the greenest towns in America. To be ahead of the curve, they achieved their goal in 2015 to use 100% renewable energy. They chose a combo special of wind and hydropower. Purchasing two hydro-plants enabled them to get 80% of their power from renewable energy, but they sought out a perfect score of 100%. Rather than build, they chose a partnership model where they now buy wind power from another state.

Having been through the initial hurdle, the cities are now happy to share their stories and models to make it easier for other cities to follow. Aspen reminds us that cities can partner to achieve their renewable energy goals.

SILO SECRET #54: A wise *sensei* taught me that an issue is either a problem that you can fix or a situation that is out of your control. Problems are awesome because we can fix them! Greensburg is an amazing example of turning what most would view as a devastating situation into a problem with a solution that has literally made the town a role model for other communities. (Rebuilding Stronger, Better, Greener, 2008)

SILO SECRET #55: While some cities think renewable energy is expensive, thinking green leads to major cost savings. Once extremely costly, wind and solar will become the cheapest sources of electricity globally by 2030, according to research firm Bloomberg New Energy Finance.

SILO SECRET #56: Greensburg saves $200,000 annually in energy costs for its largest buildings, which are all LEED (Leadership in Energy and Environmental Design) certified. (LEED Sustainability, 2019) This is a globally recognized symbol of sustainability achievement for rating green buildings, providing a framework to create healthy, highly efficient, and cost-saving green buildings. (LEED Certification, 2019)

SILO SECRET #57: There are hundreds of cities that have models to share. Earth is our only source for safe air, water, farmland, and land. Cities are partnering to share the multiple ways to transition to renewable energy. (Sierra Green Communities, 2019)

SILO SECRET #58: There is a renewable energy revolution underway. Latin American cities are leading the renewable energy charge, with much of their electricity coming from hydropower. Of the cities getting at least 70% of their power from renewables, 57% are in Latin America, 20% are in Europe, 9% are in Africa, and 9% are in North America. (Gustin, 2018)

REFLECT:

Each city is moving forward with a different flair. Did a particular city inspire you?

_____

_____

*"By working together to keep health at the center of our focus, as well as the national conversation, we can create the safe communities we all want and deserve." – **Mike Quigley*** (U.S. representative for Illinois's 5th congressional district, including most of Chicago's North Side.)

5.4 Communities Are Putting on a New HAT

On my way to a Foundation for a Healthy St. Petersburg event, I was thinking of the incredible benefits of a community adopting the HAT (High Availability Team) approach mentioned earlier, where a small team of Problem Solvers helps get to real root causes to achieve measurable results for the community. When I arrived, I could not believe my eyes when I saw the program they were sharing was called "Community HAT." Okay, it is really called CHAT (Community Health Action Team), but sometimes they call it "Community HAT." They are paving the way for an oldie-but-goodie program called Health in All Policies (HiAP), which follows key principles of interdependence where you get all silos on deck to reach holistic community solutions. (HiAP Framework, 2019) Council Member Darden Rice explained how this innovative way of thinking was so different that many had a hard time with the idea at first, but she said there are now a variety of industry sector silos on board.

Founder Randall Russell expressed how the Foundation for a Healthy St. Petersburg seeks to end disparate outcomes by race, age, gender, and geography through a united focus on health in all policies across the public and private sectors. Dr. Idehen and Heath Kirby of the Florida Department of Health shared how this broader view is intended to make decisions together to close the gap on health inequities and strengthen communities.

When the event host asked for a show of hands, an overwhelming majority were from the nonprofit world. There were a couple outcome-focused consultants in the room. In reviewing the community statistics, the speaker advised that unintentional injuries increased by over 60%. (Ulvee & Philip, 2018) You could see that the for-profit business consultants wanted to jump on board, get a team together, and focus on getting to the root cause and then the solution.

Wearing this radical HAT was already a big move, and now the outcome-focused business consultants wanted the nonprofit organizations to flip the HAT around and put it on backwards for an entirely different look?

Yes, that was exactly what they wanted. From the front, the statistics clearly showed rising issues in the community. We had no idea what was behind the scenes. What was causing a rapid increase of accidental injuries that were bad enough to get medical attention? The outcome-minded business consultants wanted to know. Even the slightly curious wanted to turn this HAT around to look at things from a different view.

One gentleman described the flood of business-minded questions that filled his mind: "What type of accidents? What if we do a Pareto chart to see which accidents are the most frequent? (Pareto Charts, 2019) Can we prevent one type of accident? How can we minimize accidents? Can we warn people via education?" Feeling alone in his way of thinking, however, he suppressed his burning questions and remained outwardly patient as the speaker went on to the next topic. Eventually, all headed home.

With business HAT teams, the team size can be small. To start, it could literally be a team of one. I know because I was that one for many years. To illustrate this view, imagine if a business had a 60% drop in customers. It would ask, "Was it a simple pothole in the street? Was it a misprint in an ad? Are we not using the latest social media to reach people?" It would flip that HAT around and figure it out.

This community HAT program is an incredible move forward with interdependence. I just hope I get to be there when they do that daring move to flip the HAT around for just a few minutes. Imagine the sense of relief and joy reflected in people's faces as they unveil even more solutions for communities.

I can appreciate how it can be quite challenging to look at something from a different view, especially a nontraditional view. Even though I consider myself a person who is open to new ideas, below are a couple stories that reminded me of the value of being open to trying on a new HAT.

A 3-year-old HAT—Senior Vice President Takes Advice From Toddler?

As a crisis resolution leader for a top global media company, I worked to separate my personal and professional life. At the time, my daughter was three years old. When I took problem-solving phone calls at home, she wanted to join me. We agreed if she was very quiet and let me focus on facilitating solutions, she could be in the room. All was fine and then it happened. I found myself juggling the mute button, trying my best to remind my daughter of our agreement, but she kept trying to interrupt. At the same time, this call was getting quite intense as high-profile clients were at risk. Just as I went off mute, my daughter stated, "But, Mommy, I think I have the solution."

As I was about to update my résumé, the senior vice president projected in this deep, authoritative voice, "Let's hear what the kid has to say." My three-year-old replied, "The same computer keeps breaking. It is time to get a new computer." After a moment of silence that felt like hours, the senior vice president confirmed, "The kid is right. We need to allocate funds for a new computer." All approved.

From that point on, whenever we had challenges where it was hard to reach a solution, someone would always say, "Let's get your kid on the phone." It prompted us to put on the hat of a three-year-old, helping us laugh, relax a little, and talk through alternatives. Being that this is the best state of mind to solve a problem, we explored and talked through options, even the ones that we assumed were not possible.

The Tiny Turtle HAT—Learning From a Turtle?

Hurricane Irma was headed right for my hometown. Our small city was all over the news. This was more frightening than most hurricanes because, well, it was headed directly for us. My daughter had just adopted a turtle. Knowing that this little guy might grow to be 12 inches, we had just purchased him a 75-gallon home and he was thrilled. But now, we were evacuating and forced to move him back to his Tupperware container. He panicked, frantically swimming back and forth, hitting the edges, splashing and banging. Sort of as a joke, I sat down on the floor next to him and went into my amateur version of a yoga meditation position with my legs crossed and my index fingers and thumbs together. As I closed my eyes and made the "mmmm" sound, little Squirt swam to the edge of the Tupperware and calmly watched.

After the hurricane passed, I could not wait to tell this story to my community service associates who help people with yoga, mindfulness, and other meditation techniques. I thought they would be so excited to hear that their techniques helped a turtle, but when I told them, they were not surprised at all. They looked at me like I was excitedly telling them "2 + 2 = 4." In their silo, it was obvious that the turtle would respond, but not being from that silo, I still feel kind of astonished that there is an untapped market for turtle yoga classes.

For years, I have been thinking how great it would be to apply the business HAT (High Availability Team) process in the community, so I am especially excited about the above Community HAT program. The challenging part will be engaging business representatives with an outcome-focused vision on the bottom line with community service professionals with a more people-focused vision. Below is a real example.

Real Example of Silo-Sharing Possibilities to Address Plastic Bags: A local city is trying to ban plastic bags, but if you ask grocery store staff in the area, they are pushing plastic over paper simply because it is cheaper. Thus, if we work together to make paper bags a fraction of a penny less expensive, *voilà*, no more plastic bags. We can talk about the water, we can talk about the pelicans choking on plastic, but stores are full speed focused on the bottom line. In interviewing 20-plus employees, their number one choice is reusable tote bags because that is no cost to the grocery store. Their second choice is plastic bags. The paper bags are under the counter because those are the most expensive choice, so the store would prefer to limit customers from viewing and selecting that option.

Simulated Solution: The HAT team would consult an environmentalist to confirm which is best—paper or reusable tote bags, considering the short-term and long-term impact on the environment. The environmentalist might even surprise us and say that getting customers to return plastic bags to be recycled may be the best option. We then would prioritize first, second, and third choices and go for the first option. If that is infeasible for now, we would go for option two, with a plan to eventually transition to the first option. When we think about judging outcome-focused people for being focused on profits, it is good to remember that profits from businesses fund nonprofit goals. This helps us respect both views and work together for the common goal of having a safe planet to live in.

Choosing the right HAT

The business HAT (High Availability Team) and the community HAT (Health Action Team) are similar, but there are still secrets to share between the two. The 24/7 HAT business model is very effective because it ensures total clarity and focus on the most urgent and important problems. Even after the excitement is over, the team digs deep into the root cause. Permanent solutions are then put in place with steps that resemble the scientific method. The team often does not sleep until a solution plan is in place.

Speaking of fatigue, the community service HAT has a different type of pressure, often called *compassion fatigue* (Smith P. , 2019), where they carry the stress of unresolved issues impacting families and children. They could benefit by learning more ways to make progress on goals versus taking on an influx of problems, where there is often no real solution in sight. As my college mentor advised, "If you really want to help people, learn about systems." The business HAT follows a system of problem-solving.

People come together in a crisis or a dream. We have the two-for-one special. Community service providers often unite two silos from the community side. There is an opportunity to go a bit further out of their comfort zone to invite a member from the business silo for a different view. In decades on the business side, my goals were always closer to 98% or higher versus 30% or higher fulfillment whether it was meeting product or service fulfillment metrics. When it came to a problem, three times represented a trend for us to get to the root cause and then focus on a solution. Many of us have that one comfortable HAT that fits us so well, but every now and then, we may be pleasantly surprised as we try on a new HAT.

SILO SECRET #59: Planning together for more comprehensive solutions, communities are proving that silo-to-silo talks are beneficial. The key value is getting input from multiple sectors.

SILO SECRET #60: This silo secret is something that I have been looking forward to. They call it CHAT (Community Health Action Team), but I like it when they call it Community HAT. From my view, it is time for us to put on our Community HAT where silos come together for better communities.

SILO SECRET #61: While the community HAT is a great union of silos, the silos mentioned are mainly from the same type of silos, meaning city planning and health organizations talking is a wonderful improvement, but city planning could still be viewed as a community versus business silo. To gravitate more toward interdependence, it may be helpful to engage a silo in the purely business district, such as finance people who make money off the problems we are trying to fix.

SILO SECRET #62: When the same people call the police or crisis lines multiple times per year, a HAT team may be beneficial. In some communities, police are starting to bring mental health professionals in their vehicles for ride-along visits, sharing knowledge to help address root causes for real solutions. If a person from an outcome silo went on the ride-along or even reviewed data trends, he or she could also brainstorm with the service providers on ways to maximize outcomes for people.

REFLECT:

HiAP (Health in All Policies) teams work together to plan cities so that people can walk versus having to take a car to go to a park, grocery store, or a community garden. Do you live in a community where you can easily walk to access food and recreation?

_____

_____

Chapter 5 Summary:

Imagine the benefits of community service leaders forming a small problem management or HAT team to continually identify root causes along with solutions to share. The nonprofit world is amazing at articulating the impact of problems. The business world values identifying and addressing root causes. We hear observations like, "We need to treat the problem, not the symptom." If we utilize the concept of HAT in our community, we can address root causes and then implement, monitor, and validate solutions.

6. GAME-CHANGER SCIENCE

*"Many of our state's most intractable multigenerational issues—addictions, child maltreatment, obesity, disease, domestic violence, school failure and suspensions, delinquency, and court involvement—could be reduced by addressing early adversity." – **Dr. Vincent Felitti*** (One of the world's foremost experts on childhood trauma and co-Principal Investigator of the "Adverse Childhood Experiences" (ACE) Study.) (Felitti V. J., et al., 1998)

*"You have to look at behavior through a slightly different lens." – **James Redford*** (Directed *Paper Tigers* documentary that offers solutions to teaching traumatized children and teens. (Redford, 2019) Cofounder and chair of the Redford Center, a nonprofit organization that shares environmental and social stories to spur action and change.)

6.1 In a Class of 30, What Do We Not See?

When I saw that a local middle school in my area had an 18% passing rate on a standard science test, I first thought it had to be a mistake. Then I thought, "Hey, I make good numbers go up for a living, so I'll just volunteer to help out with some process improvements to increase their numbers. I'll start out with some data gathering, the first step of process improvement. This will be a breeze." I joined a meeting at city hall where we had an opportunity to interview a school principal. Community leaders asked how we could help the school.

The school principal openly shared about a dozen items, but not one had to do with school. Robin Saenger, the founder of Peace4Tarpon, refers to the moment when people understand the impact of trauma as when "the nickel drops." Some call it when "the light bulb goes off." In my case, this is when I started realizing the root cause of our nation ranking #38 and #24 in science and math, respectively, was largely due to children dealing with trauma.

Here are some of the items reported by the principal.

1. Parents do not have transportation or money to take children to the doctor or to get eyeglasses.

2. One little girl presses her face against the paper trying to see her book.

3. Children do not have proper clothing to wear to school. Parents cannot afford clothes.

4. Parents are addicted to drugs, resulting in children being in survival mode, unable to learn.

5. Unconscious single moms are not awake to protect their children. Bad things are happening.

6. Parents are getting divorced often due to money, and they now have two rents to pay.

7. Children change schools multiple times as parents try to find housing or couches to sleep on.

8. Cyber bullying and online predators take children down the wrong path, impacting school.

9. Parents are in jail, and they are trying to find relatives in the area.

10. Lockdowns and stories on the news are negatively affecting children.

As I viewed the statistics on our communities, I could not believe it was possible. Below is a poem from a child's point of view.

In my class of 30, what do we not see?

Nearly 80% of us children experience a trauma or tragedy,
such as violence, unsafe touching, or a broken family.

Trauma makes our mind feel like we are being chased by a bear,
that may explain why Johnny has a hard time sitting in his chair.

Some think trauma only affects girls but do not realize or know,
many little boys also feel helpless and filled with sorrow.

A couple of my friends get quiet when we make gifts at school for Mom & Dad, I think it reminds them of love they lost or never had.

Some of my friends rebel when people come and tell us not to do drugs, I think it is because that is how they lost the people they most loved.

Some kids facing trauma act like a bully on the outside,
but most of us just hold in the pain deep down inside.

Some run away to more danger and others actually try to gain weight,
we all try to escape in our own unique way.

People think abuse is all about black eyes that show on the outside,
but words can easily make us feel worthless inside.

If untreated, trauma spreads way worse than the flu,
it could happen to me, it could happen to you.

The good news is there is help out there,
this poem was inspired by people who care.

Compared to those with no history of childhood trauma, people who have experienced trauma are: (Felitti V. J., 1998)

- **15 times** more likely to attempt suicide

- **4 times** more likely to become an alcoholic

- **4 times** more likely to develop a sexually transmitted disease

- **4 times** more likely to inject drugs

- **3 times** more likely to use antidepressant medication

- **3 times** more likely to be absent from work

- **3 times** more likely to experience depression

- **3 times** more likely to have serious job problems

- **2.5 times** more likely to smoke

- **2 times** more likely to develop chronic obstructive pulmonary disease

- **2 times** more likely to have a serious financial problem

To get a perspective on the wide range of trauma, below are some trauma statistics by age.

Young children:

- **26%** of children in the United States will witness or experience a traumatic event before they turn four.

- **40%** of children in America say they experienced a physical assault during the past year, with 1 in 10 receiving an assault-related injury.

- **25%** of children were the victims of robbery, vandalism, or theft during the previous year.

- More than **13%** of children reported being physically bullied, more than 33% (1 in 3) said they had been emotionally bullied.

- **20%** of children witnessed violence in their family or the neighborhood during the previous year.

Age 17 and younger:

- **More than 60%** of youth, age 17 and younger, have been exposed to crime, violence, and abuse either directly or indirectly.

- In one year, **39%** of children between the ages of 12 and 17 reported witnessing violence; **17%** reported being a victim of physical assault; and **8%** reported being the victim of sexual assault.

- **About 25%** of youth, age 17 and younger, were victims of robbery or witnessed a violent act.

- **Nearly half** of children and adolescents were assaulted at least once in the past year.

- Among 536 elementary and middle school children surveyed in an inner-city community, **30%** had witnessed a stabbing and **26%** had witnessed a shooting.

- **Reflecting back: 60%** of adults report experiencing abuse or other difficult family circumstances during childhood.

18 and older:

Traumatized youth grow up to join our workforce. Below are the statistics from an employer's view.

- **$246 billion per year** spent on Chemical dependency

- **$44 billion per year** spent on Depression and its work-related outcomes, absenteeism, reduced productivity and medical expenses

Impact:

- Young children exposed to five or more significant adverse experiences in the first three years of childhood face a **76%**

likelihood of having one or more delays in their language, emotional, or brain development.

- As the number of traumatic events experienced during childhood increases, the risk for the following health problems in adulthood increases: depression; alcoholism; drug abuse; suicide attempts; heart and liver diseases; pregnancy problems; high stress; uncontrollable anger; and family, financial, and job problems.

With the prison population growing at a steep rate, the U.S. is officially number one in the percentage of prisoners. According to retired Judge Sullivan, author of the book *Raised by the Courts*, girls are the fastest growing prison population. (Sullivan, 2019) One statistic that we may want to ponder for a moment is that 95% of the people in prison come out to join us in society. That reminds me of a true story that I can recall like a bad horror film trailer. It was a cold night in December, and there were just a few of us on the holiday schedule to work the night shift. We were temporarily in this trailer in the middle of this deserted area with very poor lighting.

My boss called and said, "A couple prisoners escaped, and they are headed in your direction." He went on to say, "Lock the doors," but I already had that task covered. And they said I had insubordination issues! Just kidding. Moments later, a man in a ski mask, with his face showing in the small fogged-up window, started knocking on the window. As panic was quickly setting in, the man seemed to realize that he'd scared us a tad. He yanked off his ski mask and yelled through the window, "*Lo siento!* (I am sorry) I am the new janitor."

Well, by now, the two men I was afraid of are on our streets with no mask, so let's hope they received some good therapy or training to successfully transition from prison to our neighborhood.

SILO SECRET #63: Studies are showing that bullying goes beyond the schools and impacts society. One statistic to consider is the impact on our safety. **60%** of boys who were bullies in middle school had at least one criminal conviction by the age of **24**. (Olweus, 1993)

SILO SECRET #64: The Department of Justice reports that as many as 75% of the people in prison experienced childhood violence or neglect. Some prisons such as a model used in Germany, where they mentor individuals in prison to address the past to help them move forward, are showing a much lower residual rate of prisoner's returning to prison. (Gohara, 2019)

SILO SECRET #65: Businesses can collaborate with medical doctors to optimize employee health and productivity. As an example, when an excellent employee suddenly had productivity issues, it turned out the employee's doctor was trying new medicines for his anxiety. Since the drowsy employee was unaware of the impact, I offered to provide dated feedback to help the doctor assess the best medicine.

SILO SECRET #66: To communicate with doctors and be in compliance with HIPAA (Health Insurance Portability and Accountability Act) and equality laws, I used a very simple method where I jotted down the date along with a 1 character symbol to indicate if the employee performance was better (>), worse (<) or the same (=). To ensure I treated all employees equally with no special treatment, I used this method to share feedback with all employees. They liked it as it ensured we were all on the same page.

My employee's doctor called me and said, "I checked with all my colleagues, and they have never heard of a business manager and a mental health doctor working together." He said they all loved the idea. It was a win-win-win. The doctor was able to find the medicine that helped the employee become happier and more productive at work, home and on the road.

REFLECT:

Think of someone who may have been angry or aggressive at your work or a public place.

Is it be possible that the anger may be related to unresolved trauma?

_____

_____

"I think scars are like battle wounds—beautiful, in a way. They show what you've been though and how strong you are for coming out of it." – **Demi Lovato** (American singer, songwriter, and actress. Supports charities including Red Cross, St. Jude Children's Research Hospital, Save the Music Foundation, and WE.)

6.2 The Science of ACEs—What is Your ACE Score?

Back in the nineties, an insurance company invited people to join a program to get healthier and lose a little weight. While the program was quite successful at achieving their goals, people were quitting the program. This puzzled the insurance company so much that it did a study and discovered some things that are leading to a national trauma movement. Dr. Bob Moore says the impact of this study is similar to doctors learning to wash their hands before surgery to reduce patient fatalities. With this study, we learned a relationship between adverse childhood experiences and the ability to be productive adults. It is important to know that this is not a life sentence. If people have awareness, they can use techniques to build resilience. If we are aware, we can be trauma-informed to grow stronger, healthier communities.

What is the ACE Study? (Felitti V. J., et al., 1998)

With life's deck of cards, some people are born "lucky" with a perfect hand. They have a mom and dad, a loving brother who is always looking out for them, and a grandma and grandpa who come over to make dinner and play board games. Mom works at the school, so she gets home in plenty of time to help the kids with homework and ask about each of their days. Dad comes home and takes the kids outside to throw the ball around a little before heading off to the soccer game. Even their popular golden retriever dog is stigma-free.

Some have everything, and then one card gets torn and things seem to spiral, affecting all the cards. While all of us have the same areas of life, our cards vary. Some have cards that look like they are barely hanging in there, but they keep going. Others have mended cards. There are programs like WRAP® (Wellness Recovery Action Plan®) to help people define what is in their cards when life is good and to know what to do during those times when they feel like they have a lousy hand. Last but not least, they can create a plan for when things get bad or when they feel like they are about to fold. Trauma experts emphasize that when you talk about trauma, you want to have resiliency in the same conversation. There are many tips and tools to help us mend our cards.

The ACE Study is a collaborative effort between the Centers for Disease Control and Prevention and Kaiser Permanente. Dr. Anda and Dr. Felitti led this analysis of the relationship between adverse childhood experiences (ACEs) and health and behavioral outcomes. Shocked that certain ACEs were common among the obese, middle-class population; the ACE Study followed 17,337 participants for 20 years to assess the prevalence and long-term effects of ACEs in the middle-class *general* population. (Felitti V. J., et al., 1998) Below are 10 ACE Study categories.

1. Recurrent physical abuse

2. Recurrent emotional abuse

3. Contact sexual abuse

4. An alcohol and/or drug abuser in the household

5. An incarcerated household member

6. A household member who is chronically depressed, mentally ill, institutionalized, or suicidal

7. Mother is treated violently

8. Not raised by both biological parents

9. Emotional neglect

10. Physical neglect

The ACE Score (Stevens, 2017)

The ACE Study uses a simple scoring method to quantify our exposure to childhood trauma, where exposure to one category (not incident) of ACE qualifies as one point. To calculate your ACE score, you simply add up the points. An ACE score of 0 (zero) means that a person had an unbelievably good winning hand. An ACE score of 10 indicates that a person had exposure to all ten of the trauma categories listed. Below are the official ACE questions. (Felitti V. J., et al., 1998) I shortened #3 to leave out extra details for younger readers.

	While you were growing up, during your first 18 years of life:	If yes, enter "1" in box
1.	Did a parent or other adult in the household often or very often … swear at you, insult you, put you down, humiliate you? or Act in a way that made you afraid that you might be physically hurt?	
2.	Did a parent or other adult in the household often or very often … Push, grab, slap, or throw something at you? or Ever hit you so hard that you had marks or were injured?	
3.	Did an adult or person at least 5 years older than you ever … Touch or fondle you or have you touch their body in a sexual way?	
4.	Did you often or very often feel that … No one in your family loved you or thought you were important or special? or Your family didn't look out for each other, feel close to each other, or support each other?	

5.	Did you often or very often feel that … You didn't have enough to eat, had to wear dirty clothes, and had no one to protect you? or Your parents were too drunk or high to take care of you or take you to the doctor if you needed it?	
6.	Were your parents ever separated or divorced?	
7.	Was your mother or stepmother: often or very often pushed, grabbed, slapped, or did she have something thrown at her? Or was she Sometimes, often, or very often kicked, bitten, hit with a fist, or hit with something hard? or Ever repeatedly hit at least a few minutes or threatened with a gun or knife?	
8.	Did you live with anyone who was a problem drinker or alcoholic or who used street drugs?	
9.	Was a household member depressed or mentally ill, or did a household member attempt suicide?	
10.	Did a household member go to prison?	

An associate, Denise Hughes Conlon, worked for Pinellas Ex-Offender Recovery Coalition, where she helped former prisoners transition into the real world and workplace. As part of creating a trauma-informed environment, she became a strong advocate for giving former prisoners the opportunity to take the ACE assessment and was asked to speak at many conferences to tell them about the benefits of sharing this information. She explained that the former prisoners' average ACE score was a nine and that did not include the fact that many of the adversities occurred multiple times.

Upon taking the assessment, ex-offenders understood how their past behavior had a lot to do with their childhood and realized that they had a choice to change their behavior. They grasped that they had the power to pick new cards from the deck and move on to live a better life, and they were therefore more receptive to programs to help them. To her surprise, employees were open about their own ACE score, expressing how it helped them to be more understanding and empathetic and also more aware of how their own background created stressors, formerly known as triggers, in their life and work.

With the ACE score, the higher the score, the higher the negative impact on the employer as well as the employee.

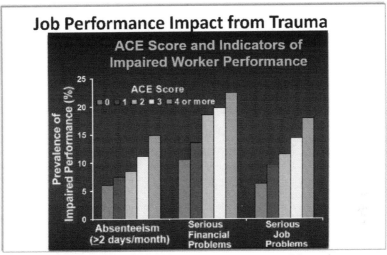

Figure 6.2 Chart illustrates how work issues increase as ACE Score increases.

One of the amazingly refreshing trends of the ACE Study is that it is helping many people see the world with a new lens. It is called a *trauma-informed lens*. I'll never forget Judge Tepper sharing a story of how she used to just tell people, "You need to be back in court at 9:00 a.m. or face penalties." She said she had no idea that some people could not physically get from their home to the court by 9:00 a.m. using the bus system. She actually had several bus map routes in her hands, showing how her team was literally trying to figure it out, and they could not find a route to get to court in time. So, now, with their new lens, they are more considerate in working out barriers like transportation. She added that it is even worse when the person has to take a three-hour bus ride sitting on the bus with their attacker, who is also riding the bus to get to court. Over the past few years especially, judges and various people are coming together to share how we can show more compassion to make it easier for people to choose the right path. Judge Tepper shares more in "Trauma-informed judges take gentler approach, administer problem-solving justice to stop cycle of ACEs." (Finkel, 2014)

SILO SECRET #67: ACE is just a tool to help you understand what past events may have impacted you. People ask, "Now that I know my ACE score, what is next?" Excellent question, and the answer is *resilience*. Simply do what works for you. There is so much evidence now that shows how resiliency activities lower cortisol in your system, which is elevated under stress. Taking steps to relax helps ensure a healthy heart rate. Having positive thoughts, volunteering, singing, or having a hobby or activity that you enjoy are all great things to do. The key truly is finding the right activity that works for you.

SILO SECRET #68: You can also find out your Resiliency Score. (McClinn, Rains, & Stevens, 2006) Just like the ACE score is not your destiny, you can always improve on your Resiliency.

SILO SECRET #69: This secret is not so much a secret as I think every silo knows how children are like little sponges, absorbing what they see and hear. One of the revelations that I had was that if we think little bullies are scary, wait until they grow up. Some communities are organizing picnics or offering free books in the park. If we can show children positive behaviors and activities to repeat, they will have a better chance of repeating good behaviors as children and adults.

REFLECT:

Think of a resiliency method that may work best for you (e.g., mindfulness, exercise, journaling, drawing, walking, etc.). You can start small like taking 3 minutes to relax your mind.

_____

_____

A while ago, one of my instructors said, "The tasks and activities on your calendar are a reflection of you." Life gets busy. Are you blocking out time to have fun and time to bounce back (resiliency)?

_____

_____

"Trauma is universal. It impacts all of us." – **Robin Saenger** (Founder of Peace4Tarpon trauma-informed community, artist, former vice mayor of Tarpon Springs.) (Saenger, 2019)

6.3 Hidden Under the Surface

Below are some short stories to illustrate forms of trauma that may be hidden under the surface.

Grocery Store Jim

When I was younger, my mom worked at a medical clinic for a few years. I remember her commenting that when you work at a neighborhood clinic, you see things that others don't see. I asked her what she meant and she explained that you know more than what others see on the surface. For instance, she knew that Jim, the nice man at the grocery store who smiled each day, was dealing with a terminal illness and had just weeks to live. The rest of us learned three weeks later, feeling like it happened so suddenly. We had no idea what Jim was going through under the surface.

Sally At Work

A few years ago, there were some rumors of layoffs, so most people were stressed. Sally was typically helpful and prompt in ordering supplies, but she frustrated Mark when it slipped her mind three times to order paper clips. Sally was distracted as her cancer returned, but she did not want to worry anyone.

Mark Had His Own Story

Mark was facing eviction with a new baby on the way. With all the stress, his doctor put him on medication for his high blood pressure. Worrying about bills generated more bills in the form of prescriptions and doctor visits.

Friends with Children in the Military

A friend of mine had twins, Dan and Dana, who signed up to serve their country when they turned 18 years old. Right after boot camp, Dan was assigned to a local military base, but Dana was sent overseas to a war zone that was continually on the news with injuries and fatalities. One day, I said, "I am amazed at how you handle everything; how do you do it?" She and her husband responded in almost perfect harmony, "We sit on the couch each night holding hands tightly, praying we will not see our daughter on the news."

Kid with an "Overmad" Bully On The Bus

Shelly dreaded getting on the school bus. Thinking she didn't want to go to school, I tried to gently ask questions to understand more, wanting to bring her smile back. Finally, she and her brother showed me the dried-up blood, advising that a girl on the bus cut them. When the girl started threatening other children, Shelly reported it to the school. Later, she described the girl as being "overmad," sharing how "she has so much anger inside her that no matter how much she cuts people, she cannot get the anger out of her." We spoke to the school counselor to make sure he knew of our concerns from a trauma-informed view. The counselor said, "We've received many complaints, but you are the first who was worried about the little girl." Eventually, the little girl's father went to prison. Since her mother was addicted to drugs, the little girl ended up moving north to live with an uncle.

Coworker You Never Had A Chance To Meet

Early in my career, there was a young man about 20 years old who worked in our office. He was not very social. I admit, I just figured he was just conceited or maybe shy. Then one day, he didn't show up. It turned out that he had died of AIDS.

SILO SECRET #70: The film *Under the Surface* helps illustrate the type of things that people may be dealing with under the surface. (Wideman & Ayers, 2014) The goal is to be more mindful and trauma-informed, understanding that people may be dealing with something that we do not know about.

SILO SECRET #71: Bullies are often victims of trauma. Some experts say that boys tend to act out and girls tend to hold in the pain. The "overmad" girl was likely doing both. All handle trauma in their own way.

SILO SECRET #72: A local Research Analyst told me that it is kind of funny that people fill out surveys saying that they have anxiety and feel depressed sometimes but do not check the box saying that they have experienced a mental disorder or illness. "Nearly 50 percent of the U.S. population will experience a mental health disorder at some point in their lifetimes. Anxiety, depression, and addiction are on the rise." – *Yes!* Magazine (Yes! The Mental Health Issue, 2018)

REFLECT:

Have you ever had something bothering you on the inside (under the surface) and maybe not projected your most positive self on the outside?

_____

_____

Can you see the value of being trauma informed and aware that people may be dealing with a situation that is hidden *under the surface*?

_____

_____

"We need to move from 'what is wrong with you?' to 'what happened to you?' way of thinking." – **Joseph F. Foderaro** (Licensed Clinical Social Worker, Diplomate with the American Board of Examiners in Clinical Social Work, Co-founder and senior faculty member for the Sanctuary Institute.) (Bloom, 1994)

6.4 What Happened to You? Mystery Solved.

There are some questions in life that kind of stay in the back of your mind, unsolved mysteries perhaps, not quite worth calling Sherlock Holmes over but enough to be on that things-that-make-you-say-*hmm* list. Well, for me, that question happened in elementary school. This boy arrived in our class without any explanation or even introduction. One day, he was absent, and I heard the teacher mumble what sounded like "Leon" as she updated her roll book. If Leon ever said a word or even made a sound, I never heard it. His body language, however, was quite clear. He did not want to be in our school or anywhere for that matter.

I could not help but notice that no matter how cold it was, he came into class with his motionless face shining from what I believe was sweat, but it made no sense that he would be perspiring. I was shivering in a portable with a heater from the 1950s and he was over there with beads of sweat dripping from his forehead. His dark eyes stared downward. His black hair was cut so close to his scalp that you could not tell if his hair was curly or straight. Even his hair had no expression.

Leon talked to no one, and no one dared talk to him. He seemed to have a permanent expression on his face, but I could not quite tell what he was projecting. Was it pure anger? Intense sadness? Burning frustration? Or some combination making him want to escape? I wondered if he knew how to read or if he even knew how to speak English or any language. Somehow, it felt like the school had no idea what to do with him so they figured, plop him in a classroom. To me, it was obvious that he was not comprehending what the teacher was saying.

Despite his large size, he walked as if he had this heavy burden. You could almost visualize chains pulling him downward. As he lifted each foot to take a step, it was as if he was pulling his foot out of quicksand with each dreadfully painful step forward. Trudging through this tremendous weight often made him late to class. One thing on his side was that he seemed to be invisible. If anyone else came to school late, we would be tardy and three strikes, you're out, or something like that, but he openly disrupted the class as his boots pounded onto the old, yellowed tile floor. Yet, the teacher kept teaching, and all of us students acted as if we could see right through him.

Then, one day, Ms. S was teaching like any other day. Suddenly, she screamed and leaped for the door in fear. She literally leapt out of the door and landed beyond the steps, so she must have fallen at least four feet. This all happened in milliseconds, but when the mad "Incredible Hulk" is in your classroom with no adult supervision, suddenly it is like a scene from a movie where time is in slow motion. It is also the one time in my life that I can honestly say that adult supervision would have been nice. Before I could even think about reacting, a chair flew from behind me from where Leon's seat (now airborne) used to be—the aisle to my right and one seat back. The chair flew, just missing the side of my cheek, and crashed into the front of the classroom, where Ms. S had been standing a moment ago. Whatever Leon had inside—anger, sadness, or frustration—it erupted at that moment. Yet, still, he remained completely silent.

No one knew what happened, but a few days later, Leon was back. The boy who had almost decapitated me was back in that same chair—the same chair that almost decapitated me. My mind was now focused on survival. I knew that Leon gave no warning, or if he did give a warning, I could not see it, other than that fearful look of Ms. S, if I could even think of watching or listening to her. She was no longer my focus. I was in the line of fire. A steel chair can take off your head, and you don't even need to aim very well. So, as the teacher spoke, whatever she was saying, I couldn't tell you; I was acutely aware of my position in relation to her and Leon. I had to be ready to duck but, like prey, I could not show fear.

My biggest fear was Leon would sneeze and I'd have to explain why I leapt to the ground. Oh man, Ms. S. was back in the center of the room, with me perfectly positioned in the line of chair fire. Every now and then, she'd move closer to the door, surely to give me a sense of some relief from this exhausting game of imaginary dodge chair. Eventually, the school year ended. Yet, for years, it was like an unresolved mystery in my head. One mystery was, "How in the world did I pass that class?" But the main mystery that stayed with me was, "How in the world does a kid pick up a clunky, heavy metal chair and fling it 15 feet like it was a flimsy frisbee?" To this day, I have never seen or heard from Leon, but 10 years later, I did get the answer on how he was able to fling that metal chair across the room.

Mystery Solved.

So, there I was, about 10 years later. I was in my first year of college, 18 years old, had my dream job with the airlines, a new-to-me car, and my own apartment. The job didn't pay well in money; it paid more in travel and cool parties, so life was good. One minor challenge was that I had started a new English class and the professor was proud of his reputation of being so tough that people dropped like flies from his class, but I was up for the challenge. He wore all black with a heavy wallet chain hanging from his pocket and arrived to class holding his motorcycle helmet with a skull prominently displayed on the back. When he wrote sentences on the board to give examples of nouns, adjectives, and verbs, he would write these strange, violent sentences. His policy was, "The only excuse for missing class is if you are dead." Oh, "You are dead." was one of the sentences he wrote on the whiteboard. He assigned one big paper that was most of your grade, so it was a lot of pressure.

You needed to have an unbelievable number of footnotes in your paper to even pass the class. This was when you had typewriters, so I had to plan out 30-40 pages of organized paragraphs and footnotes. For young people, imagine if you had no MS Word. You had to plan every word of your school papers. If you didn't get it right, you had to use this thing called whiteout to erase your mistake or retype that whole page from scratch. My strategy was using little strips of paper to write out the footnotes and then place the notes in sorted piles next to the paragraphs. I had the paragraphs all organized with little mountains of footnote piles on the table, all around me on the floor and even on top of the chairs.

Finally, I was ready to start typing the paper. It was now 2:00 a.m. With my back to the door, I was sitting at my tiny patio table (remember, I was a poor college student). Anyway, I was about ready to type up the organized piles when the door handle moved—someone was turning my apartment door handle at 2:00 a.m. I instinctively said, "Hello?" I was an 18-year-old, 122-pound college freshman saying hello to a person who was likely a burglar or up to something that was not good. Somehow, it seemed like the right thing to say. I suppose I was thinking that if I alerted this person that I was aware of their presence, they would leave. My hope was that he'd realize the person in the apartment (me) was awake and could call the police, prompting the unwanted guest to hit the road.

There was dead silence. Part of me wanted to look out to confirm he was gone, but then he answered my question, loud and clear. The man started yelling, "Open the door" and then started running and putting his force against the door like the SWAT team does in the movies to burst the door open. I put a small chair in front of the door and started putting other objects in front of the door, anything I could find. The force against the door seemed to get louder and louder, and he was getting close to busting the door open. I could see a line of light from the outdoor porch light along the opening side of the door. At this point, I visualized in my head what he looked like. He was clearly a 6-foot 9-inch wrestler, and he was aggressively mad. He did not seem to care that he was being so loud that neighbors could hear him and call the police. The fact that he didn't care was even more terrifying.

Somehow, I was able to move a large, clunky La-Z-Boy recliner chair out of the corner and put it in front of the door to hold him back. That ugly green and yellow plaid recliner chair weighed a ton, way more than the chair that Leon picked up, but I managed to get the chair in front of the door to stop my unwanted guest from forcing the door open. Somewhere in between, I called 911 to get the police. They said I needed to call the sheriff's department. I surely hope they've fixed that process by now. Anyway, the wrestler eventually became silent. I was terrified that he was going to realize that I had a window that was much easier to knock out than a door, but luckily for me, he chose the challenging route.

By now, the police or sheriff—not sure which—said, "This is the police. Open the door." I went to move the big La-Z-Boy chair, but I could not budge it. The police officer's voice was getting louder as he was clearly getting irritated that I did not listen to his request to open the door. "Ma'am, open the door. This is the police," he repeated in frustration.

Finally, I was able to push the chair away from the door enough to let him in. I literally could not recall how I had been able to move that monstrosity of a chair. I explained to the police officer that I somehow had gotten the chair in front of the door, but then could not move the chair to let him in. The officer said, "Ma'am, your brain was in survival mode—you are stronger when you are fighting for your life."

We talked, and I told him I had nothing to steal. The police officer said, "This man is coming after you, and he'll be back. I'll put you on my route to check on your apartment each night." Every night at 3:00 a.m., his spotlight moved slowly through my apartment from the outside. Thinking back, I should have gotten a little more clarity on how this method helped to ensure my safety. Was I supposed to put my thumb up, so he'd see the silhouette of a thumbs-up and know things were okay? Anyway, this did not give me a warm and fuzzy feeling, so I could hardly sleep, and I already had little sleep from earlier when I was working to finish my paper. Oh yeah, my English paper; I'd basically tossed my footnotes and papers all over the floor, so I had to stay up to sort, reorganize, and type up the paper.

Somehow, on virtually no sleep for days, I made it to English class. The professor, Dr. Ron, known for being rough and tough, took me aside and said in the most caring voice, "What happened to you?" When I told him, he gently said, "Why are you here? You should be resting."

I replied, "But you said the only excuse to miss class is if you are dead."

He said, in the politest way you could possibly make this observation, "You could pass for dead. Go home or go to a friend's house and take care of yourself."

Dr. Ron could have easily assumed I was partying all night or assumed I was an irresponsible student. He could have easily labeled me and said, "What is wrong with you?" But he didn't do that. Instead, he caringly said four simple words that meant everything to me at that time. He gently said in the most caring, non-judgmental way, "What happened to you?" He was by far the toughest teacher I had ever had, but at that moment, he just sat and listened and offered his caring support. "What happened to you?" truly was the perfect thing to say.

More Flying Chairs Among Us

Years later, I ran into the principal of my elementary school at the grocery store. As we chatted, I mentioned that Ms. S was my favorite teacher and said I would love to talk to her and say hello so she passed along my phone number and Ms. S contacted me the next day. When I told Ms. S how great she was, she said she had chills hearing about how much I appreciated her as a teacher. Then, I said, "Do you remember that time the kid threw the chair at you?"

She said, "No."

Astonished, I said, "I am amazed that you don't remember."

She replied, "Having projectiles thrown at you is part of being a teacher." Is this the new normal?

More recently, in a tour of the Juvenile Justice Facility, they pointed out that they intentionally ordered these large, heavy, oddly-shaped chairs. They said, "Does anyone know why we purchased these bulky chairs?" They explained it was to make it harder for youth to throw the chairs.

A friend of mine volunteers at her son's school. She heard from her son's teacher that they canceled a test because a young lady acted out in class and started throwing chairs around. My friend asked her son, "Why didn't you mention that to me about the flying chairs?"

His response was, "Why would I mention a flying chair? It is normal at my school."

SILO SECRET #73: The trauma-informed movement is emphasizing an adjustment in our mindset. When Dr. Bruce Perry and experts talk about trauma, they often say, "Replace the phrase 'What is wrong with you?' with 'What happened to you?'" This is published in the U.S. National Library of Medicine as "a paradigm shift." (Sweeney, Filson, Kennedy, Collinson, & Gillard, 2018)

SILO SECRET #74: ACE (adverse childhood experiences) have such a large impact on a person's health that Dr. Nadine Burke Harris is strongly encouraging a trauma movement where people understand the impact this has on the health, as well as the brain, of people impacted by trauma. (Burke Harris, 2019)

SILO SECRET #75: As far as the flying chair, the police and trauma experts explain how your body becomes stronger when you are in survival mode. Leon and many other children are trapped in that traumatic survival state of mind. I only had to endure that intense stress long enough to give me the strength to move that monstrosity of a chair. Many children are stuck in this trauma state of mind, forced to use the survival versus logical learning part of their mind.

SILO SECRET #76: Unresolved trauma impacts the brain. Cortisol levels increase like a person is being chased by a bear. "PTSD (Post Traumatic Stress Disorder) patients had 122% higher cortisol levels during [trauma] script exposure." (Elzinga, Schmahl, Vermetten, Dyck, & Bremner, 2003)

SILO SECRET #77: Flying chairs are becoming the norm. Rather than accept this as normal, many schools are working to become trauma-informed to help traumatized youth as well as others. They are getting incredibly great results, reducing detentions and increasing attendance and participation.

REFLECT:

Have you ever been in a situation where someone clearly thought, "What is wrong with you?"

_____

_____

Would you have responded better if they thought or asked, "What happened to you?"

_____

_____

"In order to effectively promote community health and well-being, services and supports must share a common understanding of the root causes of the problems and actively work across boundaries through a shared, collective mission." – **Andrea K. Blanch, PhD, David L. Shern, PhD, Clare Reidy, RN, MPH, and Leslie Lieberman, MSW** (Co-authored brief, _Building Stronger Networks_ that explores how a framework recognizing adverse childhood experiences, trauma, and resilience (ATR) can facilitate and accelerate community collaboration.) (Blanch, Shern, Reidy, & Lieberman, 2019)

6.5 Behind the Mask

Larry was volunteering, reading at a local elementary school, and the book turned out to be about bullying. Responding to the book, little Joey asked, "Why would someone hurt someone else?" Larry explained, "Sometimes when people get hurt, they repeat that same hurtful behavior, hurting more people." Joey blurted out, "It makes me angry. I don't get it." Feeling Joey's frustration, Larry added, "Things are changing. Many of the people in pain are getting help rather than spreading more pain." With Joey still looking frustrated, Larry tried to offer encouragement, saying "You have way more safety programs than when I was a kid." Both looked at the time and had to laugh as it was time to go and they only read the first two pages.

While Larry did not share his personal story with Joey, he reflected for a moment on how different things were when he was Joey's age. He recalled a neighbor telling his mother, "You are so lucky you had a boy. You don't need to worry about safety with boys." With that common myth in his head, Larry held in his shame, not telling anyone. From age 7 to age 27, he blamed himself, thinking he should have been strong enough to protect himself. At night, when no one was around, he often cried, intensifying his feelings of insecurity and weakness. It would have broken his mom's heart to know what happened so he held it in. As he put on a mask each morning, his mother would say, "There is my smiling boy."

Years later, Larry could not bear putting on the mask anymore. He tried pills, herbal tea, wine, a little more wine, whatever he could to try to get to sleep, but nothing worked. Finally, his boss said, "The EAP (Employee Assistance Program) can help you with any issue that is affecting your job performance and something is impacting your work." Being a little thrifty, Larry agreed to the first three free visits and then paid for a couple follow-up visits. They did this *trauma reduction* technique to help him process the pain that he tried so hard to mask. After 20 years, he finally realized, it wasn't his fault. For years, he didn't have too many friends, but his co-workers confessed that they had to stop referring to him as Loner Larry.

Now, he was the first to volunteer from building houses for veterans to reading with children.

Watching how Larry is starting a new cycle inspired me to include the tips in this section. I also sat next to a person from the 2-1-1 Crisis Line and she told me people often call and thank them for getting them help to address their pain to the point that they stopped hurting people. I was so excited that I exclaimed, "You need to let people know that both sides can get help!" Parents tell me this topic is hard to talk about, but it is a lot easier to have preventive talks than reactive talks. You can also adapt the tips to fit your communication style.

SILO SECRET #78: Experts advise that over 80% of unsafe touching is preventable. This impacts 1 of 3 girls and 1 of 5 boys. (DoSomething.org, 2019)

Being on the board of Peace4Tarpon, I went to about seven years of community service classes to learn tips to protect children. When I invited friends with children or parents I met, they would often say, "I am so busy, please take notes and tell me what I need to know," so here are my top five parent tips from class.

Parent Tip #1:

Communicate boundaries (safety zones)

If you are a parent, the lyrics to the Wiggles song below will likely be embedded in your mind for a lifetime, so why not add an easy safety verse? The Wiggles told me to keep my day job, but hey, it works.

Verse 1 (official tune sung around the world since the 1950s): (Nursery Rhymes, 1950; Kubler, 2002)

Head, shoulders, knees, and toes; knees and toes.

Head, shoulders, knees, and toes; knees and toes.

And eyes and ears and mouth and nose.

Head, shoulders, knees, and toes; knees and toes.

Added Verse:

These are my safety zones, safety zones.

These are my safety zones, safety zones.

Eyes and ears and mouth and nose.

Head, shoulders, knees, and toes; *safety zones!*

In some classes, instructors advise that parents can teach very young children to understand safety zones by using a bathing suit to define boundaries. The suit covers your personal space. People should respect your personal space. Other areas, "head, shoulders, knees, and toes" represent your *safe space*.

Parent Tip #2:

Talk and role-play on safety

Good news, kids will sing above verse and question you, asking "Hey, what about my arms?" This is great because it is an invitation to talk about safety. Experts want you to talk and even role-play to ensure your kids feel more confident and secure. Volunteering at a theme park event for kids, I asked one kid what he liked best. Sadly, he responded, "I like that this is the only place I don't have to worry about being abducted." One instructor suggested to talk and role-play to make sure kids know how to better handle situations. For example, if someone you do not know grabs your arm, it may be hard for strangers to tell if you are in trouble, so he suggested telling children that they can yell, "I do not know you!"

A key part of safety is open communication. Your kids need to feel comfortable telling you anything, as secrets start small but often grow to be dangerous. One of my friends told her daughter, "Safety is number one. If you are in trouble, call me, no matter what." Well, her daughter and several teens learned the power of watermelon (spiked with vodka).

When her daughter told her friends, "I'll call my mom to pick us up," the other teens said, "No way." She ended up calling. My friend picked up and drove the tipsy teens to safety. She called me and talked nonstop on how worried she was, but she kept her promise and the girls are safe. That experience helped her daughter open up to her mom and even role-play ways to get out of other tough situations.

Parent Tip #3:

Excuse me for the interruption

You know how in the movies, they sometimes show a person going on a blind date and a friend calls or stops by to interrupt just in case a character needs help getting out of an uncomfortable situation? Well, experts advise that this is crucial for kids. Experts advise avoiding 1:1 situations when a child is involved. However, when it is hard to avoid a child being alone with a person of any age, they suggest having candid conversations to let the person know that your family has a safety policy of interrupting to ensure all is okay, so "please excuse me for the interruption" if I stop by in the middle of any 1:1 event. Another approach is to always seek a "party of three."

BACA (Bikers Against Child Abuse) strictly follow this tip. As part of their mission to empower abused children to not be afraid, their policy is to have at least two established members present to assist children. For some situations like if your kid is the first to be picked up and last to be dropped off when being transported to/from school, you can still let the person know your family has a safety policy where you will often be on the phone or even FaceTime to talk with your child during the 1:1 transportation time. Most people truly have good intentions so you can approach this tip more as a standard safety tip where you simply want to stay in communication, ensuring all is okay. The safety check can actually work both ways. One child was in the back of the bus alone and let her father know that the bus driver fell out of his seat. The young girl's father beat the ambulance to the scene. The bus driver had a stroke, and this safety technique just may have saved his life.

Parent Tip #4:

Guess who is online with you

One of my associates is an expert in cyber security crime and speaks at schools to try to raise awareness. He explained that the trend seems to be that kids who are 12 years old and younger have a hard time believing that a person talking to them on the computer may not be who they say they are. Here is a game you can play with kids and maybe even grandparents to help them grasp this point.

The goal of the game is to help kids realize that kind of like little Red Riding Hood, you may have the Big Bad Wolf on the other end and not realize it. Make three cards or pieces of paper: Card #1 (Big Bad Wolf), Card #2 (Grandma), and Card #3 (Little Red Riding Hood). Then text or email questions, get answers, and try to figure out who is on the other end. Finally, the person flips the card to show you who is really on the other end. Oh! I thought you were Grandma, but you were Little Red Riding Hood. How funny! Ah! I thought you were Grandma but you were the Big Bad Wolf. Ugh, a little scary.

Seems like a silly game, but when I asked experts from police departments, Homeland Security, human trafficking, and cyber security what one tip to put in this book, they all said, "Please help parents and kids with online safety." They also advise to keep computers in a central area of the house to help look out for one another. You and your kids can be creative to come up with a more fun version of the game. The key is to be safe. By the way, this applies to us adults. We like accepting friend requests too.

Parent Tip #5:

Remember to take hug breaks

While we say, "I'm doing this for your own good," our intense love can sometimes result in the release of powerful words that don't always come across well. When the right words are hard to say, you can say,

"Hug break." It is kind of like a time out in sports. The rules are no talking, just one big hug, that conveys that our decisions are out of love. It is also hard to work on a laptop or talk on a cell phone while hugging so this helps ensure quality time versus quantity time.

Sounds ridiculous, but I recently learned that 74% of the homeless teens in my community are in that horrible situation because they had a conflict with their parents. One 15-year-old girl interpreted her parents' frustration as disapproval and disappointment of her lifestyle so she left to roam as a homeless couch surfer, not speaking to her parents for seven years. When she turned 22 years old, she returned to have a courageous conversation with her parents. Her parents said, "We can't believe you thought we were disappointed in you. Our frustration was that we were worried about your safety. We were devastated." They were so proud to learn that their amazing daughter made it through high school and a year of college on her own, but then they broke down in tears when they thought of the years they missed. It was awkwardly hard for them to hug after seven years, but when they did, it was harder to let go.

SILO SECRET #79: *Courageous conversations* are defined as "a conversation where you speak up and express how you feel about these issues that are weighing you down." (Sandford, 2019) I've witnessed police dialogues where teens and police have these conversations. Within an hour, tense officers and teens were seeing one another's point of view. One little boy criticized an officer saying, "You walk around with your hands on your belt looking so mean." The officer explained, "It is because this belt weighs 40 pounds." They all laughed when the boy shockingly replied, "That would be like carrying my little brother around all day."

SILO SECRET #80: In business, there is sometimes the view that the less you know about an employee's personal issues, the better. One approach that often works well if something seems to be impacting an employee is to say, "You can try three visits to the Employee Assistance Program (EAP) to get advice on anything that is directly or indirectly affecting your productivity at work, even if it is something like finances or a family member needing help." Another option is to let them work on a project during off-peak hours so the employee can seek help during the day. You can call it a doctor/dentist visit to maintain confidentiality. This way they can get help before things start spiraling out of control.

SILO SECRET #81: Individuals are realizing that we can change the system. A new brief, *Building Stronger Networks* (May 2019), "explores how a framework recognizing adverse childhood experiences, trauma, and resilience (ATR) can facilitate and accelerate community collaboration." It is based on interviews by Andrea K. Blanch, PhD, and David L. Shern, PhD. (Blanch, Shern, Reidy, & Lieberman, 2019)

Coauthors of Building Stronger Networks are bringing together communities as well as organizations.

1 – Campaign for Trauma-informed Policy and Practice (Dr. Blanch)

2 – Senior Science Advisor (Dr. Shern)

3 – Health Federation of Philadelphia (Clare Reidy, MPH and Leslie Lieberman, MSW)

REFLECT:

In one class, the experts showed how even strong, wealthy people are vulnerable. Do you think there is any tip that could help you or one of your loved ones be more proactive in terms of safety?

_____

_____

Chapter 6 Summary: *Trauma is universal, and it impacts everyone directly or indirectly. It has a negative impact on people and profits. Businesses and communities are working together with a common vision of community wellness. Trauma experts say that the key is to transition our thinking from "What is wrong with you?" to "What happened to you?" It seems hard to believe, but that minor adjustment to thinking with a trauma-informed lens will help improve the health and wealth of our communities.*

7. RESILIENCY IS KEY

"Once you choose hope, anything's possible." – **Christopher Reeve** (Best known for his role as Superman. Founded Christopher Reeve Paralysis Foundation to promote research on spinal cord injuries.)

"Smile and let everyone know that today, you're a lot stronger than you were yesterday." – **Drake** (Canadian rapper, singer, and songwriter.) (Smith J., 2017)

7.1 Evan's Earth Angel

When I think of resiliency, I think of a wonderful lady I met at the gym by the name of Janet. From the outside, Janet appeared to have a beautiful, happy family of four. They did everything together. One day, we got into a deeper conversation with others as we were in the waiting room (waiting for the Zumba class to begin), and the news came on. Several people openly sighed, commenting on how the news program was upsetting them. A gentleman asked, "Okay if I just turn off the nonsense, I mean, the TV?"

About four people said, "Sure, please turn it off," and several thanked him.

That was when Janet confided in me and said she "worked hard to stay positive," explaining that she often felt like a "Cuban sandwich being compressed on both ends." She shared that both her mom and son suffered from depression, making her feel like a hot mess caught right in the middle. I shared that, from the outside, she seemed to handle things very well. She happily replied, "I have Evan to thank for that."

Curious what she meant, I said, "We have 15 minutes, if you'd like to share more."

Janet explained, "Well, I didn't always come to work out. I didn't even know what mindfulness was until recently." She said that Evan introduced her to a new way of being.

Another lady, Marsha, said, "Do you mind if I join the conversation?"

Janet commented, "Marsha knows all about how I used to be, so she already has the background of me sitting at home eating comfort food but not getting much comfort." Janet explained that one positive step seemed to lead to more positive steps. She shared, "Working out at the gym got me meeting new people who knew tricks to eat healthier and feel better" and added, "But really it was learning things like mindfulness that helped a lot because it helped my mind feel more relaxed and in control."

Janet went on to say, "This one lady who comes to the gym knew I didn't have a lot of patience to learn all these new steps, so she taught me this easy thing called tapping." (Tapping, 2019) She was clearly excited to share this with me. Showing me with her hands, she said, "With both hands, you just take the tip of your index finger and thumb and tap them together; next you do the same thing with your flippin' middle finger and thumb." Laughing, she continued, "Then you tap your shoulda-putta-ring-on-it finger with your thumb, and last you tap the tip of your sophisticated pinkie finger with your thumb. You just rotate doing that and science shows it helps; go figure."

With a smile, I said, "Janet, thank you so much for showing me your technique. That is awesome. But I am still a little curious. Who is Evan, and how did he get you to change your view to get stronger mentally and physically?"

Janet, with a friendly grin, said, "I get a little off on the tangents, but yes, I would love to tell you about Evan." Janet went on to share how she was standing in the line at the grocery store, kind of in a daze, not really noticing things around her, and a little boy, about four feet tall, said, "It is going to be okay."

She looked over at the little voice and realized the little boy must have been going through chemotherapy as most of his hair had fallen out, with just a few strands of white-blond frail hair draping over his eyes. While his hazel eyes had dark sunken circles around them, he still looked filled with positive energy as he said, "Whatever it is that is bothering you—it is going to be okay." Janet explained that she was feeling overwhelmed, but now she was looking at this little boy and suddenly her problems seemed insignificant.

When Janet and the boy talked a little more, she asked how old he was and he replied, "Seven years old." She shared her name and he replied, "My name is Evan, and this is my mom. Her name is Alicia."

Perhaps not wanting Janet to say anything like, "You'll be fine too," Alicia tried to discreetly let Janet know that little Evan had been given one week to live. Janet could feel her mouth start to quiver as she held back the tears. She could not imagine the right words to say. Just then, Evan smiled and touched Janet's forearm gently, saying, "Now, don't you worry about me. I have been chosen for a very important job. I will be an angel, and my job will be to help the people on Earth."

At this point, I was trying to hold back the tears. Janet stated, "Since then, when I feel like things are getting unbearable, I remember I've got a little friend named Evan looking out for me." Janet paused, clearly to reminisce on her time with Evan. As she glanced away, she added, "Now you know how I manage to keep on smiling."

SILO SECRET #82: One person can make a big difference to inspire others. One of my mentors used to say, "I can light and hold one or two candles, but I can inspire others to keep sharing and bring thousands of candle light to others."

SILO SECRET #83: Experts describe mindfulness as the number one factor that influences our success, even more than income and intelligence. A key reason is that it enables you to be more in control of decisions, whether it is choosing a healthy or not-so-healthy food or taking steps to ensure safety when traveling from one place to another. (Kabat-Zinn, 2017) (Altshul, 2019)

SILO SECRET #84: The tapping exercise that Janet shared is an abbreviated method that seems to work for so many people. It started out with therapists having people do this while they prompted clients to repeat positive sentences. Some felt that was a lot to do and not easy to accomplish at work or in public, but people are thrilled with tapping because you can do it anywhere, anytime. If people notice you doing it, it is likely because they do it too! (Tapping, 2019)

Shannon Krukonis, Behavior Specialist at the YMCA, has kids of all ages tell her all about how they do their tapping at home and at school to help them relax. It is an easy resiliency exercise to teach children.

REFLECT:

Note one word to describe how you feel. _____

Try the tapping exercise that Janet describes.

Note one word to describe how you feel. _____

Some adults are comfortable helping kids with tapping but feel strange doing it themselves. As they mentor children, the adults benefit too.

Note: As mentioned, the key is to explore to find the resiliency techniques that work best for you. If you are comfortable with breathing exercises: inhale, count to five, and then exhale, counting to six or more. A friend of mine used a HeartMath earlobe monitor and computer display to illustrate how we have the power to control our own vital signs via breathing and visualization. (McCraty, 2019)

"Assume good intentions; never take it personally." – **Dr. Carol Lewis** (Psychologist at the University of Florida, cofounder of Peace4Gainesville, researcher, and trainer of easy-to-administer treatment models.) (Lewis, 2019)

"Trust your gut and be aware." – **Master Sergio Haritos** (Three-time Olympic gold champion in mixed martial arts.) (Haritos, 2019)

7.2 Running into Danger

Back in middle school, I had a tendency to hang out with latchkey kids. They wore their house key like a necklace of freedom. My one friend Gina and I had so much fun at her house. She had the power to cook fried bologna. Her dad, Vern, had this rugged John Wayne look like he should have been in the cowboy movies, but he hardly spoke, so maybe not. His wife, May (a.k.a. Gina's mom), was the extrovert of the family with her country accent and bright red hair. She worked as a waitress and kind of reminded me of Wilma on the Flintstones cartoon because she was always helpful and looking out for Vern. Both worked a lot of hours, leaving Gina and me to crank up the tunes and fry bologna all day long. We were living the good life.

Vern worked for a bug spray company. I always felt bad that he had to drive around in a vehicle with a big, dead cockroach on top of it. You could tell it was dead as it lay on its back with its two-foot-long dangly legs in the air. Imagine John Wayne driving a vehicle with a gigantic dead bug on top. As I put it in writing, I think he cherished the idea of getting another car. Since it was their only vehicle, they had to park the bug mobile in front of their house at night. Thank goodness they did not have a Home

Owner's Association back then. Of course, it was even worse when they went out to a restaurant, so they stayed home most of the time.

Staying home helped them save money. One day, Vern came home with a brand-new car. He now left the bug mobile at work most of the time. Even though he was not a man of many words, you could tell he was proud of that car. It was "grabber" blue, which is a funny but appropriate color description. When this car was in your peripheral vision or even in your rearview mirror, your eyes would be drawn to it; it was so bright. The inside of their new dream car was white leather, so Gina and I had to remove our shoes when we went for a ride. They protected that car like it was Gina's newborn brother.

A week later, they excitedly announced that they were going on vacation. They went on vacations about every three years or so, and they let Gina invite a friend. By this time, Gina and I were buds. We hung out all the time after school and bonded as we conquered minor kitchen fires with Gina's amateur bologna-frying skills. I was never sure if she was allowed to cook. Since I never heard Vern talk, I always feared that his first words would be loud yelling if he ever caught wind of the minor fires in his kitchen, but his eyes were only on that new car, so he didn't seem to notice the charcoaled kitchen towels or trimmed kitchen window curtain that we had to shorten out of necessity.

That night, May said she wanted to talk to Gina. While Gina always feared she was going to get busted for something, it turned out her mother just wanted to let her know that she could invite a friend on their vacation. Gina let me know it was down to me and Nadine, the friend she took last time. Finally, the suspense was over, and she invited me. Wow, we were going to travel in their new car up the East Coast, stopping in Georgia, Alabama, Tennessee, and West Virginia. My mom said, "Yes," and gave Gina's family some spending money for me.

Soon, we were officially on the road. For the first 500 trucks we saw, we did the horn-blow gesture and had them beep back at us. For Gina, one beep was not enough, so we usually got two or three good, loud horn beeps. Honestly, I was annoying myself and was amazed that the adults, Vern and May, did not make us stop. I wrote a note to Gina on the Etch-a-Sketch pad that I could use some fried bologna about right now. We cracked up laughing. Her parents were so relaxed. They just sat and enjoyed the drive, almost like they didn't realize they had a couple looney tunes in the back seat. This went on for hours. They just listened to eighties music, tapped their fingers every now and then to the tunes, and drove.

Suddenly, it was like this cold, dark cloud seeped into the car. The mood drastically changed. Vern and May's body language was clearly different. They sat up very straight, and you could actually hear the tension in them as they exhaled. As we got closer to Vern's hometown, where we were going to visit some of his family, May was clearly nervous. They started talking about the car, strategizing on how they would protect the car from being stolen. May suggested they schedule family members 24 hours a day to watch the car to make sure it was not stolen or vandalized. Vern nodded in agreement.

With all the tension, Gina and I were a little nervous about asking to stop to go to the restroom. Finally, Gina asked. May abruptly blurted out, "Hold it." Reluctantly, Vern pulled over at a truck stop. There was only one stall. Gina joked like she was sliding in first and then quickly leapt back out. "Holy ----, that is the biggest spider I ever saw!" she exclaimed.

I looked, and there was this furry black spider the size of my hand. We both ran out of there but with so much tension in the air, we were afraid to tell her parents that we'd chosen to skip using the restroom. Eventually, Gina told her mom she had to go again. They were clearly annoyed but stopped at the next stop. I thanked Gina for taking one for the team.

While I thought a furry spider would be the scariest thing I'd see on this trip, I would soon be introduced to a world that was scary in a whole new way.

We arrived in the small town to stay at Vern's cousin's house. In front of the house, there was a group of about 12 people walking in a circle with their backs hunched over and their faces pushed into paper bags. In the background, they had a radio playing the song "Keep on Smilin'." It was so strange. It was like they were walking aimlessly in a nearly perfect circle. I asked May what they were doing. She nonchalantly said, "They are sniffin' glue." She didn't offer any opinion or say it was wrong. Normally, she was like Wilma on the Flintstones cartoon, all sweet and proper, so I thought she might add that we should avoid this activity. She was still tense as she and the family immediately jumped into a discussion on protecting the car. It was clear all felt the car would be gone if they did not have a 24-hour watch on Vern's prize possession.

A lady with a Southern belle accent, Martha, brought Gina and me upstairs to show us the room we would sleep in. She directed us to an upstairs loft-like room. It had a large window on the top where a man was looking in with extreme curiosity. Martha acted like he was a fixture, saying, "Oh, never mind him."

Gina and I rushed down to tell the other adults. I'll never forget the response, "Girls, just ignore the strange man looking in the window." Gina tried to talk to her mom, but they were all focused on planning the all-night stakeout to ensure we had a car to drive home.

So, Gina and I wore the same clothes for the two days, seven hours, 32 minutes and 15 seconds that we had to stay there. Every now and then, the large, dark object lurking in the window would disappear. While we should have felt relieved that the man was not in the window, it somehow made us less comfortable not knowing where he'd gone. By the way, Martha also said, "Girls, you have a shared bathroom" as she showed us the door handle on the other side of the bathroom. We never stayed there long enough to find out who was on the other end of that door.

While the outside was clearly dangerous, the inside was actually a warm environment. Vern's cousins and family were all so nice to us. I loved how

Vern's family had so little but they were so thankful and happy. Despite their surroundings, they were such good people. I mean, if you looked up "good people," *Merriam-Webster* would have a picture of them. They lived in a fixer-upper that wasn't fixed up, but they were so grateful.

When Gina's Aunt Bea went to cook, I noticed that she had tin cans with no labels. Curious why they would remove labels from food cans, I asked her about it and she said, "Oh honey, we buy it with no labels because the food is cheaper."

Then I asked, "How do you know what to cook?"

She smiled and said, "Honey pie, every day is a surprise blessing; we don't know if we are going to get corn, potatoes, beets, or pears." She jokingly added, "Sometimes we even get peas, peas, and more peas for dinner." We laughed, and I told her it kind of reminded me of how my kindergarten teacher used to say, "You get what you get."

To be honest, I was starting to get a little homesick, but they started treating me like one of the family. Even the guy looking in the window seemed to be taking a liking to me—like the really weird uncle that I am so glad I never had. Then, Gina had some of her younger cousins come over. We were playing board games and running around the house and then, suddenly, Gina got angry. She always described herself as jealous, so it was not surprising when she said, "My cousins like you more than me." Then, she looked directly at me and yelled, "I wish I brought my other friend. I hate you!" She paused and said one more time, as if to make sure I knew she meant it, "I hate you!"

Feeling hurt and maybe wanting to show Gina in a strong way how much that hurt, I ran toward the door. As soon as I rapidly ran out the door, I was reminded that we were not in Florida anymore. They lived on this hill, so the side of their house was like the second story. I somehow leapt to the ground, landed on my right leg, and just kept going. The adults were all to my left at the picnic table. For a dinner table, they had a worn picnic table covered with a red and white plastic checkered tablecloth that gave it a Martha Stewart, hometown-magazine look.

Jessie looked up from the picnic dinner table and yelled, "We got a runner," and the younger adults scurried from the table to chase after me. At first, it was kind of nice to have so much attention; not as much as the shiny car on 24-hour watch but still, all eyes were on me. By this time, I was thinking, "Man, I run a lot faster than I thought I could run." Then it hit me; gravity was taking me faster down this hill, which seemed to get increasingly steeper. There was no way I could even try to stop. Terrified of falling down and tumbling to my death, or at least a very painful drop, I focused intently on landing one leg at a time. It was like a scary Olympic pole vault—let right leg touch the ground briefly to launch left leg straight; then let left leg touch the ground briefly to launch right leg. Gravity took care of speed while I focused every ounce of energy on landing my beanpole legs enough to support the rapid downhill pole vault.

A key part of this story is what was at the bottom of this hill. We were continually warned that we were not to go near that hill. The adults warned us that, "The bottom of the hill is a very dangerous part of town." Vern's cousins even gave him directions on how to avoid the crime-infested horror zone when it was time to leave. So, I was basically running into a place I was not allowed to say: "H-e-double hockey sticks."

I finally made it to the bottom of the hill, and there were three men standing there, looking at me. If they had phone cameras back then, I am pretty sure the terror on my face alone would have gotten a million hits.

Even though it was about 50 degrees out, one of the men had sleeves torn from his shirt as if to flex his power over the others. There was another guy with long straight black hair covering the entire right side of his face. The third guy had dark glasses on, so I could not see his eyes, but he stood facing directly toward me. He said to the sleeveless leader, "Pretty little thing, huh?" Then he said to me, "I bet you would like a drink of orange soda." Sleeveless added, "How about some mac-n-cheese?

How 'bout you come with us—we'll get you some orange soda and mac-n-cheese." While orange soda and mac-n-cheese were two of my favorites things, it somehow seemed terrifying as they kept trying to lure me to go with them.

While it was likely only a minute, or maybe even seconds, it felt like an eternity for the good guys, Vern's cousins, to get down that hill. Big Jim was the first guy to join us at the bottom of the hill. In the two days I'd known him, he always seemed kind of quiet and nice, but when he saw me, he came right up and stared right into my eyes. He was breathing heavily and his eyes looked like they were filled with water. Probably not the best thing to say, but I said, "What took you so long?"

He looked at like me like, "You inconsiderate brat!", but my comment was more because I felt like I was about to be devoured by ferocious piranhas. Big Jim paused, holding back the flood of swear words accumulating in his head, and then said, "We ran down a _____ hill to save you."

As he caught his breath, Big Jim just started yelling, "Do not ever run away again!" His dark brown, almost-black eyes, were glistening. At the time, I could not imagine he had tears in his eyes, but then I realized, those really were tears. His eyes looked like the eyes of a gentle deer, but his mouth was firing out the harshest words I could have imagined. He exclaimed, "If you run away again, you will be eaten by dogs. Do you understand that? You will be eaten! Eaten by dogs!"

Honestly, I think I am the only person I know who can say the exact moment in time when I was converted from being a dog person to a cat person. That was my moment. That visual was frightening. I could not even speak. I was thinking, "People here sniff glue—never saw that before. Men sleep on top of houses looking in at kids—never saw that before. Is it possible the dogs here eat people?"

Finally, they brought the car down to pick us all up. We headed back to the house. Kind of ironic that the runners all beat the person in the car.

Thanks to my adventure, the dynamic in the house changed. It was no longer warm and friendly. They were frustrated. No one chatted over dinner. I could hear May trying to console Vern, which confirmed my perception that they felt insulted that I'd run away from them. I felt terrible that I'd hurt all these good people. No matter how much I tried to explain that while I did run out the door, I meant to stop, but gravity turned me into a robotic beanpole vault. With their own eyes, they had seen this girl run, and technically I was headed away, so I was without a doubt a "runaway"—no doubt about it in their minds.

On the way home, May and Vern seemed relieved to be off 24-hour car surveillance. Their grabber-blue shiny baby was now nice and safe. While they were happy to be free again, it was a long, silent ride. No more getting trucks to blow their horns. As annoying as it was, I kind of missed doing it. Finally, Gina, who cherished every horn-blowing event, could not hold back any more and gave me the sign to start signaling those truckers to blow their horns. Vern almost swerved off the road—it had been silent so long that the sudden blow from the truck horn next to him startled him, causing him to jerk the steering wheel. Soon the superficial mood returned to almost, but not quite, normal.

When I tried to talk to Gina or her mom, they would get upset and say, "I can't believe you ran away." Each time I tried to clarify, they pushed back, not wanting to be hurt again by what they thought I'd done. To this day, I wish that group of truly good people could hear what was in my head to know that it was a mistake. I also never got to ask Gina about how she really felt when she yelled, "I hate you!" Did she really mean it? Was she just feeling left out and frustrated? We've talked a lot since, and had fried bologna together, but never really "talked."

SILO SECRET #85: Sometimes people with good intentions have very poor delivery, while people with bad intentions are quite smooth. With good intentions, pent-up fear and worry can come across as anger. In contrast, people with bad intentions don't have a worry in the world, so they can focus on saying the right things to achieve their harmful mission.

I have actually applied this lesson to coach people who have conflict in the workplace. I prompt them to share what was in their head. Nearly every time, they show how they had good intentions, but it came across as mean or inconsiderate. A key tip is the word "why." It can put people on the defensive, feeling insulted when the person did not mean it that way. For example, asking a person, "Why did you cut your hair so short?" is the same as "What made you cut your hair so short?" but the use of the word "why" tends to come across as judgmental.

SILO SECRET #86: Some labels like "runaway" really stick—even when the label says the wrong thing. A recent trend is to adjust labels. For example, rather than call someone a "homeless person," say a "person without a home." The purpose is to show it can be temporary versus placing a permanent label on someone. (Rich, 2017)

SILO SECRET #87: There are some very sad statistics in our community that likely stem from misunderstandings. When people are hurt or frustrated that someone they love is putting themselves in danger, they sometimes say or do things that lead those young minds to run directly into danger. In meetings with nonprofit organizations, this is a common situation, but kids are not as fortunate as I was to have eight adults on standby ready to come rescue them. They run into danger and never get out. One suggestion is making sure the kids in your life or your circle know of a safe place to go in the event that they feel frustrated to the point of running. Show them how to run into safety versus danger.

SILO SECRET #88: Between 1.6 and 2.8 million youth run away in a year. If I had disappeared, I would have for sure been labeled as a runaway, but really, my situation was closer to the 1.2 million tragedies where no one really knows what happened. If all of these young people lived in one city, it would be the fifth largest city in the United States. Many of these young people will end up on the streets. (National Runaway Safeline, 2019)

SILO SECRET #89: The teenage mind is being "rewired" up to about 26 years of age, so when you hear that a teen made a bad decision, know that it is part of their development. They are at the youth development stage where they are supposed to take risks and prepare to go out on their own. Unfortunately, the opportunities to get into serious trouble are more complex with more dire consequences. (Jensen, 2014) Katie Forster shares answers to some Frequently Asked Questions in her article "Secrets of the teenage brain." (Forster, 2015)

SILO SECRET #90: "Shark" seems to be a growing term that is used to describe kids recruiting kids into danger. At various meetings, I have heard of situations where kids are lured away to get their hair or nails done or to go off in a nice car. The story endings are too horrifying to put in this book. The key seems to be helping the kids feel valued. Over and over, I see kids go from F's to A's and from hopeless to excelling. With a little encouragement, they can be kids and go on to be great grown-ups.

SILO SECRET #91: "TXT 4 HELP is a nationwide, 24-hour text-for-support service for teens in crisis." Be sure children in your circle know if they are in trouble or need help, they can "text SAFE and current location (address, city, state) to 4HELP (44357) for immediate help." (Safe Place, 2019)

REFLECT:

Do the children in your life know they have a safe place to run?

_____

_____

"Effective cybersecurity should be considered an investment." – **Mike DeWine** (Former U.S. senator).

7.3 Cover Your Assets

Liz and Dave were living the American dream. Everyone said they had it all together. Liz started out as a teacher, and Dave was in technology and engineering. Wanting more time together, they decided to combine their talents to help teens and people of all ages learn about careers in science, technology, engineering, and math (STEM). Actually, Liz taught art, so they even added art to the mix. Liz was proud to be one of the first to officially teach STEAM; STEM with the added "A" for including art.

Word of mouth had their business growing leaps and bounds. While many couples may have a hard time working together, Liz and Dave loved that they got to spend time together and even traveled to conferences and competition events to support their students.

One week, they were invited to speak at a big event in California. This was an incredible opportunity. Over dinner, they discussed how they could mentor some of the older teens to help, as they expected a big increase in work. About to book a flight for them, Dave found it odd that his credit card was declined. He thought for sure it was a mistake. He called the bank only to find that their entire business account had been hacked and depleted overnight. The nice lady on the phone informed him that nonprofits and small-to-midsize companies are often a target because they do not have departments dedicated to system security.

Imagine being a small-to-midsize business owner and waking up one morning to find that all your finances were taken overnight. With thousands of businesses impacted each year, below are small business trends cyber security statistics that "Small Businesses Need to Know." (Mansfield, 2018)

- 60% of small companies go out of business within six months of a cyberattack.

- 66% of small businesses reported that their greatest concern is customer data.

- 55% of businesses who participated in a 2016 study experienced a cyberattack in the past year.

While Liz and Dave did have it all, they made a big mistake of having it all in one place. They joked about being "one bucket," and now their bucket was empty. In shock, Dave neglected to call the conference contact back to say that he could not afford to travel to present. The host of the conference was quite upset because she was counting on Liz and Dave as the keynote speakers. Dave apologized profusely and explained that he was just devastated. His mind was on trying to figure out how to pay his bills to keep his home, cars, and business. While they only had a few employees, they were filled with guilt knowing that they did not have the funds to pay the employees who counted on the payroll checks to pay their bills.

Ms. Rhodes, the conference host, was understanding. She said, "Just the other day, one of the conference attendees closed down their business due to a similar situation."

Feeling powerless and exasperated to learn that attackers frequently wipe out payroll accounts overnight, Liz and Dave felt naïve and frustrated that they thought their money was safe in their bank. As they talked, they could not help but feel a desire to spread the word so others were more aware of ways to protect themselves. They spoke to a friend of theirs named Jeremy, who worked in cyber security. Jeremy showed them a screen on his computer that revealed multiple attempts to hit their business each and every week. He worked for a large company, so they had a team monitoring their systems 24 hours a day. Jeremy explained that nonprofits and smaller businesses are targeted because they often cannot afford to investigate the crime or put in safeguards to prevent or react to the crime.

Dave asked if there was one thing they could do and teach others to prevent this from happening. Jeremy said a simple but very effective suggestion is to spread out your assets. That way, if criminals hack one account, you still have a backup. He said, "Having all your eggs in one basket is risky these days."

Liz and Dave learned that lesson the hard way, but it inspired them to use this new knowledge to help others. They now incorporate basic cyber security tips into their training program. They had a great relationship with the bank, so they were able to get a loan to keep their home and business afloat. Turns out there is a high demand for this knowledge, so

Liz and Dave are bouncing back. While it was a painful lesson, they are able to illustrate a real-life example to help others learn through their experience.

SILO SECRET #92: Diversifying assets is a valuable protection tip. Recently, there was a local charity that collected toys to give to children. All the toys were stored in one place and then stolen from that single place on Christmas Eve. People doing good deeds often neglect the step of identifying and addressing risks. An easy risk to think about is location of assets. If you have all your valuables in one place, it makes it easier to lose everything, whether it is a cyberattack or a natural disaster or a thief with poor timing.

SILO SECRET #93: Large businesses place a high emphasis on backing up their data (customer data, payroll data, etc.) in the event there is an extended power outage or other issue. Whether it is data or belongings, it is good to have a backup plan in place. In case of a widespread natural disaster like a hurricane traveling across multiple states, businesses often store backup data in a location at least two states away.

SILO SECRET # 94: In helping out after recent hurricanes, I saw how many people were more devastated by the loss of their photos than the loss of their home. Imagine losing all your baby pictures, holiday photos, etc. Individuals can have a data backup plan with key information like a video of belongings with serial numbers for insurance along with photos stored on a password-protected flash drive.

REFLECT:

Do you have your photos, important files, and finances stored in more than one place?

_____

_____

*"Music is one of the most powerful things the world has to offer. No matter what race or religion or nationality or sexual orientation or gender that you are, it has the power to unite us." – **Lady Gaga*** (American singer, songwriter, and actress known for her unconventionality and visual experimentation.)

7.4 What Song Is Playing in Your Head?

In interviewing and reading about people who entertain across different countries, artists have a common theme where they say that music, dancing, comedy, and art cross national boundaries and bring people together to laugh, dance, or just simply have fun and enjoy life. Bono, a well-known philanthropist and performer, describes how "music can change the world because it can change people."

Similarly, many artists talk about how songs help people through a rough time. Opus Peace is an organization that helps veterans essentially release pain. (Grassman, 2019) An artist volunteered to write a song for their cause. It is a real tearjerker, but they explain that it is crucial to relinquish pain stored in the body. Many times, art is the only avenue that some people feel comfortable using to lighten that pain. So, on that note, no pun intended, sad songs can be quite therapeutic but, like everything, we may want to be aware of what is playing in our head to ensure a healthy balance. Chris Martin, lead singer of Coldplay, expressed that, "Going through something difficult in your life, music, for me, is always a friend and something that helps you to figure things out."

Looking at the trends in Top 40 songs from the 1960s to the 2000s, it is interesting to see the change over the years. While there are many other songs, I thought it would be fun to pick out most popular songs that related to views on life like "I Will Survive." While all of the songs below through the decades are quite upbeat, you can sort of see the trend. I mean, the sixties were known for Woodstock, but the songs were more like "I'm a Believer." Then, by the seventies, we were singing about being strong, belting out, "I will survive—hey, hey!" By the eighties, we were "Livin' on a Prayer" and then came Ricky Martin in the nineties, encouraging us to dance like no one was watching, or watch him, whichever you preferred, as he sang "Livin' La Vida Loca" (living the crazy life). By the 2000s, we were openly singing "Wanna New Drug."

Topic:	60s	70s	80s	90s	2000s
Life	I'm a Believer	I Will Survive	Livin' on a Prayer	Livin' La Vida Loca	Wanna New Drug
Relationship	I Wanna Hold Your Hand	Killing Me Softly	Tainted Love	I Will Always Love You	Single Ladies

In an article titled, "Psychology of Music," (Christenson, de Haan-Rietdijk, Roberts, & ter Bogt, 2018) the writer points out how the proportion of songs referencing sex-related aspects of relationships, along with references to violence, death, dancing, alcohol, drugs, and status/wealth increased substantially, particularly in the 2000s. The article discusses how earlier song references to hate, hostility, suicide, and occult matters were very rare.

In the 2000s, a rapper known as Logic shook things up a bit with a slightly radical move. His team reached out to partner with the National Suicide Prevention Lifeline on a strategic idea to title a song as the actual phone number of the National Suicide Hotline. The album that included this suicide hotline number, 1-800-273-8255 (1-800-273-TALK), ranked No. 1 on Billboard's Hot 200. As listeners heard Logic's new song about emotional hardship, they also heard a message of hope. As they heard words like, "You don't gotta die, I want you to be alive," the number to call for help showed on their radio display. To me, this is an example of the simplicity and power of interdependence. These two diverse groups came together to work toward a life-altering solution. (Billboard.com, 2020)

So, is art reflecting reality, or is reality reflecting art—or some combination? I was thinking about leaving this section out of the book, but then I heard the song "Hey Ya!" on the radio. Everyone in my car started dancing, and this was a somewhat conservative group, so I thought, "Hmm, maybe this music silo secret is worth mentioning."

SILO SECRET #95: Music can change your mood. A person commented online that "Hey Ya!" brings her out of depression. 13,000 people liked that comment. Find what music helps to pick up your mood and helps when you need time to think or deal with a sad situation.

SILO SECRET #96: I think stores and employers may be on to this music inspiration thing. My friends and I still joke about songs we used to sing when we worked together 20 years ago. They used to play the music lightly over the speakers. One song was "Don't Worry, Be Happy." When we had a tough project with all kinds of obstacles and deadlines, that song always seemed to come on and get us all laughing. I also think my biggest shopping spree was in a store playing the drum solo from "Wipe Out!"

SILO SECRET #97: Learning music has also been shown to help people with math. Math, specifically algebra, is taught in schools to help us with problem-solving. So, if I have my algebra right, music helps you with solving problems.

REFLECT:

With this reflection, try to find the decade(s) that move you. Using your preferred method (YouTube, iTunes, or another method), take one to two minutes to play a song from each decade. As you listen, jot down the first adjective that comes to mind. Below are a couple sample songs to make it easy to search. In the blank below, write how you feel as you listen to the song.

1950s: Tutti Frutti or Why Do Fools Fall In Love: _____

1960s: Wild Thing or Twist and Shout: _____

1970s: Stayin' Alive or I Will Survive: _____

1980s: Tainted Love or Girls Just Wanna Have Fun: _____

1990s: Jump Around or Livin' La Vida Loca: _____

2000s: God's Plan or I Gotta Feeling: _____

So, which decade(s) moved you the most? _____

The good news is you have an easy way to play the oldies but goodies if you choose. This exercise may help you pause a moment to ensure you are listening to the best station for you.

If you are in a mood to be intense and think about deep topics, you can find that song that inspires you to ponder the world. If you are in the mood to forget your problems and jump around, well then, you can travel back to the nineties and "Jump Around." Lately, I have noticed at some of the conferences I have attended that they are using music in a strategic way. They play a certain song and talk about the meaning. Conversely, I was at a conference once where we were given the lyrics to popular songs and asked to translate the verbiage. The goal was to help parents be more aware of the meanings behind songs that kids are listening to. Turns out "Cake By The Ocean" has nothing to do with cake, although I still think an actual ice-cream cake by the ocean would be quite refreshing.

Speaking of music on the ocean, remember how they instructed the band on the *Titanic* to keep playing music to calm the people as the ship sank? Let's not do that. Instead, let's find music that inspires us to take our ship forward. Full dream ahead!

*"When it comes to friends, it's not about the number of friends you have, but it's the quality of your close relationships that matters." – **Robert Waldinger*** (Psychiatrist and professor at Harvard Medical School; director of the Harvard Study of Adult Development that is considered one of the world's longest studies of adult life, aimed at identifying how our experiences link to health and well-being.)

7.5 The Friend You Can Call at 3 a.m.

Hitting the trifecta at 17 years old was not a good thing. First, a friend called to say he was driving to Florida and asked if he could stop and visit while he was in town. I wasn't home so my mom relayed the message for me to call him. She said, "Give him a call, he really values your friendship," but I said, "No, I will surprise him." Well, he surprised me when a car went through a red light and he was gone. Second, I got a call that a close relative was hit by a car while he was walking. I had a hard time processing that he could have been saved, but the car pushed him from the city side of the street to the unincorporated side of the street. This apparently caused a few seconds of delay in deciding which ambulance to dispatch to the scene, abruptly ending his life at the age of 16. Last but surely not least, there was a five-year-old girl named Melissa.

Melissa and her family came into the restaurant that I worked at all the time. With her strawberry-blonde curls, her family often called her Strawberry Shortcake. One time, she giggled as she revealed that her older brother had a crush on me and that was the reason they chose to eat Chinese food three times a week. As I walked away from their table, she said, "I love you," and I smiled back at her as I took the food order at the next table. I guess I thought there would be plenty of times to say "I love you" back. Her family stopped by weeks later to tell me that there had been a freak accident at a carnival. They said, "Melissa loved coming to see you at the restaurant but she is in heaven now."

While the moral of this story for me should have been, say "I love you" because you never know when that window will end, I went another direction. I officially became the social butterfly, mingling and being friendly to everyone, but not getting close to anyone. A friend asked if I was okay. I explained that I was able to turn off my emotions, not letting myself feel too much. I simply fluttered away when anyone got too close. A formerly close friend, Michael, sat behind me in psychology class. One day he said in frustration, "Just in case you are wondering, this next chapter is about you." The chapter was about people who go into isolation and push others away. My subconscious knew he was right, but people described me as having "so many friends," so that is the opposite of isolation, right?

About a year later, I was taking one of my first college classes, Sociology. Being a social butterfly, I figured it was a good fit, but on the first test I got an "F." As my husband would say, "Here comes the justification." Well, as I took the test, it seemed that 80% of the answers were "all of the above." In my head, I could hear my high school teachers saying, "Do not pick all of the above" as they urged us to "pick the best answer." At the last minute, I rushed to erase most of my "all of the above" bubbles and feverishly filled in what I thought were the best answers.

Learning my lesson from the strikingly large red "F," an image that filled my head, I got A's on all the other tests. At the end of the semester, the professor said, "Everyone wait in a line to get your grade." I had already accepted that my overall average was a "B." However, the professor showed me that he had given me an "A" and said, "Clearly you deserve an 'A.'" I replied, "No, I messed up on the first test so I have a 'B.'" After watching me convince the professor to lower my grade, a lady from the class whom I had never spoken to before exclaimed quite loudly, "What are you, an idiot? Take the A!" Well, that was when I first met Beverly. With that commanding but caring personality, Beverly knocked my solid brick emotional barrier wall down and I didn't even realize it. We went out for pizza after class and we laughed and talked for hours.

Beverly has now been one of my closest friends for decades. Knowing her powerful personality, I will surely not mention how many decades. Now, for the real moral of the story. Beverly is among the few cherished friends who I know I can call at 3 a.m. In fact, she was the friend I called at 3 a.m. when that not-so-gentle man tried to break into my apartment (earlier in section 6.4). Beverly insisted that I stay with her until I found a new place. It truly felt like home. She actually had the same blue floral pattern curtains and bedspread that I had growing up. Even though I called her in the middle of the night, she welcomed me into her home like it was a relaxing afternoon.

Later, as I went to events and parties, I turned off the butterfly switch and thoroughly enjoyed the company of family and friends. I was so thankful to relinquish the butterfly and enjoy true friendships and family. Yet, I hear more and more about how the world is changing where many people are working to get more and more online friends. As I read studies of how people feel more disconnected as they increase their number of online friend connections, I can definitely understand.

While networking and online connections are great, Harvard University is reporting that after 80 years of study, they have discovered that true happiness is just what Beverly taught me. True happiness is in having those friends who you can call at 3 a.m. I do not say it nearly enough so I am putting this in writing for the Library of Congress to keep on file: Thank you, Beverly and Phyllis, for being my amazing friends like family whom I can call at 3 a.m.

SILO SECRET #98: The Harvard Study of Adult Development is the longest study of its kind. Starting in 1938, the researchers followed two very diverse groups and did everything from brain scans to asking individuals and their families a broad range of questions. While most thought money and power would be on top, it turned out that our close connections are the most important thing in our lives. The director, Robert Waldinger, shares the three lessons we can learn about relationships from the study. (Mejia, 2018; Mineo, 2017)

1. Social connections are "really good" for you

2. When it comes to relationships, pick quality over quantity

3. Good relationships actually protect your brain

In an interview with CNBC on how to be happier and have stronger, positive relationships, Mr. Waldinger recommended "replacing screen time with people time." He suggests going on long walks, date nights, or reaching out to a family member who you haven't spoken to in years. Sometimes I find myself texting my grandma, thinking that I am not sure if it is okay to call. Seriously, let's remind each other that it is more than okay to pick up the phone or meet for coffee or a smoothie or to just talk a few minutes. Your friends and family will love it and you will both live longer, happier lives.☺

REFLECT:

Think of a friend or family member you have not talked to in a while. Imagine living a longer, happier life by simply reaching out. Text, I mean, give them a call.

_____

_____

Chapter 7 Summary: They say a broken bone is stronger than the other bones. Similarly, people who have overcome trauma demonstrate immense resilience. They are often filled with inspiration to apply their experience to help others. Experts agree a support network is key. Having a safe place to go, a friend you can count on, and a song you can play are all forms of resiliency. The key is to find what works for you on your schedule.

8. THE SECRET INGREDIENT

"The best and most beautiful things in the world cannot be seen or even touched—they must be felt with the heart." – **Helen Keller** (Author, lecturer, and first deaf-blind person to earn a bachelor of arts degree.)

"Fear is contagious, but so is courage." – **passiton.com** (The Foundation for a Better Life creates public service campaigns to communicate the values that make a difference in our communities.)

8.1 The Silent Child Who Had So Much to Say

Back in college, one of our first Delta Sigma Pi business fraternity community events was to go to a park and spend a couple hours with foster children. When we arrived, the fraternity guys said, "Lisa, you are in charge of all the sport activities." Not realizing that they were joking, I grabbed the sports equipment and soon had 19 adorable little foster children running toward me.

As I showed the children how to serve a volleyball, there was a petite six-year-old girl hiding behind a large tree. While the other children had worn-out clothes, this little girl was dressed in expensive clothing, and it was evident that someone spent a lot of time styling her hair. To me, she looked like a miniature Whitney Houston and was even dressed like a famous singer on a stage. She had tiny little beads delicately woven into her hair, matching her beautiful turquoise and pink, sparkling clothes. It seemed odd that this little girl with strikingly vibrant clothing clearly wanted to be invisible as she hid behind a tree. I could barely see her head as she periodically peeked out from behind the tree to watch me show the other children how to serve a volleyball.

While it was clear that she did not want to be seen, it was also evident that she wanted to learn to play. She simply wanted to be a kid. To help her come forward without having to speak, I announced, "I am really busy teaching, so if anyone wants me to show them how to play volleyball, tug my shirt two times. If you tug one time, I'll just think I have an itch." A few minutes later, I felt two tugs. Being a silly 18-year-old, I acted like I only felt one tug and pretended to have an itch. This time, the little girl's pronounced dimples showed as she focused intently on making sure I felt two very distinct, deliberate tugs. I said, "Oh, oh!" and jumped into showing her how to serve the volleyball. No eye contact, no talking, just showing her how to play ball—how to be a kid.

Next, I guided her and the other kids over to the volleyball court and explained that I'd pass the ball to her and the other children and let them volley the ball over the net. When I passed the ball to her, she spiked the volleyball and as I turned away, the ball hit my back. Trying to boost her confidence, I facetiously remarked, "Who was the big person who spiked me with the ball?" She was so proud; she jumped up and raised her hand. I said, "It had to be a very big person to spike a ball that powerfully now, who was it?"

She leapt up and thrust her tiny little arms in the air in excitement, exclaiming, "It was me! It was me! I did it! I hit the ball!" It was like she became a child for the first time. She suddenly started smiling, talking, playing, and laughing with the other children.

Afterwards, the foster care director pulled me aside and said, "Do you realize what just happened?" He advised me that this little six-year-old girl had such severe trauma that she had stopped talking and interacting for over two years. He told me that I was a natural in social work and helping children and asked why I was pursuing a business degree versus social work. I explained that when I took my career test, there was a handwritten note strongly recommending that I avoid social work.

The foster care director explained that he might know why the person wrote that note. He went on to say that the little girl that I'd just helped speak, after two years of silence, would likely be sent back to the environment where she'd experienced trauma and that she'd likely stop speaking again. He then went on to share additional statistics, stating that many of these beautiful children would go on to repeat the same cycle of trauma that they'd experienced. I wanted so much to help, but I didn't know how.

The director said those words that many of us have heard before. While he was strong in appearance, he appeared powerless as he looked into the distance and said, "The system is broken." I was so frustrated that it felt like the words would be etched in my mind forever. Then, my college professor, Dr. Munyan, advised, "If you want to help people, study systems." I did just that. I studied systems, majored in management information systems, and then went on to get certified in every system improvement tool I could find.

After over 25 years of applying global best practices, I know that those words "the system is broken" simply mean our current way of doing something is not working. A system is, by definition, "a way of doing something." And we can adjust how we do things. Since I was a kid hearing the adults talk about this "broken system," I imagined it to be this Godzilla-like system that had control over all the people, but after years of study and experience, I know that is not the case. Humans are supposed to design systems to make our lives easier. Systems are not supposed to take over our lives, and they surely are not supposed to take our lives.

While people still talk of broken systems, I am thrilled to hear more and more about how nonprofit agencies are using proven, evidence-based practices to help young people and families identify and use their strengths to set and achieve goals that are most important to them. This is a very exciting time where we have multiple movements going on in parallel: the trauma-informed movement, the peer support movement and the roll-out of wellness recovery action plans using high fidelity Wraparound principles. Each of these movements is working toward uniting for more holistic solutions.

SILO SECRET #99: A system is simply a way of doing something. We can change the way we do it.

SILO SECRET #100: Pay attention to body language. The little girl had an unmet need to play and be a kid. That need had to be met before she could go on to her next need. This is actually a technique covered in the River Phoenix Center for Peacebuilding training. They have a long list of needs so you can assess unmet needs, enabling you to focus on addressing that pressing need before moving on to another. Once we addressed the little girl's unmet need to play and be a kid, she was ready to speak.

SILO SECRET #101: Kids really do need to be kids. There are key milestones. This little girl was at the age where it was important to develop social skills and play. For that moment, we were helping her simply be a kid, which is critical to her development to be a great grown-up. Each age has key developmental milestones. Parents can check with their doctor, library, or even online for tips to create an ideal environment for development milestones.

SILO SECRET #102: There is a growing focus on "increasing normalcy." It is kind of what it sounds like—letting kids do normal stuff. Basically, our minds purge connections that are not used. This purging peaks at adolescence, so it is critical that teens are able to do teen activities during this time, where they have part-time jobs, go on field trips, do community service, and engage in other things that help them develop skills that they will need for adulthood and for getting a job. Otherwise, they can lose up to 30,000 brain pathway connections per second. (Bianca Rey and Cyd Oppenheimer, 2016)

REFLECT:

Think about a time you changed the way you did something to make it a little faster, better, or easier.

This is an example of how you can refine or even fix a system.

_____

_____

A local teacher jokes with her students that she is worried that they will be caring for her when she is older. Do you think it is important that we help young people have the tools to develop into productive members of society?

_____

_____

*"Integrate purpose into your for-profit business model through a long-term commitment to a cause that is aligned with our core values and those of your community." – **Simon Mainwaring*** (Founder & CEO of We First: How brands and consumers use social media to build a better world.)

8.2 The Compassion Experiment

Throughout the hallways, the white noise turned into a rumble as everyone watched live reports of the devastation from Hurricane Katrina. Consulting for a top media company, my role at that time was overseeing the programming to phone millions of people across the nation. We agreed to suspend all phoning to New Orleans as it faced flooding and the loss of many homes, but then I got a call to attend an urgent meeting.

An executive client from the New Orleans area had called the meeting. He was practically begging us to resume phoning for New Orleans. We explained that people were furious that we would be so inconsiderate to call that area and explained that we agreed, so we'd stopped phoning. Still, he persisted. He then added, "We all realize that New Orleans is going to essentially fail when it comes to the ratings, and we realize that cooperation rates will surely be zero," but he insisted on the importance of New Orleans being part of the demographic ratings.

Finally, I had to ask, "What is motivating you to have us call New Orleans?" I will never forget his answer.

He explained, "Many of us have lost our homes and nearly everything— we are just trying to keep our city's name on the map." He was fighting for the survival of his city, his hometown.

This was no longer a typical project. This was now a humanity project—a project with an intense purpose. We agreed to phone the citizens of New Orleans to help with their mission to keep their city on the map. Even if they showed as a zero rating, they would consider that a step forward in helping to save their city. After we hung up the phone, we talked amongst each other, still concerned with how we would be upsetting the people of New Orleans. At that moment, I said, "What if we let the research interviewers show compassion?"

The statisticians, scientists, and everyone in the room, were 100% sure that the city would fail in terms of cooperation and ratings. Since all agreed that the people of New Orleans would hang up the phone or, best case, tell us they did not want to answer questions in the aftermath of a natural disaster, all agreed to let the interviewers deviate from the phoning script. We were letting them simply be human, with the freedom to show compassion. When we called people, we would start the call by asking how the people were doing. Then, we would explain that we were actually working to help New Orleans. One gentleman responded, "You are in luck—Hurricane Katrina took everything I own, but I still have a TV. It is underwater, but I still have a TV."

Research interviewers actually requested to call New Orleans. While it was intense and often involved laughing and crying with the citizens of New Orleans, the interviewers loved being part of this meaningful project. They cherished being able to do something to help out and show their empathy and compassion.

About a week later, the results were all compiled and ready to be published. All were stunned to see that New Orleans had gotten the best results ever. All expected them to fail. After all, they were literally underwater, and we were asking them to answer the phone and provide all this data to us. Yet, they did it. They kept their city on the map! The research interviewers asked, "Can we call New Orleans back and tell them the great news?"

Management smiled and said, "Sure, you can call them back with the wonderful news." Below is a photo of the area impacted by the hurricane. (Katrina Destruction, 2005)

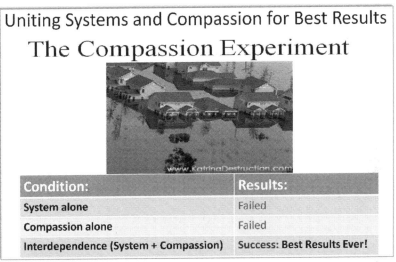

Condition:	Results:
System alone	Failed
Compassion alone	Failed
Interdependence (System + Compassion)	Success: Best Results Ever!

Figure 8.2 Individually, the silos failed. Together, the silos were successful.

With "The Compassion Experiment," everyone expected failure. The systems team, the scientists, the statisticians, the business people, and even the people of New Orleans expected failure. However, the combination of systems and compassion resulted in the best results ever!

SILO SECRET #103: Combining outcome-focused objectives and people-focused attributes can generate amazing results. The unintentional experiment showed how two focus areas or silos combined are better than one. The people-focused silo alone failed. The outcome-focused silo alone failed. However, when we combined the two, the experiment was a major success.

SILO SECRET #104: Even clunky systems can work with a personal touch. While the author of the interview script described the verbiage as being 30 years old and ready for a rewrite, the interview system worked incredibly well once we added the element of compassion.

SILO SECRET #105: Compassion is a strength rather than a weakness. For nearly 20 years, I have heard comments that compassion in business is a weakness, but I always suspected it just might be the secret ingredient. The Compassion Experiment shows how compassion is a key ingredient in getting amazing results. (Doty, 2008)

SILO SECRET #106: According to Stanford University's Medicine's Center for Compassion and Altruism Research and Education, "The Best-Kept Secret to Longevity is Love." While "having social-relationships predicts a 50% increased chance of longevity," studies showed that "those who engaged in helping others and supporting others ended up living longer lives." While "volunteerism lengthened lives," this is only the case when "volunteerism was done for selfless reasons." (Seppala, 2013)

REFLECT:

Think of a project where you had compassion. Do you think it helped get better results?

_____

_____

"I went skydivin', I went Rocky Mountain climbin', I went two point seven seconds on a bull named Fumanchu. And I loved deeper and I spoke sweeter and I gave forgiveness I'd been denyin'. And he said someday I hope you get the chance to live like you were dyin'." – **Tim Nichols** and **Craig Wiseman** (Cowriters of song "Live Like You were Dying" sung by **Tim McGraw**, American country singer-songwriter and actor.) (Evans Price, 2017)

8.3 Roaring River of Judgment

At the wise age of 13, I got to spend a summer vacation in Colorado with family and friends. With us arriving right after a serial killer had just been caught there, that not-so-subtle reminder of danger somehow seemed to elevate the sense of adventure as we delved into the forests and mountains. We went on what seemed like 180-degree mountain climbs, but mostly we just had fun being independent teens walking a fine line between being rebellious and exploring the wild.

On the radio, the news seemed to continually make announcements about people drowning in three feet of water. Trying not to be too critical of a person who just faced a tragic death, I just thought to myself, "Why don't these people just stand up?" It made no sense. One day, I accidentally voiced my opinion out loud at a community get together. Somehow, I felt reassured as I realized that I was not alone in being judgmental. Others voiced that they were just like me, questioning the people who no longer had a voice. Seriously, couldn't they figure that out? Couldn't they just stand up?

A couple weeks later, we realized we had climbed nearly every mountain in the area so we decided it was time to take up river rafting. Given our miniscule budget, we had to downsize our plan to river tubing. The challenge was the only nearby river was appropriately named the Roaring Fork River. Even before you saw the river, you could hear the commanding roar from a distance, making it quite clear how it earned its name. Yet, we were not sure how it earned the "fork" part of its name. Was there a fork in the river where one part went towering down a steep waterfall? We had no idea what was ahead, but being a fearless 13-year-old with the common sense to stand up, I was ready.

Entering the water reminded me of the movies where people have to do the impossible task of jumping onto a moving train, but we had to do a synchronized leap onto this tube aboard the moving river train. Our adrenaline was high as we maneuvered our way onto the tube and soared down the river, each holding onto the handle as if it was our lifeline. It was not like a carnival ride where you can press an emergency exit button if you realize that you made a monumental mistake. I had never pressed that button, but with this ride, it occurred to me that there was no turning back.

All three of us hung on with all of our might as the river was clearly in the driver's seat. It was like the river was like us, an irresponsible teenager wanting to take risks, have fun, and show us who was in charge as it flung us on an unexpected sharp turn to the left, then a swift right, and then into a spin. It wasn't like the planned spin that you expect on the Congo River Rapids ride at the Busch Gardens theme park, where you just kind of wonder who will get soaked. This ride was filled with unpredictable spins that took us flying backwards as piercing 40-degree water spouts sprayed us like an out-of-control fire hose. We quickly learned that with each large rock, we had to hang on extra tight and even then it was like we could barely hang on.

Already feeling like we put our lives at risk, I could feel my heart rate climb as I saw that my aunt's adorable sheep dog had managed to get free and was now running along the edge of the river. He wanted to join in on what he believed to be a great time, but I feared that he would not survive if he got too excited and tried to join us. Worried that Bubbles the sheep dog would dive into the dangerous waters, I got distracted as I tried to encourage him to go back to the house. At that moment, we hit a boulder that jolted our tube into a rock like a car crashing into a wall, yanking my hands from the tube.

While my hands throbbed with this hot rope-burn sensation, that was the least of my worries. I was now in the roaring river without a paddle, without a boat—without anything but me. It was ironic that I landed in a driving position as if I was in total control with my legs extended out as if I had one foot on the brake pedal and the other foot on the gas pedal, but I had never felt so out of control. Instinctively, I tried to grab at the rock formations underneath me, but the sharp-edge rocks covered in algae felt like slimy razor blades slicing my hands at the slightest touch. Still, I kept my hands on the bottom of the river, trying to only touch it gently to help stay upright and keep my balance.

While I had suspected before that there was a fork in the river, now I knew for sure that we had reached the fork. My friends went soaring down the river to the right and I was now taken abruptly from them and headed to the left. Our explorations on foot always seemed to take us east so I was now headed into uncharted territory, heading west with no idea where this journey would end.

So I was alone in water that I would estimate was only three feet high. Recalling each announcement on the news of how a father of three, a captain of the swim team, and two teenagers died in just three feet of water, it all made sense now. My judgment turned to empathy as water rushed into my face. I tried to stay face-forward with my legs extended in front of me. That way, I could try to maneuver to steer my body left or right, convincing myself I had some control over the situation. The only thing I could do was literally try my best to keep my head above the water.

The height of the river shifted up and down, sending me plunging under the water periodically at the deeper parts. Observing that the chances to grab air mainly happened in the roughest waters where the shallow water crashed against the rocks, I had to go against every ounce of logic I had in me to strategically take a breath at each white water opportunity. When I could see nothing but white water, it was the time to gasp for air.

Squinting as the water pressure was like needles piercing at my eyes, I managed to see a lone tree ahead with branches hovering over the water. The river apparently decided that the ride was over and it was time for me to disembark. By this time, my friends got to the end of their ride. They came over and pushed the tree limb down so it would be within my reach. I grabbed the tree branch, pulled myself over, and exited the river ride.

The experience was like the Congo River ride and the Sky Rush roller coaster all in one. From deep excitement to dire hopelessness and then ending with intense joy as my friend's hand pulled me from the branch over to the shore, it was a day that I will always remember. It could have been me that people heard about on the news. The short news clip would have probably simply stated, "Teen from Florida drowns in just 3 feet of water." Now and then, I still catch myself thinking, "Can't that person just stand up?" and then I recall the Roaring River of Judgment. Sometimes we take risks by accident or on purpose. Hey, those are often the stories we'll always remember. The story may even be a chapter of our life story. For me, it is a reminder that there may be a deeper, meaningful story behind each and every shallow, surface judgment.

"I looked at her and said to myself, I am not going to be judgmental. Instead, I just thought, she must have a really interesting story." – Sylvia Sanctious (70-year-old peer support recovery specialist who has been in recovery for 37 years. She wants to continue working to help others move forward.)

Judging the Judges

Decades after the river incident, I was driving to the courthouse. You are likely wondering, perhaps even judging a little, so what did she do this time? Well, this was perhaps the most life-changing part of that Juvenile Justice Citizens' Academy training that I mentioned earlier. Remember when I went to jail as part of the 10-week training of what happens from a kid's perspective? Well, this was the day that we went to the courthouse to hear what happens in that building that looks like an expensive, untouchable marble-tiled museum but feels more like a cold, over-sanitized, unbreakable cement structure.

On the way there, a news story interrupted every station on the radio. I know, because I tried changing the station several times as I found myself getting frustrated, asking myself, "How could this happen? Why didn't the legal system do its' job?" Driving a car illegally for the fifth time, these two little girls went off a bridge, drowning in the accident. Every station had a different twist on who was to blame. The girls had a long rap sheet. They had been to court many times. I wondered if one kid was the instigator and the other just got stuck in a bad situation, but mostly I formulated questions in my mind on what to ask if I had the opportunity to inquire, perhaps even interrogate, the lawyers in the courtroom. Of all the days to have the court tour, it was the day that everyone seemed to be judging the system. Part of me felt like it was an incredible and rare opportunity and it was, but not in the way that I imagined.

Arriving early, I recognized a sweet, friendly lady from class and said, "Hello." Her carefree disposition reflected her childlike kindness. Tonight, she looked like she had been crying, and she asked if I had heard the news about the young girls drowning. She added, "Those were my girls." She was a volunteer, devoting her own time and money to help kids "in the court system." These two little girls were among the 30 girls that she visited each week after working 50 hours in her day job. She wouldn't take any money for what she did because, as she put it, she wanted these kids to know that she "does this out of love and not for the money." As we walked slowly into the courtroom to learn about the justice system, she leaned over to me and softly shared, "You know, they truly were good kids."

The courtroom was filled with the 27 of us sitting tensely in our seats looking ahead at the judge, two juvenile attorneys, and another lady who turned out to be the court psychologist. I didn't ever really think about having a psychologist in a courtroom, but she was the first to speak. Like me, everyone was filled with the facts on all that had gone wrong—17 arrests by this one, 30 cumulative arrests. We were filled with questions, but I think mostly filled with anger and judgment. The psychologist paused and stated, "You know, I have two little girls the same ages as the little girls who just drowned in the accident." She said, "If my little girls went through the horrible hardship those girls went through, they could have ended up in the system too." What she was clearly envisioning in her mind was that her little girls could have drowned if they had no love, no family, no one to stand up for them—other than, of course, the lady sitting next to me who was juggling a full-time job, her own four kids, and 28 other foster children.

Next, the defense attorney spoke. Tears began to roll down her face as she asked us to, "Please excuse us. This day has been very hard on us." While we in the judgment seats were well-informed on the numbers, she explained, "We knew those little girls personally. We knew their stories. We knew them all too well." She sipped her water bottle, working hard to pull herself back together, back to being the highly professional, sophisticated woman that society expects of an attorney. She spoke of how it looks so simple to watch from afar, judging and asking ourselves why these girls were not put behind bars or something. After all, would that have saved them?

Since I had carpooled with my acquaintance-turned-friend on an earlier juvenile justice visit, it prompted me to realize that I knew firsthand exactly where the two little girls lived. My friend pointed it out on our drive to the jail. The house that the little girls lived in was known by different names. Some called it a halfway house. Others called it a temporary or transitional residence. Conveniently, it was halfway between the jail and the courthouse so I guess the "halfway" description seems appropriate. However, it looked more like an abandoned old office building converted to jam in 20-plus kids with nowhere to live, so calling it a "house" seemed like a bit of a stretch.

Finally, the prosecuting attorney had the closing words as he had the last presentation topic. Now, this guy looked like society's version of an attorney. He wore an expensive suit and tie, shiny shoes, and even slick, impeccably combed-back, shiny hair. He exuded experience and professionalism as he spoke on the facts. He asked if any of us knew the reason that they assigned these kids to do community service. While nearly everyone thought it was to punish them or force them to give back to the community, he explained that "Community service is often the first time these kids hear the words 'Thank you.'" He said that they were trying to help these kids have a sense of being valued, a sense that just one person cared enough to say those two words we perhaps take for granted. I tried to imagine my life without those words. I tried to imagine never saying "thank you" to my child and wondered how she might be a different person without those two simple words. Honestly, I wanted to erase that terrible vision from my mind.

The most surprising and shocking part of the visit was when I saw how amazingly caring the people in "the system" were. I could not help but think of how I had been brought up in a time when men didn't cry and now I was watching the toughest of correctional officers and lawyers in tears. The prosecuting attorney explained that "no one chooses to be a juvenile attorney." He said, "It chooses you. It is a calling." While he managed to hold his emotions in for a good seven minutes, he then broke down too. It was not a typical closing argument filled with a well-thought-out script. Instead, he truly spoke from his years of pain, watching hundreds of kids and families drown over the years. It was like an impromptu plea for help as he appeared to almost beg for us to listen as he stated his final words, "These kids have no one. They just need someone to stand up for them." All we have to do is stand up.

SILO SECRET #107: Recently, I noticed a common theme, even within the nonprofit sector, of how judgment can hinder solutions. A nonprofit case manager who works with young expectant moms inspired me to share this experience. She said, "If people only knew the whole story, maybe they would not judge," explaining how homeless shelters to hospitals are human just like I was in slipping into the judgment mode. She said, "People do not wear a sign of the horror they have been through but they do wear a big belly for all to see the baby on the way," expressing, "If we can suppress judgment, we can help mom be a better mom and help baby be a contributing member of society." 93% of homeless mothers have a lifetime history of trauma. (Grandin, 2019)

SILO SECRET #108: Surprised when a man told me that he "did not know how to raise a child in this country," I naively responded, "but you have health and wealth." He explained that the phrase *"It takes a whole village to raise a child"* originated in his birth country of Africa. He shared how children play freely in the neighborhood, knowing they have a bunch of adults looking after them, and added that grandparents are always around for advice and support, especially to new parents. Australia is showing how we can apply the spirit of villages in our neighborhoods. Moms take turns, helping each other with tasks from cooking to carpooling. They stand up for each other. (Rhaiti, 2016)

SILO SECRET #109: A teacher named Erin Castillo created and shared an idea to have a mental health check-in board for kids in her class. Kids put their name on the back of a sticky note for confidentiality and then place the Post-it on the board next to the description of how they are feeling. Then the teacher confidentially follows up based on how the children feel. There are six rows to choose. At the top is "I'm great" and "I'm okay." In the middle, there is "I'm meh" or "I'm struggling." At the bottom is "I'm having a tough time and wouldn't mind a check-in." At the very bottom is a broken heart symbol that says, "I'm not doing good." Even with Ms. Castillo working to stand up for her kids daily, she still finds that she often has a few broken hearts to help mend each day in her class. (Reneau, 2019)

SILO SECRET #110: The "check-in" concept can be done in different ways and used in a variety of settings. I've been in meetings where the facilitator has each person do a quick check-in stating how they feel. I've seen how it enables people to offer support to adults too. Adults sometimes say, "I'm feeling great," but then often share a pressing concern like, "I'm struggling with a parent with Alzheimer's disease" or "My car just got totaled in an accident." We then continue the meeting, but it allows us to be more considerate and understanding. It also helps to not misinterpret body language or a lack of participation. It gives us a tool to stand up for one another or at least be a little more understanding.

SILO SECRET #111: If you met someone with multiple arrests, would you perhaps judge? Yet, increasingly I meet people with long rap sheets who turned things around when they connected with positive people and activities. Tonier Cain, arrested 83 times, is an example of a success story. She speaks all over the nation talking about how she changed her path. (Cain, 2019) Some respond to equine therapy, others like talking it out, others like expressing and releasing through art. Tonier shares how her spiritual beliefs changed her life. Trauma and recovery are both unique to the individual. The commonality seems to be that in almost every recovery story, individuals seem to mention one person who did something seemingly small like say "It is so nice that you came today." From the recipient's view, that comment felt like one person was standing up for them and it made all the difference.

REFLECT:

Think of the last time you felt judged even for a brief moment. Do you think if others had more information, they might have been less judgmental?

_____

_____

Have you ever been in a meeting where it was hard to focus? Would a check-in have helped?

_____

_____

"Short, loving nonprofit 501c3 silo enjoys sunsets and long walks on the beach—seeking tall, strong silo with 401k for sustainable relationship." – **Anonymous**

8.4 Silo Seeking Silo

Going from silo to silo, I sometimes wish I could create "silo seeking silo" personal ads. I go to a nonprofit meeting, and they say, "We need more men at these meetings." Then I go to a STEM (science, technology, engineering, and math) meeting a few hours later, and they say, "We need more ladies at these meetings." I want to have a matchmaker dinner and invite the two groups together.

While some diversity is easier to identify, like the obvious comments above (e.g., "need more of the opposite sex"), it may be less obvious forms of diversity that are creating the barrier. This relates to the four personality cards covered in the first chapter. Below are real examples of the less obvious lack of diversity in terms of personalities.

Real scenario – Nonprofit event table with seven people-focused personalities and one outcome-focused personality.

One table was assigned to discuss solutions for affordable housing. A key suggestion was that a major department store raise wages so people could afford housing. The one outcome-focused person at the table said, "While that would be nice, that store is replacing people with automation." All agreed that was true, but they wanted to see the department store be more people-focused like they were. They insisted the store needed to raise wages.

The outcome person tried to explain that money needed to come from somewhere else to go to those wages and asked where it would come from, but the people-focused group didn't want to get into the finance stuff. They said, "The store just needs to realize that they need to give people higher wages so they can afford housing."

Result: No change. The store continued on the same path.

Real scenario – Business meeting with one people-focused personality and four outcome-focused personalities.

When a group of high-level business executives met, they were asked to agree on the best way to cut costs to increase net income. Four outcome-focused personalities immediately proposed that the company do layoffs with "people being the most expensive resource." The one people-focused personality kept saying, "But people are the most valuable resource." There was not a lot of discussion because the majority took a quick vote, agreeing on the simple solution to do layoffs.

Result: Layoffs occurred. One of the outcome executives was among those impacted by the layoffs.

SILO SECRET #112: Partnering to combine differing silo views helps ensure a balance of people-focused and outcome-focused considerations. Ensuring equal consideration of for-profit and nonprofit views is valuable because there are often different skills that each silo can bring to the solution. Even the same role, such as a CFO for a nonprofit or a business, often has different viewpoints, tools, strategies, and goals. Having both people look at the same problem can help offer a more complete view in order to reach solutions.

SILO SECRET #113: When viewing the very important issues that nonprofits are working to address, business silos could help offer a perspective to optimize things like efficiency. Likewise, nonprofits could help offer businesses guidance on the impact of decisions on employee morale and motivation. For example, the above-mentioned layoff negatively impacted the productivity of those who stayed at the company. While they were not directly impacted, their morale and loyalty declined. Several expressed resistance to continual improvement efforts as they feared efficiency gains might result in further job cuts.

SILO SECRET #114: We have the opportunity to ensure that nonprofits have access to tools that businesses have to save them time and money and help improve quality and service goals. Many nonprofits are seeking changes for more efficiency and sustainability. Example: Some mental health providers are now utilizing technology to send out reminder appointments via text. They learned by observing their own dentists and doctors use this service. They saw how they could use that silo secret for their agency to reduce costly no-show visits. While doctors tend to charge for a no-show visit, many mental health providers still try to just absorb the cost.

REFLECT:

Can you see the value of ensuring a balance of the people-focused and outcome-focused silo views?

_____

_____

"Fire Prevention Is Our Intention." – **The Fresh Quotes** (45 Fire Safety Slogans, 2019)

8.5 Fire in the Silo—Firefighters Unite

Robert, a CEO who brought me in to boost quality, introduced me at a company meeting where he screeched, "No more overtime for putting out fires. We need solutions." While this added a tad bit of flame to the fire, it inspired people to clearly vocalize their feelings when I met with staff to learn their views and identify common denominators to address. As I had one-on-one meetings with staff, it was clear they wanted the same thing as the CEO. They wanted to go back to delivering high quality, but perhaps even more, they wanted to feel valued. Yet, even as I interviewed them, alarms were going off with "another fire to put out." They felt trapped in a vicious cycle of emergency issues.

To show we were listening and respond to their input, we had a follow-up meeting. While we all agreed that we needed to address the urgent priorities, I asked, "Could we possibly allocate one or two people to work on preventing just one of the issues?" They smiled and one person commented, "Eric and Jan keep suggesting a simple idea to secure the cables." All agreed to take Eric and Jan off the emergency on-call list for two days while they focused on securing cables.

On day 3, they implemented what they all described as Eric and Jan's "simple adjustment" to secure the cables and devices, reducing the risk of accidental loss of power and minimizing issues (a.k.a. fires). Even Robert, the CEO, noticed a visible improvement as alerts declined. Next, we had a milestone meeting where he rewarded the team. Robert announced, "I want to recognize not just Eric and Jan for implementing the solution, but also the rest of you for covering for them to make the solution possible."

The team radiated with energy. You could almost see the cultural transformation as they shared stories of how they would finally be able to make it to their kid's soccer game or family dinner without the cell phone going off. Eric then added, "You know, Luis and Mark have been working on an idea to give us proactive alerts when we are running out of storage on the computer. Maybe we could give them some time to get that idea in place." The team kept this culture of continual improvement going until eventually they were back to producing like the good ol' days where the cell phone hardly ever went off.

Emergency Fire Hazard Alert – seriously, now is not the time

Ironically, as they were joking about saying "goodbye" to their 'firefighter' hats, I got an emergency call of my own. Caitlin, my out-of-town guest called exclaiming, "So sorry to bother you, but this is urgent." She was planning a relaxing couple days at my condominium with her two-year-old son and baby on the way. Once I was done with my work, the plan was to go sightseeing. All was fine until Caitlin wailed, "Lisa, I can't take it. It is burning up. My baby is miserable. The air conditioner is not working." She cried, "Normally, I could handle this, but being very pregnant, I cannot handle it any longer."

Ugh, I felt terrible. My mind went into "just fix it" mode. Knowing I was busy, Caitlin had already taken the initiative to call the A/C maintenance phone number listed on the unit. She said that they could send someone out immediately. I replied, "Yes. Definitely. Let's get this fixed." On break from my training, I called back as the A/C guy was finishing up his inspection. He got on the phone and said, "Ma'am, you got yourself a fire hazard. You got sparks coming out of your A/C unit."

Feeling like I had exposed my friend and her babies to a fire hazard, I felt terrible. With my lunch break about to start, I said, "I will be right there." Wanting an immediate fix, I told him, "I will write a check to correct this. Do you have parts to fix this right away?" He replied, "Yes, ma'am, it will cost you about $3K for a new unit." While I was not thrilled, price was no object. On top of a baby crying and a pregnant friend about ready to have heatstroke, I had a fire hazard putting my guests, neighbors, and self at risk.

Visualizing my overheating guests, I rushed home. Upon arrival, the A/C guy boasted, "If you want, we can turn on the A/C switch and see the sparks fly." I suppose the right answer would have been, "No, that is fine," but I said, "Sure, that would be great, let's turn it on to see the origin of the spark." As Caitlin flipped the switch, I could almost hear my science teacher advising, "You really should be wearing protective eye gear." Anyway, too late now. Sparks were flying! The A/C guy shouted, "Shut it off!" as we watched sparks surround one panel. He went to loosen the screw to look behind the panel and realized it was already quite loose. He said, "Ma'am, it looks like the spark is from the friction of the screw vibrating against the metal. Hmm, looks like you got a loose screw."

For me, my "loose screw" was a reminder of how we can sometimes, especially when emotions are involved, get pulled into the "just fix it" mentality. Ironically, it was my emotions that led me to also focus on the prevention side where we looked at the problem logically to get to the root cause and ensure we had a permanent solution in place. I didn't want any more sparks and surely did not want a fire. So, it turned out the $3,000 solution would have cost me literally 100 times the $30 maintenance fee and might or might not have solved the problem, depending on whether they tightened that one screw.

Now, there is definitely a time to think "just fix it" and a time to allocate a little more time to say "let's prevent it." If the spark had caused a fire, we would definitely have wanted all firefighters on deck with the "just fix it" mentality. Later, the firefighters would have suggested ways to prevent or even do early detection. Einstein suggests that we invest in getting to the root causes to prevent or minimize issues. If we just keep reacting to sparks and fires, things eventually get out of control.

While the chart below represents extremes for illustrative purposes, it can help you assess whether you are being aware and flexible to adapt to the best silo view for the circumstances.

FIREFIGHTING 'SILO' view	FIRE PREVENTION 'SILO' view
"Just fix it"	"Get to the root cause"
Short-term thinking (immediate solution)	Long-term thinking (permanent solution)
Problem = situation to diffuse (i.e., stop spark)	Problem = incident to prevent (get to root cause)
Reactive mode (problem focus)	Responsive mode (solution focus)
Put out the fire (get rid of unit that sparks)	Prevent future fire (address source of spark)
Decrease problem of heat in house	Achieve goal of safe, cool air in house
More is more – work harder (i.e., replace AC unit)	Less is more – work smarter (tighten the screw)
Do it yourself view – jump to fix problem on own	Partner view – tend to unite on solutions

SILO SECRET #115: While it is easy to go into firefighting mode, even the fire department has a philosophy to continually focus on prevention and reduction. In a local firefighter presentation, they explained that they spend over 80% of their time educating on prevention or ways to reduce the severity of their calls. They install smoke detectors and train people on proper use. This helps notify people when there is smoke versus waiting until it is an uncontrollable fire.

SILO SECRET #116: When we are thinking more with the emotional part of our brain, it is easy to get pulled into a single focus to just fix or stop the problem. There are situations where this mindset is great and even a natural reaction for survival. The phrase "put out fires" is a visual term to describe this type of focus. You can still use the logical part of your brain to do all the planned and unplanned steps to put out the fire, but you can also use the logic side of your brain to ask yourself, "How can we prevent fires?"

SILO SECRET #117: In my experience, it gives everyone peace of mind to be candid, acknowledging that "fires happen." Some people, often the fun Change Agents, love the thrill of being near fires and being the hero who puts out the fire, so I often allocate roles so they can be primary responders in emergencies, but am sure to rotate staff to give them needed breaks. Their front-line experience gives them great insight on ways to prevent fires and even fun ways to inform people on how to prepare, prevent, plan, or if needed, react to a fire.

SILO SECRET #118: When you are surrounded by fires, it is easy to feel like you are going to suffocate. This book is really to inspire a mindset of possibilities. *Permaculture* is a solution-focused training designed to grow the analytical and creative skills needed to design innovative solutions. "Some ideas change how we see the world, and then we change the world." (Hardie, Problem-Focus vs Solution-focus, 2015)

REFLECT:

Do you tend to jump into action or prevention? Is there anything you could do to adjust your view?

_____

_____

Chapter 8 Summary: *Over the past decades, I have been asked the secret to achieving world-class results. Well, we did the experiment, and it showed that a blended focus on people and outcomes creates optimal results. Compassion and empathy often serve as the inspiration to work past our most challenging barriers to achieve outcomes. The combined view helps us work toward lasting solutions.*

9. OUR PLANET EARTH

"We have reached a new milestone as a human family. With seven billion of us now inhabiting our planet, it is time to ask some fundamental questions. How can we provide a dignified life for ourselves and future generations while preserving and protecting the global commons—the atmosphere, the oceans, and the ecosystems that support us?" – **Ban Ki-Moon** (South Korean diplomat, eighth secretary-general of the United Nations.)

"As I looked down, I saw a large river meandering slowly along for miles, passing from one country to another without stopping. I also saw huge forests, extending along several borders. And I watched the extent of one ocean touch the shores of separate continents. Two words leaped to mind as I looked down on all this: commonality and interdependence. We are one world." – **John-David F. Bartoe** (American astronaut, master of science in physics, and PhD in physics from Georgetown University; astrophysicist at the Naval Research Laboratory, currently serves as manager for ISS at NASA JSC.)

9.1 My Earth, What Is the Big Deal?

Fernando and Sarah were seated at the captain's table aboard the *Queen Mary* with fellow passengers from all over the world. For sure, this was one of the high points in their lives. A couple days into the trip, they were enjoying dinner when suddenly a group of passengers scurried toward the port, looking curiously at the water. Excited that it might be a whale sighting or maybe an island, Fernando and Sarah rushed over to check it out. Looking out, it was so strange. A huge dock, the size of a tennis court, was floating in the middle of the ocean. The dock surface was filled with unrecognizable sea life.

As passengers questioned how a massive dock ended up in the middle of the ocean, a scientist named Dr. Kwan described how an older dock would have broken up into pieces and decomposed. He explained that newer materials are not biodegradable, so they last and float longer. He shared a story of how he and a team of scientists in California had studied a similar dock that floated from Japan to the U.S. Apparently, it was loaded with hundreds of strange-looking invasive species that they had never seen before. (Fackler, 2017) He said they wore biohazard suits because they were not sure how much radiation had floated over with the decaying creatures.

Fernando looked increasingly concerned as Dr. Kwan explained, "With more natural disasters projected in the future (hurricanes, tornadoes, tidal waves), more garbage will float or blow to new destinations."

They were all dressed up, with the best food and entertainment money could buy. Yet, they had a view of toxic waste floating from a natural disaster thousands of miles away.

Astronauts explain that when they go to space, they realize how special and unique Earth is and express that when you have been in space, you realize that there really is no place like our earth. Gaining this intensified appreciation for Earth, some astronauts are speaking and writing books to try to encourage us to unite to protect the air, water, land, and space that we share. Looking at our planet from an objective view, below is a summary of our shared planet quality indicators.

Planet Earth Quality Index:

Air: 4.2 million deaths every year from air pollution (World Health Organization Health Topics, 2019)

Deaths per year due to pollution: 300,000 in China; 527,700 in India; 25,000 in California.

Land: 2.6 **trillion pounds of garbage** (Thompson, 2012)

Water: About 8 million metric tons of plastic are dumped into the ocean each year (Earth Day, 2019)

Forecast: By 2050, six million people will die per year due to air pollution (Kelland, 2016)

Prior Warnings: In 1952, the great smog of London killed 8,000 people (Klein, 2018)

Some say part of the problem is that we talk in millions and trillions of tons, and people can't quite relate to that, so it is just a number on a page and doesn't feel real. To try to appreciate the impact we each have on the earth, let's imagine you have a 3D printer that makes a stunning replica of you. You like it so much that you order five of the 3D models. They look and weigh the same as you. Well, pretend the manufacturer puts in an automatic order and sends you five of these replicas every year for the rest of your life. While these models are admittedly quite appealing to the eye, you may start to wonder, "Where in the world am I going to put these beautiful replicas of me?" Well, that silly analogy represents a very real challenge that we face.

Each year, a typical 175-pound person in a developed country generates approximately 2.6 pounds of garbage a day. (Thompson, 2012) So, an average man of 175 pounds will produce about five times his weight (nearly 1,000 pounds) of trash each year. Just like you would likely ask yourself, "Where in the world will I put these strikingly appealing 3D replicas of me?," world leaders are trying to figure out where in the world they will put the nearly 1,000 pounds of trash that we each generate every year. China in particular is saying it doesn't want the world's junk anymore, handing the world 111 million tons of garbage to cram somewhere.

These numbers do not include the five multi-ton piles of garbage in our oceans. Imagine sitting at the beach watching a garbage truck dump 1,440 truckloads of junk into the ocean each and every day. This adds up to eight million tons of waste that we pour into our ocean. When we clean up the oceans, will we plop those piles into the landfill, saying, "Hey, what is a few more million tons?" The intent is to recycle the plastic from the water, but the globs of plastic mixed with sea salt, seaweed, decaying creatures, and other garbage may not meet the tight criteria of our recycling plants.

Viewing the gigantic piles of waste somehow reminds me of John Candy's comment, "C'mon, a little toxic waste never killed nobody" in the movie *Armed and Dangerous*. It seemed funny at the time, but not so much now.

SILO SECRET #119: Some very smart people say that humans will become extinct if we continue down the same path. There are also many people showing how we can turn things around, but we need to have more people on the "Earth wagon." Below are excerpts from a few highly respected individuals on this topic.

Richard Branson (highly successful business leader, investor, author, and philanthropist) has stated, "The earth cannot wait 60 years. I want a future for my children and my children's children. The clock is ticking." (Dauncey, 2009)

David Pimentel (Cornell University Department of Ecology and Evolutionary Biology PhD) published "Soil Erosion: A Food and Environmental Threat" study in the *Journal of the Environment, Development, and Sustainability,* concluding that "Soil is being swept and washed away 10 to 40 times faster than it is being replenished." (Powers, 2019)

Margaret Wheatley (global speaker, teacher, community worker, consultant, and leader with a doctorate from Harvard with a focus on organizational behavior and change) states, "Our best path forward is to be warriors for the human spirit as we create 'islands of sanity' in the chaos we see around us." (Wheatley, 2019)

SILO SECRET #120: With more natural disasters projected in the future, scientists have explained that more garbage will be spread because it does not degrade. It just floats or blows to a new destination until eventually you have to figure out what to do with that pile of junk or, in some cases, pile of toxic waste. The key is for us to share and implement known solutions.

SILO SECRET #121: The Oceanic Society has posted seven ways we can help. On top of helping with beach and river cleanups and recycling activities, they ask that we avoid products with microbeads (they start with 'poly-' and end in '-lene'). Just as we are getting people to stop using plastic straws, now we are putting eight trillion of these tiny plastic balls into our water every day. Back in 2015, my dental hygienist told me that they were trying to figure out why people had all these tiny balls stuck in their teeth and were relieved to hear that President Obama signed a bill to ban plastics in toothpaste. However, we are still putting the microbeads into other items like cosmetic products and detergents. (Microbead-Free Waters Act, 2015)

REFLECT:

United we stand. People tend to feel great when they are part of achieving something bigger than themselves. Is there a sustainable goal that you would be interested in improving?

_____

_____

"It is not the strongest of the species that survive, nor the most intelligent, but the one most responsive to change." – ***Charles Darwin*** (English naturalist, geologist, and biologist, best known for his contributions to the science of evolution.)

9.2 The Straw That Made a Big Stir

Shelby, a 16-year-old Girl Scout at the time, saw a commercial that inspired her to do her part to help save our oceans. Below is an excerpt of her thought-provoking letter to a company CEO. This is the note about the one straw that created a big stir. (Jr. Ocean Guardians, 2018)

> *"With all due respect, the company's 'Human Kindness' commercial had a glaring flaw: it depicted the casual use of a disposable plastic straw to blow out a birthday candle.*
>
> *Did you know that straws are one of the top ocean polluters? Scientists are predicting by the year 2050 there will be more plastic in the ocean than fish if we don't start making drastic changes with our plastic pollution. I'm urging you to stop using this specific commercial."*

Well, Shelby's note undoubtedly raised awareness. Dignity Health's vice president of environmental sustainability, Sister Mary Ellen Leciejewski, was especially inspired that a 16-year-old had taken the initiative to elicit positive change. They cut the use of plastic straws, stirrers, and cup lids from eight million to four million per year, meaning that Shelby's letter led to the company cutting its plastic usage in half.

Shelby was on a roll. The chief executive officers of Farmer Brothers coffee and Alaska Airlines personally responded. All three companies went into action to reduce the use of the items mentioned by Shelby. Dignity Health, which has 39 hospitals in California, Arizona, and Nevada, looked at its operations and decided to go beyond reducing straw usage. It took extra steps to eliminate plastic stirrers and lids. Positive changes continued. Alaska Airlines plans to swap out their yearly 22 million plastic stir straws and citrus picks with stir straws made from white birch and citrus picks made of bamboo. Last but surely not least, Farmer Brothers wrote to Shelby, saying it would replace plastic stirrers with wooden ones.

When asked, "What have you learned from being a Girl Scout?," Shelby replied "I know that I can make a difference in the world!"

SILO SECRET #122: There are things we can do personally. We too can take action like bringing our own utensils in a pouch or purse versus using plastic utensils. When going out to eat, we can bring our own container versus taking home plastic throwaway containers. Like Shelby, we can be role models and inspire others to protect our oceans.

SILO SECRET #123: More and more places are discontinuing straws and finding ways to inspire change. In Singapore, a nonprofit called Zero Waste SG did a campaign to encourage consumers to bring their own utensils to food outlets in exchange for discounts and freebies. Within four months, they eliminated 2.6 million pieces of disposable plastic. (Hicks, 2018)

SILO SECRET #124: The average life of those plastic bags we say "yes" to at the grocery store is 15 minutes. When grocery stores say, "Plastic okay?", we can help by using reusable tote bags. We can also reuse or recycle plastic bags.

SILO SECRET #125: Some are debating whether we need to focus on cleanup or prevention. Richard Thompson, a marine biologist who has studied plastic waste at Plymouth University in the UK , stated, "Imagine you get up to make some tea and you leave the bathwater overflowing; do you start cleaning up or turn off the tap?" Shelby is working on turning off the tap, but we also need to clean up our flooded home or we'll be up to our knees in water. We need a two-part plan: Operation Cleanup and Operation Prevention. Lucky for us, our next story will share plans to help with cleanup.

On a funny note, a nurse friend has us laughing as the inside of her refrigerator looks like a wine storage rack. She believes it is healthier to store filtered water versus buy bottled water to drink. Orb Media did not test the impact of containers, but they found that 93% of 250 plastic bottles across nine countries had signs of plastic and 83% of 159 tap water samples from around the world had signs of plastic. (Morrison & Tyree, 2018)

REFLECT:

Think of a step you can take to help the environment. You can select from the list below or add one.

____ Store a couple tote bags or plastic bags in your car to use when you go grocery shopping.

____ Carry a spoon, fork, or spork into fast food restaurants versus using plastic utensils.

____ When you go to conferences, skip putting a plastic lid on your coffee.

____ Drink out of a glass using filtered water when possible versus using plastic bottles.

____ Bring a container to a restaurant to take home leftovers versus using plastic.

____ Other: _____

*"Looking out at the ocean, it's easy to feel small and to imagine all your troubles, suddenly insignificant, slipping away. Earth's seven oceans seem vast and impenetrable, but a close look tells another story." – **Ted Danson*** (Actor, winner of a Golden Globe Award, advocate for oceans via Oceana.)

9.3 The Dive That Changed His Life

While 16-year-old Shelby was working on Operation Prevention, then-18-year-old Boyan Slat, a Dutch high school student, began his cleanup operations. He founded The Ocean Cleanup after he went on a diving trip to Greece and discovered that below the surface of the water, he was surrounded by plastic waste. Boyan shared his story in an interview with MNN.com, the Mother Nature Network, a news website that includes information on topics such as sustainability, health, lifestyle, technology, money, food, home, and family. He expressed to MNN, "There were more plastic bags than fish" and "That was the moment I realized it was a huge issue and that environmental issues are really the biggest problems my generation will face."

Young Boyan figured someone was developing a solution, but learned that many of the proposed efforts risked harming animals. Wanting a better answer, he put his personal life on hold to find an answer to this urgent issue impacting every country, every person, and ultimately every creature on Earth. He was determined to design and develop a solution. What worried him most was that there are large pieces of plastic that are close to decay. He explained how the large objects will break down into small and harmful microplastics over the next few decades, increasing the already dangerous levels of plastic waste in our oceans. He urgently stated, "We must defuse this ticking time bomb."

Laurent Lebreton of The Ocean Cleanup Foundation in The Netherlands warns that the results of the ocean study indicate that "The vast dump of plastic waste swirling in the Pacific Ocean is now bigger than France, Germany, and Spain combined—far larger than previously feared—and is growing rapidly."

Boyan's design is a series of autonomous and energy neutral surface floaters that each have skirts below the water. The goal is to use the natural ocean tides to move the floaters along, capturing plastic along the way. To make the floating device more flexible, he plans to have 60 smaller systems about a half mile wide in the ocean. One goal is to make it more scalable, less risky, and easier to implement in stages as funding comes in. The Ocean Cleanup plans to make periodic trips to collect the captured garbage. Boyan and his growing team of over 80 engineers, researchers, scientists, and computational modelers are diving together into this uncharted turbulent territory and learning along the way. They are ready to tackle what will surely be a wave of challenges ahead, but are determined to save our oceans.

SILO SECRET #126: Scientists are saying we need a two-sided global focus. We need to follow Shelby in her mission to stop adding plastic to the pile and also follow Boyan in his mission to clean up our mess. As The Ocean Cleanup's research found that nearly 80% of river plastic emissions into the ocean comes from 1,000 rivers, they began to deploy their latest design, The Interceptor™. While the systems look more like yachts, they route river plastic into bins versus oceans.

SILO SECRET #127: Each ocean has its own multi-ton pile of plastic. We are intelligent life forms. Rather than let the saying be "the straw that broke the human's back," we have the opportunity to focus on prevention and cleaning up our water.

REFLECT:

Seeing how two teenagers took the initiative to lead high-impact ocean cleanup and plastic prevention initiatives, does it give you hope that each of us can make a difference?

_____

_____

Chapter 9 Summary: *A dock floating all the way from Japan to California helps us to see that we are truly connected and interdependent. Together, a 16-year-old American girl and an 18-year-old Dutch boy are demonstrating how individuals and countries can come forward to be a part of solutions. If we each take small steps, it adds up to significant results. It is okay that we are learning. The key is to continually improve and work to improve our world.*

10. TOP TIPS FROM EINSTEIN AND CONFUCIUS

"The world is being reshaped by the convergence of social, mobile, cloud, big data, community, and other powerful forces. The combination of these technologies unlocks an incredible opportunity to connect everything together in a new way and is dramatically transforming the way we live and work." – **Marc Benioff** (Internet entrepreneur, author, philanthropist, and co-CEO of Salesforce.)

"We need to identify who is not in the room that needs to be in the room to achieve the goal." – **Dr. Sandra Whitehead** (Director of program and partnership development for the National Environmental Health Association; appointed to the National Environmental Justice Advisory Committee by the EPA.)

10.1 What Would Einstein Do?

Have you ever had a decision to make between two options (a risky, fun option and a safe, not-as-fun option), and decided to consult a friend? Do you notice a tendency to ask the friend who will give the answer you want to hear? Well, Einstein might have suggested that you ask the other friend or better yet, ask both friends to get two views and learn what you might be missing.

Einstein believed in getting input from others to look at a challenge from different angles. The more diverse views, the better, as it helps to see different angles on the problems and solutions. He suggested that we:

- **Raise new questions and possibilities with a new view.**
  *"To raise new questions, new possibilities, to regard old problems from a new angle, requires creative imagination and marks real advance in science." – **Albert Einstein** (German-born theoretical physicist and one of most influential physicists of the 20th century, earned a Nobel Prize in physics, developed the theory of relativity, influenced the philosophy of science.)* (Einstein & Infeld, 1938)

- **Seek to understand.**
  *"Peace cannot be kept by force; it can only be achieved by understanding." – **Albert Einstein*** (Albert Einstein Archives 48-479)

Even though Einstein was viewed as brilliant, he valued thoughts from others. Over the years, I have met people who go into locations of extreme conflict and even war. With them having a 90% or higher success rate in facilitating peaceful solutions, I always ask them their secret. They each describe how they simply help the two groups understand each other's views.

I often hear people make comments about how they have the answer but they believe they have to "stay in their lane" versus speak up. Inspiring people to share their unique set of skills and experiences offers us a fresh perspective that can often help us formulate a better path together.

SILO SECRET #128: Einstein believed that his strength was related to his focus on understanding the problem before jumping into the solution. There is a technique called the 5 Whys where you keep asking why until you get to the root cause. (iSixSigma-Editorial, 2019)

SILO SECRET #129: It is easy to jump to a single root cause of an issue when there may be multiple root causes or points of failure. In problem management, people work to identify all the possible points that could cause a failure and then prioritize them by which are most probable and which have the highest impact. If we break down problems to understand the different root causes, as well as the possible points of failure, we can work to prevent or minimize reoccurrences.

SILO SECRET #130: Using the four personality types will help ensure you get the right people in the room. Getting a comprehensive view from the finance and problem-solver view is often more complicated because the same job titles in the business and nonprofit world typically have access to different tools and approaches that are extremely helpful in reaching solutions. A way to overcome this challenge is to have these members reach out to their counterpart in the other silo for a second opinion.

REFLECT:

Is there something in your life that you would like to improve? Think of how you could learn from an existing solution.

_____

_____

"A single conversation with a wise man is better than ten years of study."
—**Chinese Proverb**

10.2 Top 10 Tips from Confucius

A funny thing happened on the way back from getting my driver's license. I had just turned 16. It was July, so it was quite hot. My mom was among the 5% of Floridians to be proactive in saving the polar bears, so we only had air conditioning in a dire emergency. Her definition and my definition of a dire emergency differed. The only option was to get a job over the summer, a place with, you got it, air conditioning. On the way home, we passed by a gigantic red and yellow "grand opening" sign at a new Chinese food restaurant. That seemed like an invitation so I put on a beautiful white dress (as if I were dressing for a school dance—okay, it was the dress I wore to the school dance) and headed to the restaurant.

When I walked in, this incredibly tall man pointed and guided me to talk outside. When I say tall, I mean this man had to lean forward and tilt his head to go under the front door as we headed outside. To this this day, he is the largest man I have ever seen. He started speaking at a rapid pace, but in Chinese. Every now and then he would say a word in broken English. He kept talking, so my thought was there was a chance he had a job opening, and I listened intently. When I'd say, "Hostess," he would say, "Waitress." I felt confident in telling adults where to go, but serving adults food and drinks seemed way too hard. With some irritation in his voice, he said, "Want job? Waitress," so I didn't say that "hostess" word anymore.

As he rambled more in Chinese, my neck was getting a little strained from looking up, but I kept eye contact and nodded periodically to give evidence I was listening—not quite understanding, but listening. Now and then, I wondered, "Does he think I speak Chinese?" He might be mad to find out I did not understand about 99% of what he said, but he said a couple words that I did understand—"five o'clock"—and then went back to the rapid-fire Chinese. I picked up a menu and motioned to get approval to take it home. He nodded and headed back to get ready for the grand opening.

Life is really simple, but we insist on making it complicated. – Confucius

When I arrived back home, my mother said, "So, did you get the job?" I said, "Not sure, but I'm going to show up at five o'clock and see if they pay me." To be a waitress in a place where everyone spoke Chinese, I figured I would have to write down what people wanted in Chinese symbols, so I practiced for the next few hours, replicating the Chinese symbols, copying the items from the menu to practice for the big night. It was hard because I could not tell if tiny marks were an optional style or if the mark would change the meaning of the word. I didn't know how to say "hi" in Chinese, but I could write a mean "sweet and sour chicken."

At 4:00 p.m., I headed over to the restaurant. There were a few people waiting at the door to get in, but they did not open until, you got it, five o' clock. Being a VIP employee, I walked right in. A lady with a strong Chinese accent crinkled her face and said, "Who you?"

I responded with confidence, "Me waitress." She lifted her hands in the air with a look of disgust and walked briskly out the door. I never got a chance to ask her, "Who you?", so I cannot say for sure who she was.

Soon customers started coming in. I looked around and, other than the customers, I was the only person in the room. I smiled and said, "Welcome to our Mandarin Chinese restaurant" and let them know that I could take their order when they were ready. My first table had three people. Luckily, two of them ordered the same thing—sweet and sour chicken—and the other ordered General Tso's chicken. I went to another table, sat down, and intently copied the Chinese symbols onto an order sheet to give to the cook. Whew, longest seven minutes of my life.

Eager to get my masterpiece to the cook, I hurried to the kitchen and gave the order to Mr. Lou. He yelled in a very masculine voice, "Two number four; one number three." Realizing he had just used the sequence number from the menu, I took the paper back and wrote next to my Chinese symbol masterpiece "2 – #4" and "1 – #3" and showed it to him with kind of a questioning look on my face—like seriously, this is all you need? He nodded. He made some comments in Chinese, and the other cooks cracked up laughing. Fine with me—whew, this job had just gotten a whole lot easier. Good thing, because when I headed out of the kitchen, a line of people had showed up waiting to be seated. That was when I truly gained an appreciation for *Tip #1: Simplify.*

Not to complain, but I just got promoted to hostess/waitress— apparently, I was the floor manager too. I honestly never had a chance to ask about that lady who left after I said, "Me waitress." Was she supposed to be my boss? Head waitress? Only waitress? I never got the answer to that one. Definitely could have used her help. Things were nonstop, and it was just me. Fortunately, they noticed after a couple weeks that I could use some help and hired a very nice, hardworking Italian busboy named Antonio. He was 15 years old and fit in as well as I did. He spoke English, so it was great having a buddy. He was intimidated by Mr. Lou when Mr. Lou got stressed, which was pretty much daily. The kitchen was about 120 degrees, and so was he.

Consideration for others is the basis of a good life, a good society. – Confucius

One night, they asked me to help at another Chinese restaurant. Of course, they did not ask directly; it was more like a game of charades. Using creative sign language, they asked if I could go help another restaurant with a big party. A baseball team had come in, and they needed help serving them. Even though I had trained Antonio to back me up, I was concerned that I was not familiar with the other restaurant's menu or the way it did things.

"Oh—all same," they replied. The other restaurant had the same menu. I was so relieved to learn how they did ***Tip #2: Standardize across all locations.*** Great, now I just had to worry about having a hungry baseball team that had been waiting through our 15-minute charades game plus 10-minute drive time.

Luckily, I got to the new restaurant. So, I was working to help their waitress, who did not speak English, get caught up. A person on the baseball team said to me, "If you can just bring us 16 chow mein bowls of soup, that would be great." They were actually quite patient considering the wait time, but I wanted to ensure we served customers in order, and the place was packed. I ran in and out of the kitchen, back and forth, with large trays. Mr. Lou came over to help. As I was rushing out the kitchen door, I said to him, "Sixteen chow meins next."

One of the cooks mumbled, "Sixteen lo mein?" Carrying a heavy tray of entrees, I was in a rush and just said, "Yeah" as I headed out the double doors. I figured they knew what I meant as it was the only order with 16 items, so he could see it was chow mein versus lo mein. When I returned just moments later, Mr. Lou had 16 bowls of lo mein ready. When I gently said, "It is actually chow mein," he shouted, and I mean shouted, "You know difference between boy and girl?"

Seriously, the only words I had heard this man say in English were "no hostess, waitress" and now, he suddenly exclaimed at the top of his lungs, "You know difference between boy and girl?" We worked through it, got the right soup to the baseball team, and they all had quite a laugh as they had heard the loud question coming from the kitchen. Everything worked out fine. It was also educational. I don't think any of us will ever forget the difference between chow mein and lo mein.

Even at 16 years old, I thought it was amazing that the restaurant owners followed the philosophy of **Tip #3: Support versus compete with peers.** They united to help one another. They used the same vendors and standard menus and supplies. Being able to jump in and help at a moment's notice showed that making tasks simple made it easy to standardize, which then made it easy to help one another and save money. In addition to the benefits of sharing resources between restaurants, I learned about **Tip #4: Unite to save costs.** They basically got volume-purchasing discounts and shared everything from ordering to shipping costs.

Wherever you go, go with all your heart. – Confucius

Believe it or not, other Chinese restaurants started requesting my help as a waitress. I know, I was just as surprised then as you are now. So, I was now working at various Chinese restaurants in the area. There was a group of senior citizens that ate out a lot. This one sweet lady said to me, "We could not help but notice that no matter what Chinese restaurant we go to, we see you there." She whispered to me, "Are you Chinese?"

I got this question a lot. I'd tell customers, "No, I am not Chinese, but please don't tell the boss; he doesn't know." They would always smile and laugh. It never occurred to me that you had to be Chinese to work in a Chinese restaurant, but many people seemed astonished. It never occurred to me that they would treat me differently and they didn't. I enjoyed experiencing *Tip #5: Treat all as equals.*

Ironically, I used to run from one restaurant to another without a lot of time to eat. Even Mr. Lou didn't have time to eat until about 10:00 p.m. His large family came in late each night to eat at the restaurant. One night, Mr. Lou came over to me and said, "You skinny; you eat." He motioned me to come over and join him and his family for dinner. I was impressed as clearly he had been working on broadening his English vocabulary.

Not wanting to impose, I said, "You eat with your family; this is your time with them." He looked at me and did this quirky but kind smile. It was like the first time he had tried to pull the sides of his mouth upward. As he kept the smile in place, it turned into a real smile and he said in the kindest tone, "You family." He truly made me feel like part of the family.

Excited to finally get to taste the awesome food I was serving to others, I eagerly joined the table. It was at that moment that I learned that American Chinese and real Chinese food (at least what they ate at the restaurant) were quite different. No sweet and sour sauce here. They had duck and rice almost every night with some form of soy sauce. It was at that moment that I learned how to fake eat—hmmm, pretending to load up on duck, but just putting a tiny bit on the plate and surrounding it with a mountain of rice to make it look like I had a big helping.

Mr. Lou was onto me. He just did that quirky smile. The food part was painful, but the family part is one of my best memories. Being invited to be part of Mr. Lou's family taught me lessons that you can read in a book, but not really grasp until you experience it. Their showing how they cared made me feel even more loyal to them. **Tip #6: Treat employees like family** was the tip I cherished most. For years, customers kept coming back for the sweet and sour sauce and fried rice. Listening, Mr. Lou continued to give the customers what they wanted, even though it would not be his choice of food. This was essentially *Tip #7: Truly listen to the voice of the customer (VOC).*

Education breeds confidence. Confidence breeds hope. Hope breeds peace. – Confucius

Late in the evening, Mr. Lou's very wise grandfather would come in to help. I never asked his age, but I figured he was one of the oldest people in the world. We called him Confucius because every night, he would gather the busboy and me together to share his wisdom. He tended to save up a lot of wisdom for the weekend. With us being 15 and 16 years old, this was not quite our idea of a great Friday night, but we listened as attentively as we could. To be honest, we wanted to go party, but Confucius was so intent on passing down his wisdom that we stayed and listened. He didn't make any money for doing this, yet he came in to help teach us everything he knew from life lessons to restaurant best practices and even ownership tips. We were kids, but he still gave up his time to teach us the business. To this day, I still find myself realizing the value of **Tip #8: Pass on generational knowledge.**

When I went on to college a few years later, the college students were studying FIFO (first in, first out) and LIFO (last in, first out) inventory methods. I'd already learned all that stuff from Confucius, so it was a breeze for me. He showed us how FIFO was very important to ensure fresh food and to make sure nothing expired. To this day, I do not know his real name. He smiled when we said, "Thank you, Confucius; we have enjoyed your wise lesson for the night," so we continued calling him that.

Another practice that Confucius taught us was to share the tips (money) equally. Being wise, he could see I was not totally bought into the splitting the money idea, but said it was important to "share and make sure all have money for food and home." He shared the importance of **Tip #9: Share the wealth** so all of us were okay. He said, "Someday in life, it may be you who is the one needing help; this will be the day that this practice will make sense." I agreed with that part, and the busboy kind of liked feeling like the Karate Kid, so we went with the flow. In the spirit of his master, Antonio repeated, "Wax on, wax off" as he cleaned the tables.

While my waitress career and Chinese impersonation skills were soaring, high school exams were coming up, and I didn't study. I was quite proud of my exam-cramming skills, but I needed some extra time to study for this one test. Mr. Lou seemed to be expanding his English vocabulary, so I was hoping I could get his permission to reduce my hours one day to have a little time to study. No such luck; the game of advanced charades began.

"I have a test that I need to study for." I tried to act out studying with the menu. Studying was not a role I played often, so I may have been a little rusty in acting out the process. He had no clue what I was doing. When I used the words "study for school," though, his eyes got wide when I said the word "school."

He said, "School important, me waitress; you school … me waitress, you school." Mr. Lou literally put my education above his business, illustrating his high regard for *Tip #10: Value education.*

As I imagined nearly seven-foot Mr. Lou as a waiter, I visualized customers running for the door. He sort of scared people. Okay, he really scared people. Since he had to duck at every doorway entrance, I think he got tired of putting his hands and head both out, so he just bent down and pushed through the two doors with his head to save time. When his head pushed through the double doors, I could always tell because customers had this look on their face like Godzilla had just walked into the dining room. He was really a good person. He just startled people, and while I have mentioned his growing English skills, he had some phrases that made the customers a little nervous.

He would yell to the busboy, "Make doo doo on table." Translation, "Please put bowls of noodles on the table." Another goodie was "Mop table!" Translation, "It is almost our high volume time; please ensure all the tables are clean and ready."

Finally, with charades, we were able to work out a solution where I could bring my books in and study in between waiting on tables. Everything worked out fine and Mr. Lou was able to stay in the kitchen.

While I have spent over 20 years working with top companies who use best practices from around the world, I really think Mr. Lou and his network of restaurants helped me experience multiple global best practices firsthand. Below is a summary of real-life best practices from Mr. Lou and Confucius.

Top 10 Tips from Confucius	Real-Life Example:
1 **Simplify** – make the non-value-added processes as easy as possible; focus on value-added tasks.	Rather than write out the menu selection, I learned to simply write the menu number and quantity ordered.
2 **Standardize across all locations** – create consistent methods to make things easy and repeatable for customers and employees.	Standardization of the menu enabled customers to easily order from any location. Consistent processes enabled employees to help at any location.
3 **Support versus compete with peers** – build a support network to help one another; realize there are plenty of customers for everyone.	Restaurant owners and staff supported each other. Customers went to a convenient location, sometimes going to different owner locations.
4 **Unite to save costs** – collaborate with others on common needs and then purchase together to get volume discounts; share expenses to keep costs down, especially on administrative items.	Restaurants bought the same supplies so they could get volume discounts (e.g., same fortune cookies and noodles). Menus were the same except for the name and location printed at the top.

5 **Treat all as equals** – treat employees and customers all as equals regardless of age, race or other differences, creating a great experience for both employees and customers.	Customers were surprised that a non-Chinese person could work in a Chinese restaurant. Elderly people often asked, "Are you Chinese?" Mr. Lou and his family welcomed me and treated me like an equal.
6 **Treat employees like family** – treat employees with kindness; not expecting anything in return. This also aligns with the service-profit chain as happy employees provide better service that generate increased profits.	The owner showed he cared about my health by saying, "You skinny; you eat." He treated me like family, saying, "You family," inviting me to eat with his family. His caring inspired me to reciprocate with more loyalty to his restaurant.
7 **Truly listen to the voice of customers (VOC)** – listen to customer wants. This is a best practice to ensure the needs and wants of customers are met.	Even though the owner and the family preferred to eat duck and rice, they continued to cook the version of Chinese food that customers enjoyed and made it easy to order.
8 **Pass on generational knowledge** – invest in growing children and create a culture of learning, taking time to help and grow those around you.	Each night, Confucius would take time to teach us a new lesson. He passed down generational knowledge of life and business lessons that seemed to be tips he got from his ancestors.
9 **Share the wealth** – take care of the community; finance experts teach three buckets (spending, savings, and charity).	Confucius' philosophy was to share tips to ensure everyone had enough money for food and a home.

10 **Value education** – value and invest in education and growing employees; listen and show compassion and empathy to help employees continually grow via education.	The owner said, "School important," putting education as a top priority above his restaurant business. Together, we figured out a way for me to balance work and school.

SILO SECRET #131: Henry Ford used Lean practices years ago, even down to repurposing sawdust so it did not go to waste. Today, Toyota uses the Lean model to enable 90% of their employees to submit and implement small changes for significant results. Even though I studied and have years of experience in Lean workflow optimization, the Chinese restaurant seemed to be the epitome of Lean, simplifying and standardizing in all areas, resulting in an intuitive flow for both customers and employees.

SILO SECRET #132: Mr. Lou and Confucius were walking examples of the value of passing on knowledge to help future generations. Below are Chinese proverbs that summarize what I learned through experience versus words.

If you want 1 year of prosperity, grow grain.

If you want 10 years of prosperity, grow trees.

If you want 100 years of prosperity, **grow people**.

—Chinese Proverb

If you want happiness for an hour, take a nap. If you want happiness for a day, go fishing. If you want happiness for a year, inherit a fortune. If you want happiness for a lifetime, **help somebody**.

—Chinese Proverb

SILO SECRET #133: If you look at the top five list on the United Nations sustainability list, Confucius pretty much covered them all. Below is a Chinese proverb that seems to show how their philosophy can ripple from individual to society.

If there is light in the soul,

There will be beauty in the person.

If there is beauty in the person,

There will be harmony in the house.

If there is harmony in the house,

There will be order in the nation.

If there is order in the nation,

There will be **peace in the world**.

—**Chinese Proverb**

SILO SECRET #134: Two of the top choices for food orders are often Chinese food and pizza. If you notice, you'll see competitive pizza ads, but you will rarely see Chinese food ads. They mainly just send out that same menu with the only difference being the contact information for the local restaurant. From my experience, they do not compete and they have no need to advertise. They have the best form of marketing, consistency, and word of mouth along with a natural support network. By helping each other, they make it easy for us to be consistently happy customers whether we buy their food locally or are out of town. Likewise, it is easier for employees and owners.

REFLECT:

Was there one insight from Confucius that you can apply to your life?

_____

_____

*"You have to be able to talk about your mental health in order to be mentally fit and therefore be happy and healthy for the rest of your life. You have to talk about your mental fitness." – **Prince Harry** (The younger son of the British royal family Prince and Princess of Wales; launched,*

along with Prince William and his wife Catherine, the Heads Together campaign to end stigma around mental health.)

10.3 Emotional Fire or Physical Fire—Who You Gonna Call?

A few years ago, I was asked to speak at an event called the Great American Teach-In. They opened the dividing doors so that I could entertain about 100 kids at once. Yeah, no pressure. I was to present to young kids who were about 10 to 12 years old. I think they said something about the average attention span being a minute, and I had to keep their attention for 90 minutes. Again, no pressure. Anyway, they asked me to present on careers in process improvement and systems design.

Despite my amazing personality, I brought props so they could build and improve upon paper airplanes to make them fly faster and better. The teachers seemed slightly hesitant about me inspiring the kids to build projectiles with an easily accessible supply of paper, but they kept inviting me back. It was inspirational to observe the students go from being insecure and holding back to exuding confidence and asking if they could test a new and better design. It was also fantastic to hear what they learned.

One boy said he made a mistake, but then the mistake made the airplane fly all the way across the three classrooms with ease. The teacher actually called an engineering professor over to check out this accomplishment. We set up a runway for the kids to test their latest creation. They rushed to get in line and show off their soaring airplanes. In some cases, they somehow made boomerang planes that flipped and came right back to them. The room was filled with high energy, laughter, and excitement.

As we were having fun building and tweaking designs to go faster and further, one young girl asked me, "So, tell me about your passion." To my surprise, the kids shut down the airport for a moment to hear my response.

I explained, "On a recent project, I designed a solution that generated over three million dollars." I tried to have my voice crescendo at the end to convey passion, but she didn't buy it and neither did I. So, she repeated her question, being a little more specific, with sincere determination in her voice, "Really, tell me what makes you passionate about process improvement."

I then said, "Okay, let me ask the class a question." I asked, "With a show of hands, how many of you have heard of the phone number 211?" Not one teacher or student knew. Out of 100 kids and four teachers in the room, only one person thought he might have heard of 211. I then asked a follow-up question: "How many of you know about 911?"

Before I even finished saying the last "one" in "911," hands were going up, with 100% of the class, kids and teachers, raising their hands. All were eager and confident to tell me how 911 was used in an emergency.

I responded, "My passion is that I want to use my process improvement skills to help kids and families. One example is I would love to use my skills to help ensure that everyone knows about 211 as well as 911. By knowing, they will have knowledge if they have a friend or family member in need or if they themselves need help."

A little boy asked, "So, when do you call 211?" Another asked, "What is the difference between 211 and 911?"

Being that it was a young audience, I wanted to be careful to not be too harsh with my wording. I said, "If a person or family is about to lose their home or if they do not have access to food or if—" I paused, wanting to be careful, so I said, "It is kind of like if you have a fire, but it is not a physical fire in the house—that is when you call 211 versus 911."

One little girl said, "So you call 211 for an emotional fire, but you call 911 for a physical fire."

The little hands of the bright minds started going up to ask questions. The first question was from a boy in the back of the class. He asked, "So if I have a friend who is always hungry and does not have hardly any food in his house, I can let his family know about this 211 number?"

I answered, "Yes," and also added that I had just been in a meeting where they introduced a fast-track program to help families with children. The hands kept going up. Next question: "If I know someone who is very sad and hurts themselves, can that person call 211 to get help?" At this point, the kids shut down the airport, suspending all paper airplane flights, and the room got very intense.

I said to Ms. McDonald, the primary teacher, "We kind of went on a tangent. I hope that is okay."

Ms. McDonald had tears in her eyes and said, "Clearly, this was a much-needed topic." I could sense that Ms. McDonald also had someone in mind who needed that 211 number.

SILO SECRET #135: The 211 crisis line is like the help desk for our community, just like many businesses have a help desk area for their customers and employees. Best practices in business are to centralize help desk requests versus having people go person-to-person trying to find answers on their own. The same best practices can be used to optimize efficiency and effectiveness in responding to communities.

SILO SECRET #136: In a recent hurricane warning, an urgent task force was put together to teach people to take 211 calls. We can share best practices with 211 to help such task forces be fully positioned to serve our community. For example, we can use the 5 Steps to Success (from Chapter 4) to develop volunteers to be ready to jump in and help in an emergency. This will also help foster collaboration between community service agencies by expanding their knowledge of one another's roles. Broadening their understanding of provider services will simplify and facilitate referrals.

SILO SECRET #137: Just like firefighters can teach people to minimize fires, the 5 protective factors can help reduce emotional fires by building (1) parental resilience, (2) social connections, (3) knowledge of parenting and child development, (4) concrete support in times of need and (5) social and emotional competence of children.

SILO SECRET #138: 211 is a great source to share proactive updates and training opportunities. One grandfather was suddenly on his own raising four grandkids. When he called 211, they connected him to a kinship program to help grandparents and people in his situation. In just 20 minutes, he learned how one child needed a quiet space to study, another studied better with music playing, and the other two children performed better when studying involved an activity. The grandpa said this new knowledge fostered harmony within his new family. Nationally, relatives or family friends are raising nearly 2.7 million children because their parents can no longer care for them. (Foundation, 2019)

SILO SECRET #139: Another great tool covered as part of restorative justice training is "family circles." Families can apply the "Cool WHIP" approach. "Cool" reminds us to stay cool, calm, and collected. The "WHIP" stands for "**W**-hat **H**-appened? Next, each person answers, "What was the **I**-mpact on you?" Last, you discuss tips to **P**-revent it from happening again. For example, a son was upset that his parents yelled when he got home late (**W**hat **H**appened). The father explained the **I**-mpact is that they worry as they love him and want him to be safe. They talked about ways to better communicate to **P**-revent the worry by sharing that he was okay. This technique helps focus on the objective versus getting caught up in emotions.

REFLECT:

Do you and your loved ones have an easily accessible emergency contact list (i.e., on the refrigerator)?

_____

_____

"Learning to see waste and systematically eliminate it has allowed lean companies such as Toyota to dominate entire industries. Lean thinking defines value as 'providing benefit to the customer'; anything else is waste." – **Eric Ries** (Entrepreneur, wrote the *Lean Startup* book on the lean startup movement.)

10.4 Standardize Menu—Maximize Greatness

What if emotional fire help was as easy as ordering Chinese Food?

After the 211 conversation, I went off to watch a friend's two kids for a couple hours because she had an emergency and her backup babysitter was ill. It was dinnertime, so I figured I'd order a pizza or Chinese food. Her five-year-old ran to the drawer, pulled out the one-page Chinese food menu, and handed it to me, saying, "I like sweet and sour chicken." Later, we were on a business trip, and my friend brought her five-year-old son along. We only had an hour to grab food, so we discussed ordering. Without a menu, all of us were able to jot down our Chinese food order. It was so easy, even being in another city.

While it is simple for a child to request Chinese food, most children and even adults have difficulty figuring out how to request help when they feel down, depressed, or need mental health services. "Either the resources aren't available or, sometimes, people can't figure out how to navigate the system to find the resources." (Santich & Kunerth, 2019) The key reason they give is the inability to navigate the system. Even therapists I know talk about working on their days off to try to come up with a flow, or maybe a document for people to use. Seriously, if I have a headache, navigating the safety lid on the aspirin bottle is enough for me. Yet, when people are suffering from depression or anxiety or another condition, we are asking them to follow these long IF-THEN instructions that closely resemble the pseudocode I used when I did software engineering. It doesn't make sense that a child contemplating self-harm has only a 30% chance of knowing how to ask for help, but he knows how to order Chinese food.

So, what if we followed the spirit of Einstein and took a working solution and applied it to mental health? You can pick another model, but for simplicity, I'll use the Chinese food model. What if we applied some of the basics from the top 10 tips from Confucius? To start, create a simple, shared mental wellness menu to make it easy for patients as well as staff. Below is more of a humorous menu, which illustrates how we can come up with a basic menu to share among multiple locations. This saves on money, saves on educating between sites, and enables sites to back each other up in emergencies such as natural disasters, shootings, and issues that affect large groups where they need therapists from other areas to come in and help. It would help to be able to say, "We could use 20 therapists to come in and help with #1 (where people just need a mental fitness checkup), but we need five senior therapists to come in and help individuals at the #4 level (where they need urgent help now)."

Sample Menu to Illustrate How You Could Apply Chinese Food Menu to a Wellness Menu

---

Wellness Menu

#1. Appetizer (Try some relaxation tips—check out our mental fitness checklist)

#2. Sweet & Sour (Feel happy with some sad—a brief therapist chat may help)

#3. General Tso's (Feel anxiety—some resiliency or stress-management tips may help)

#4. Kung Pao (Severe trauma—need urgent help now)

#5. Family Special (A family session would be helpful)

* Combo Special: Could use a weekly #3 and a monthly #5.

Just as restaurants have free water or bread, wellness centers could offer free stress toys or pocket-size leaflets to share easy ways to relieve stress. Inviting pamphlets could be left on the Buddy Benches, Friendship Benches, and Yellow Benches popping up by the thousands for people to help each other connect and grow their mental fitness. They could have a quick menu to see the offerings along with a list of local places available for more advanced help if needed.

In my college courses on efficiency and defect management best practices, one of the first steps taught was to assess how important it is to have high standards for efficiency and quality. The main factor is typically the impact on humans. As an example, we had to evaluate how important it was to have bottles of shampoo have exactly the same amount with little variation. While customers could look at bottles and possibly choose not buy the shampoo due to the variance, it was not life-threatening, so it was not considered critical to invest in the highest standard. An airplane, however, involves the safety of humans, so even when the number of defects was one out of 1,000,000, students still believed it was worthy of continual investment to optimize that quality ratio due to the potential impact on lives.

Lack of access to a strong mental wellness system is causing lives to be lost every day, every 40 seconds to be exact, so this is an area where experts in best practices would say Lean Six Sigma should be used to the highest level, yet this silo often does not have knowledge or access to those tools. I typically avoid mentioning that I can use my Six Sigma Black Belt skills to help because many nonprofit agencies are not aware of best practices in this area, so they wonder why I am mentioning my black belt in karate. This is a big area where business best practices can help nonprofit organizations. The great thing is you can take an easily viewed model like Chinese food and ask, "How can we make accessing our nonprofit service as easy as accessing Chinese food?"

SILO SECRET #140: Many solutions are interchangeable. It is kind of like that Mad Libs game you may have played as a kid where you fill in blanks of a story with nouns, adjectives, or verbs. Even when you fill in outlandish words to make the story funny, it still works. Solution models work in the same way. For example, if you take the model for delivering pencils, you can likely swap out the word pencil for eraser. Now if you want to deliver glasses, you would think, "Well, it is similar but breakable," so you may want to check if there is another successful model in place to deliver small, fragile products. Often, you can simply mirror a solution in place and make minor adjustments to apply it to your area.

SILO SECRET #141: The nonprofit world has various statewide program implementation goals, but they are often using a complex and time-consuming model. Many successful global and national businesses have success by simplifying first and then replicating versus trying to train using a complex model. These statewide programs are an opportunity to look at business solutions that have been rolled out statewide, nationally, or even worldwide to see what tips and tools to apply to more easily expand.

SILO SECRET #142: Consistency is measured as part of the Six Sigma best practice, measuring the ability to deliver the same way regardless of who is delivering a service. Think of a meal that you may like from a franchise restaurant. You want to have consistency regardless of the purchase location or the person preparing the meal. The restaurant likely takes steps to ensure consistent details from the portion to the preparation.

SILO SECRET #143: Hand-off points or transition points, where an activity transfers from one person to another, require extra care. Phrases like "fell through the cracks" and "dropped the ball" are sometimes used to describe the impact of inconsistency, where something or someone is damaged because there was not a smooth transition from one person to another to ensure success.

SILO SECRET #144: High inconsistency is a sign of enormous opportunity. To illustrate, the Child Welfare site mentions a wide range of case management turnover from low turnover to 90% turnover. This is an incredible opportunity to identify and share successful practices across locations. Ohio alone estimates that inconsistency (case management turnover) is costing $24 million a year. Pursuing that multimillion dollar savings will naturally help us improve our success rate for unifying children with families by up to 59%. That is my kind of two-for-one special. (Stewart, 2016)

REFLECT:

Imagine you are a child and you have a friend who has hardly any food. Would you feel better if you had a three-digit number to share to help your friend's family access a local program?

_____

_____

"Coming together is a beginning; keeping together is progress; working together is success." – **Edward Everett Hale** (Clergyman best remembered for his short story "The Man Without a Country.")

10.5 Statewide Solutions—It's All In the Delivery

Have you ever had a moment when you knew you bit off way more than you could chew? My moment was my freshman year of high school. It started out so innocently. We had a fundraiser where students could earn money toward a trip to Washington, D.C., by selling light bulbs and candles. Soon, neighbors and even strangers were singing "You light up my life" when I was near. The vendor actually offered me a job selling light bulbs, saying I could make six figures.

Before I had time to contemplate this career move, my teacher called me in a total panic, "Come to the school immediately. These light bulbs you sold are filling up the auditorium stage and we need it cleared for a big school event." As I walked in, my jaw dropped. There were rows of boxes piled at least five feet high. While sales seemed to come naturally, I had not thought through the daunting delivery requirement. Caught up in the joy of "lighting up" lives, I sold way more than required to pay for my trip.

Even though it was a Saturday, the principal came in and shared some creative words that most do not get to hear out of a principal. He was clearly not happy with my prominently displayed accomplishment. While I knew that what I was about to ask was against the rules, I went ahead and asked if I could split up the load and share the wealth, the fundraising dollars, with some friends. Eager to get those boxes out of the school fast, he blurted out, "Do what you gotta do."

This was officially my first experience with mass distribution. To start, I called my friend Sue who had broken her leg and was really bummed about not being able to go on the trip. I offered her a chance to earn money by helping from her home as our official distribution coordinator. She maintained the master list and kept track of deliveries. She ended up tracking what time to try again when customers were not home and details like what day people said to come back after their paychecks got deposited. She definitely earned her trip.

For the heavy lifting, I recruited a couple football players, Derek and Rico, who had low light bulb sales but a lot of muscle. Apparently light bulb sales was not their thing, but they were thrilled to lift and load boxes into cars and trucks. In fact, both went on to work for the United Postal Service so apparently they discovered their calling. Sue gave them the list and they went into high gear, loading up vehicles to prepare for deliveries.

For the actual door-to-door deliveries, I enlisted my competitors based on the neighborhood area that they lived in. I knew where they lived because they'd complained earlier that I infringed on their turf. They were quite happy because with this plan, they got the money without having to sell. They just had to help with deliveries. Sue organized everything into Delivery Area A, B, and C and even mapped out the best routes. For safety, another thing I did not have in my original plan, we had groups of two go to each neighborhood. Within a week, all deliveries were complete and all had enough money for their trip.

Let's get Real – Bringing Light Across the State

While my trial-by-fire high school distribution plan could be labeled as small potatoes, I used that same basic model for years in the real business world. Just substitute the word "light bulb" with a process or product and the plan was fundamentally the same. When the implementation plan seemed too grand, I imagined that auditorium where we simply needed to define the logistics. In the real world, we found a person to fill Sue's role as our project coordinator and hired Two Men and a Truck to deliver to hub sites. When we needed a little extra muscle for local deliveries, College H.U.N.K.S. Hauling Junk & Moving® provided extra support to get products into each neighborhood.

When you have a great product—whether it is a spinning toy that the world can't seem to get enough of or a service that could benefit people everywhere—there are delivery models to enable your solution to be shared enterprise-wide, county-wide, statewide, nationwide, country-wide or even worldwide. While community service organizations, in theory, have access to the same methods, the tools are sometimes viewed more as a business-type tool, but when you have incredible light to bring to neighborhoods, why not leverage available techniques?

Since the job positions that lead statewide implementations typically earn salaries and benefits in the $80,000 per year and above range, funding is often perceived as an obstacle. Ironically, reinventing the wheel often costs more than designing and implementing a simplified, repeatable solution. This may be an area where it may help for nonprofits to knock on the silo door of businesses to check out how they rolled out a training program or service to large groups of customers or employees across many cities or even across the world. There are organizations that have people who would love to share their expertise to help strengthen their community.

Opportunities around every corner

Recently, St. Petersburg College held a collaborative lab session where both business and nonprofit organizations voted real-time on career skills that are in demand. Leaders agreed that a key need was to develop employees with skills to coordinate statewide program implementations. In discussing the topic, we agreed that we could add so much more value in communities if we had people to coordinate the sharing of great programs throughout the state. If you search top issues, you'll likely find that there is at least one location that is somehow doing better than the others. By working together, we can share those best practices to get a handle on the growing demand on community resources.

There are wonderful programs that have been around for 10 years or more that many people do not know about even though the knowledge benefits them or someone they know. Zack Gibson travels around Florida doing his best to spread the word on the protective factors to strengthen families. Jo Dee and others from the Florida Children's Mental Health System of Care drive all over to engage Florida organizations to implement evidence-based ROSC (Recovery-oriented System of Care). Retired Judge Cohen travels from Ohio to Florida to share how concurrent planning can be implemented in courtrooms to get better results for families. The list goes on of people working hard to get the word out. This passion to share great programs is all around us.

As you see the incredible benefits of using available tools to magnify the positive impact of community programs, you too will want to bring the business and nonprofit silo skills together. This is perhaps the greatest "low-hanging fruit" (within our reach) benefit of interdependence. Sometimes people-oriented community service organizations express a preference for more organic versus structural growth. They can still apply a personal, organic growth approach, but they will have tools to help broaden their incredibly valuable impact.

Dr. Mimi Graham, Director of Florida State University Center for Prevention and Early Intervention Policy, invited a wide range of leaders, setting the stage for interdependence. Dr. Andrea Blanch, who has been working on a national level, commented on the intense energy in the room, saying this truly represents "endless possibilities." With the guidance of Dr. Felitti, this think tank, entitled "Expanding Trauma-Informed Systems in Florida," is striving to initiate a movement of statewide collective impact by sharing innovative trauma methods and strategizing on how to leverage trauma science across Florida systems. Watching the news from this trauma-informed lens, I cannot help but think, "This is a job for the business silo." There are all sorts of statistics on the multibillion dollar impact to our global economy. Aside from the human impact, "The ACE Study revealed that the economic costs of untreated trauma-related alcohol and drug abuse alone were estimated at $161 billion in 2000." (Rosenberg, 2019) By partnering to help community services, we'll be helping our businesses, communities, and our economy.

SILO SECRET #145: To implement community service solutions statewide or across a large area, one technique is to leverage existing best practices and models to implement enterprise-wide, nationwide, or even worldwide solutions. Solutions are often interchangeable with just minor adjustments.

SILO SECRET #146: When it comes to the community, businesses realize it is their community too. When I presented a college paper on how we could use Lean Six Sigma to help foster children and case managers, nearly the entire class offered to take vacation days to help out on the project. Nonprofits are used to giving versus receiving help, but businesses could offer their expertise to help by providing support from certified project managers, certified help desk support staff, and other implementation experts.

SILO SECRET #147: In my county, multiple nonprofit organizations set out to reduce travel time and the expense of driving to meetings 30 to 90 minutes away. In contrast, businesses often get so used to virtual meetings that sometimes we have to remind people to go in-person to meetings in their own building. The key is to figure out which is best to achieve the goal. There may be great opportunities for the nonprofit world to utilize virtual meetings and technology to share tips and reduce costs. Likewise, businesses can sometimes improve results by forming stronger relationships gained by more in-person meetings.

SILO SECRET #148: One organization that is working to tap business silo tools to spread the word is Emergency Services. In a recent emergency management planning meeting in our area, the team announced that it is getting the message out for people to build a support network. They are working to have an infrastructure ready to provide real-time data to help during disasters like hurricanes or storms. This includes creating a database so that, during a disaster, they know who has beds, charging stations, cooking facilities, electricity, etc. This is excellent because they are working proactively to have the database ready and updated with roles prior to a disaster, along with a plan to adjust roles as needed.

REFLECT:

If someone had a proven solution to an issue impacting you, would you want them to share it?

_____

_____

Chapter 10 Summary: *Adding more perspectives enables us to be closer to interdependence, creating more holistic solutions. Many times, we can take a solution from another area and apply it to our world. We can also share knowledge between silos. What if requesting mental health services was as easy as ordering Chinese food? What if businesses started increasing profits and productivity using tips from nonprofits? What if we realized we could reduce our budget deficit by being more trauma-informed?*

11. ENDLESS POSSIBILITIES—FROM HERE TO THE UN

*"Our world faces difficult challenges, but no more so than in the past. Working together in a constructive spirit, we can assure our children the future they deserve." – **Paul Kagame** (President of Rwanda; previously commanded the rebel force that ended the 1994 Rwandan genocide.)*

*"Everything you can imagine is real." – **Pablo Picasso** (Considered to be one of the greatest and most influential artists of the 20th century and the cocreator of Cubism, along with Georges Braque.)*

11.1 Going Global

As an information technology leader, my philosophy was always to have goals that people got excited about. My boss used to say, "Why do you choose to climb mountains when you would get the same paycheck if you climbed hills?" For my team, climbing mountains was exhilarating, and when you climb with a team, you are sort of family for life. My guideline was to have goals that were feasible but big enough that you looked forward to sharing the goal over Thanksgiving dinner.

Our small but mighty team of 10 climbers had just celebrated a major accomplishment, where all the executives came to celebrate how we'd achieved record-breaking heights. We had started with a backlog of requests and improved processes to the point that we were able to guarantee 100% of requests within 24 hours of receipt for over 25,000 requests per month. The president, customers, and managers all came to celebrate with us. We did a sports-themed party and presentation to demonstrate, in a fun way, all the work that had gone on behind the scenes to transform us into an A+ rated, top site to tour. We even showed how our customers jumped in to help. Excitement was at an all-time high, but now what? Where did we go from here? What mountain did we climb next?

Well, periodically, the company had organizational restructures. Word in the hallways was that my team was taking on an added responsibility. We were kind of excited about it, and then leadership decided that our team was doing so well, and information technology was so important to the company, that they wanted us to stay focused on ensuring record speed turnaround on requests. We were mountain climbers, so I had to think of a big mountain for us to climb that still fell within our area of responsibility. I remembered the president saying at a recent meeting, "We plan to go global in the future." That sounded interesting. Yes, that was it! That would be our goal. I made the announcement, "We are going global."

One employee said, "What exactly does that mean?"

I smiled and answered, "I'm not sure, but we're going to have a blast going there."

Word traveled fast. Energy was in the air and the team was motivated—for what, exactly, we didn't know, but we were ready to get started. No department had gone global before, so we would be the first to climb this mountain. Thinking I could learn from other companies in the area, I met with large organizations, but it turned out this was truly uncharted territory. While I really thought my boss would be thrilled as he was from Europe, he exclaimed, "You can't go global! You don't have the infrastructure; you don't have the telephone system; you don't have people who speak multiple languages; and you don't have funding." He knew that would just motivate me more and smiled.

Things just started happening. One of the help desk analysts said, "Can I be the French liaison?" "Sure," I said, and she was off studying French. Another employee said, "Can I be the liaison for Latin America?" "Sounds good," I replied, and he went off to study Spanish and Portuguese. That day, a funny thing happened. We started getting unusual phone support requests from people with sophisticated French accents along with callers who frequently used the expression "Aye." I called the manager of the help desk in Canada and said, "Is it possible your calls are routing to us?"

He said, "Oh, so sorry, aye. We had a meeting, and I must have accidentally routed the calls to the U.S."

"That is awesome," I replied. "That means we can route between countries and I just need to figure out how."

Next, Charlie, who was in charge of the telephone system, came to me with a sample of the code used to program the telephone system routing. He said, "Lisa, you used to be a software developer, do you understand this?" Between his knowledge of the telephone codes and my knowledge of programming, we were able to set up the system to take calls from other countries. Since no one, even the vendor, had experience in doing this, we came in during off hours (2:00 a.m. – 4:00 a.m.) to test it out, emailing coworkers in other countries to give us a call, and it worked!

A couple days later, Jim, a manager from the computer network department, came to me and said, "I heard you are going global—did you know the network managers from other countries are here this week for network training?" My eyes lit up. He said, "Do you want to meet with them?" I said, "Can I have just five minutes with them?" and he said, "Sure, I'll add you to the schedule."

The next day, Jim and I headed into the conference room with about 15 network managers from various countries. Knowing English was their second language, I found myself speaking with my hands, trying to supplement my English. I told them, "We are looking to create a global knowledge database to store the best solutions." I then gestured over to the gentleman from Sweden, saying, "So if Sweden has the best solution for a server problem, we would put that solution into the database." Then I gestured over to the two gentlemen from Latin America, saying, "If Latin America has the best solution for a printer problem, we would put that solution into the database."

Interlocking my fingers as if that was the international sign language for integrated shared solutions, I said, "We would then share this database, so we would all have a central place to go to for global best practices and solutions."

Then, something concerning happened. About five men got out of their seats and spoke in another language to each other. I was worried my interlocking finger gesture could have meant something bad— you know how that president did the peace sign and accidentally flipped off a country. *Oh boy, what do they think I said?*

Then one gentleman from Portugal said, "We think we understand what you are saying. Is it okay if I translate to ensure we interpreted correctly?"

I smiled and said, "Yes, that would be wonderful."

He carefully stated, "If we hear you correctly, you are saying that you value input from all countries to define best solutions to share with all countries." I nodded yes. He then said, "We will then agree and update global best practices into a common database for all countries to share." I nodded yes again. He said, "We're used to being instructed on what to do; we like this idea where we are all invited to exchange ideas to make things better, creating global best practices." He enthusiastically smiled and said, "We'll go global with you!"

They asked if they could meet the liaisons that I'd mentioned and, of course, my team was thrilled. Immediately, the network managers started sharing access to their individual spreadsheets and solution databases so that we could start working together to build a common knowledge center to identify and store the best solutions. I'd always heard that if you try to learn another country's language, the people of that country will appreciate it. It was especially tricky with technology words that meant something else. For example, we had to be careful that automatic translators did not convert the technical word "server" (data storage) to mean "server" (waiter/waitress or maid). However, I have to admit that made solutions a little more entertaining.

To help others follow our exciting path, the Help Desk Institute asked me to present "How to Build a World-Class Global Support Desk" at its HDI conference. While it looked fancy on paper, it was really about bringing people together. Though we were in different locations all around the world, we simply connected, realizing that we were, after all, on the same team.

SILO SECRET #149: Having an inviting goal with a purpose tends to generate enthusiastic energy that naturally grows as people share their excitement and invite others to participate. People volunteered and actually had fun doing tasks like coming in at 4 a.m. to test the launch of a new idea. They loved knowing that their input and actions were truly valued and making a difference.

SILO SECRET #150: World-class support is often surprisingly less expensive than common support practices. Sharing solutions enabled people to solve problems faster and set up customer access faster. This had the added benefit of enabling customers to order products sooner which increased revenue.

SILO SECRET #151: Each time we evolved to a more goal-focused view versus a problem-focused view, we were viewed more as an investment versus an expense, enabling us to further increase ROI (return on investment) and benefits.

SILO SECRET #152: Working together enabled us to relieve each other. Rather than have people be on-call or have to work late hours, we applied the *follow the sun* model. Support schedules were designed to consider time of day. If a call came in at 3 am, a support person in a time zone where it was currently standard business day hours would take the call and only escalate if needed to the sleeping technician.

REFLECT:

If a small team of 10 can share solutions and best practices globally for a company, could a small team share best practices for one of the sustainable goals on the United Nations site?

---

*"Issues transcend national boundaries and cannot be resolved by any one country. The world today is more interconnected than ever before. The SDG [Sustainable Development Goals] can only be realized with a strong commitment to global partnership and cooperation." – **United Nations***
(© 2019 United Nations. Reprinted with the permission of the United Nations.)

11.2 United Nations Dashboard—Sustainable Goals for All

Below are the United Nations' top 17 sustainable development goals. With more tools than ever to communicate across the world, there is so much opportunity for us to use our tools and technology to unite on addressing our shared sustainability goals. This is an interesting opportunity to virtually connect our silos. We all work in our own areas, our little piece of the world (silos.) We watch the news and think things are worse outside our walls, but in some cases, there are great tools and solutions in the silo next door.

The great thing about interdependence is each of us get to choose the topic that matches our passion. Looking at the chart below, some people will choose #15 (Life On Land) and pick up a few pieces of paper or trash to clean up a local park. Others may choose #8 (Decent Work and

Economic Growth) and help people learn about basic finances so they have a little saved for a rainy day. Still others may love the idea of creating an at-a-glance dashboard for #17 (Partnerships for the Goals), to help all 16 areas share ideas and implement best practices across the world, enabling us to achieve these goals together.

When I view the dashboard below on the United Nations screen, it reminds me of the global dashboards we used to share the real-time status of worldwide goals in the business world. Currently, the issues affecting our entire world are articulated very clearly. What if we added a link to each of the buttons below to share solutions? Perhaps even more exciting, we could watch real-time to visibly see how our actions are making a difference. (United Nations, 2019)

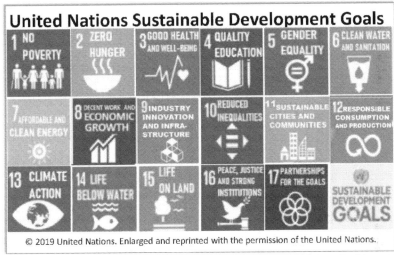

© 2019 United Nations. Enlarged and reprinted with the permission of the United Nations.

Figure 11.2 The United Nations has posted our top 17 world sustainable goals.

SILO SECRET #153: The above United Nations dashboard is very similar to online displays that we used to share global goals for Fortune 100 organizations. The UN has already agreed on the top 17 goals. We can use technology for people to view the top best practices in the different areas just like we did at Tech Data when we agreed to "Go Global!"

We simply updated the top two or three best ideas for solving a given problem and shared those ideas across the world. When someone came up with an even better way with better results, we tested it out. If it got better results, that became a higher standard to share. Before we even knew there was a "world-class" rating, we exceeded best practices and leaped to world-class practices. We can do the same for our United Nations goals. United we stand (period).

REFLECT:

Looking at the 17 United Nation sustainable goals, is there a goal that you would like to be a part of?

_____

_____

*"Real, sustainable community change requires the initiative and engagement of community members." – **Helene D. Gayle** (President/CEO of the Chicago Community Trust, a leading community foundation.)*

11.3 S.S. Interdependence Is About to Depart

Peter, Miguel, and Elisha were honored to be selected as UN Youth Delegates. Participating in United Nation intergovernmental meetings inspired them to envision the incredible possibilities. These brilliant, enthusiastic, and computer savvy teens truly want to make a major difference in the world, so why not empower them to make a difference? Let's invite these talented youth from various countries to join or perhaps organize the S.S. Interdependence team.

Clearly the UN already has a great webmaster to update its website. The UN Youth Delegates could come up with ways to update the website to empower citizens to more easily contribute to our shared world goals, making it fun as all are invited to climb aboard. Local hub sites could post the EPA Air Now numbers to show how we are improving air quality. Likewise, we could post Fish and Wildlife water samples to show how we are improving water quality. We already collect much of this data across the world. The difference is we would now be able to see an at-a-glance dashboard to view how we are doing on goals and assess the positive impact of our efforts and actions we can take to further excel with our sustainable goals. Together, we can create a culture of learning and continual improvement to ensure lasting solutions for our shared planet.

What if – in the spirit of our World Olympics

Isn't it odd how a low point can propel us upward? For me, it oddly happened right after my team earned an A+ rating in support services. After customers exclaimed, "We love your team," I could not help but think it was an ideal time to ask for funding, but my boss stated, "No matter how great your team is, your department will always be viewed as an expense versus a department that adds value," explaining that the reason was that we fixed problems versus achieving goals.

Inspired to flip our thinking, we transformed our mindset with just one word. Rather than help with "problems," our new mission was to help with "*goals*." To start, we volunteered to handle goal reporting for all the departments, giving us a clear picture of the top goals worldwide. Believe it or not, people are quite willing to give you their paperwork. Similar to the Olympics, we posted an electronic scoreboard to display "wins" (goal accomplishments) for all the countries.

With this approach, we naturally came up with Olympic themes to celebrate accomplishments because it felt like the Olympics as departments cheered for one another. Since our team was involved in all testing and implementation, we made sure to recognize those teams who made the wins possible. I suppose this part was more like the Emmy Awards where we recognized the script writer who came up with the project idea along with the coaches who provided their expertise and the crew who came in at 4 a.m. to ensure the set was just perfect. Departments who had never seen their name up on the big screen were excited to be a part of the big Olympic wins. Below is an illustration of how seven departments helped with three continual improvement projects, together making a $2 million win possible.

Project Name	Department	Idea by:	Contributions by:	Financial benefit
Rapid Client Setup	Sales	Support	Account Mgt	$1,200,000
Warehouse Savings	Distribution	Support	Desktop Support	$500,000
Volume Purchasing	Purchasing	Support	Systems Support	$300,000
				$2,000,000

Writing this book has been inspirational as I learn more about great things happening across the world.

Imagine if we had a dashboard to make it easy to share solutions between countries.

Peter, Miguel, and Elisha and the newly formed S.S. Interdependence Team could help us have fun learning and achieving sustainable goals together. To start, they could share quick links from countries who have had great success. Below is an example of how we could start with fun two-minute webinars.

Sustainable Goal Projects:	2 minute Webinar to learn more:	Country Sponsor:
Bioenergy	Bioenergy - dream come true?	Finland
Geothermal	HOT stuff - check it out	Iceland
Hydropower	Water view - energy for you	Latin America
Micro-generation	Europe's macro micro leader	Portugal
Renewable Partnerships	You had me at Hydro	United States
Solar Power	The Future is so Bright	Croatia
Wind - Opportunities	Kenya use Windpower - you ken	Africa
Wind - Job Growth	A wind win - 31,000 jobs in wind	Denmark
Wind - Efficiency	Soarin' with Wind - 25% of energy from wind	Romania
Wind - Transformation	The Big Shift - 53% renewable energy	Sweden

In our case, we actually did a scoreboard, but our score was last year versus this year. People could easily see the growth as countries went from three to 20 on the scoreboard. While we could tweak this model for the UN goals, below is an example of how we could use a point system to display on a website dashboard or scoreboard, rewarding countries for creating, implementing, and sharing world solutions.

- Create idea: Earn one green point for coming up with best practices to help with a country goal.

- Implement idea: Earn five green points for implementing a best practices in your country.

- Mentor idea: Earn three green points for helping another country implement a best practice.

Countries could easily see if there was a country that was strong in an area that they sought to improve, such as renewable energy. Both countries would earn points for contributing toward improving Earth. Having all the data in one place, it was so easy to see and unite on the big picture goals. Would it be possible to do this for our world goals? An easy example is plastic. One small country has a solution where they virtually eliminated plastic utensils. What if we give them points for sharing their solution and then give those countries that hop on board points for implementing the solution? All countries would earn points for our world team.

What if – in the spirit of Einstein thinking

What if we had a knowledge center of best practices for our world to share? We could easily start small and then expand. This is an opportunity to use technology to share solutions. At Tech Data, we had the same number of customers as the number of people in my city. We had one person who set up links for the different sites to update and automatically display on a shared master website. We could create hub locations and field locations to make it easy for everyone to participate. Many colleges and schools are already onboard with improving and collecting data on sustainability goals so it is mainly expanding to coordinate our efforts using steps below.

1. Have a central website to serve as a dashboard (similar to the UN site with links to top goals).

2. Get a few liaisons from a few different countries who are excited about planet Earth.

3. Let liaisons pick areas that are easy to measure, monitor, and improve.

   a. Air we breathe (already have growing number of apps to measure air quality)

   b. Water we drink (already have site with water samples; i.e. Florida Fish and Wildlife)

   c. Land used to grow our food (do existing E. coli test before versus after we eat food)

4. Have a change review board where representatives from various silos review suggested actions.

   a. Environmental representative could validate solutions from a sustainability view

   b. Finance and economy experts could ensure solutions are financially sound

   c. Nonprofit representative could ensure the various people needs are considered

5. Once above suggestions are agreed upon, update website of how global citizens can help.

SILO SECRET #154: Organizations with subject matter experts in best practices already have a global presence. Below is a sample of organizations with globally accepted best practices. The experts below, along with related organizations, would be great advisors or additions to our S.S. Interdependence team.

- Project Management Institute (PMI): Ensure project best practices and coordinate meetings.

- Business analysts: Help define problem and document proposed solutions.

- Problem management: Analyze trends, identify root causes, and address failure exposure points.

- Change management: Review proposed changes to ensure all views, back out plan, etc.

- Lean: Look at efficiency and add input to make it easier and ensure smooth workflow.

- Six Sigma: Measure quality improvement and consistency and minimize defects.

- Risk Management: Help keep us safe along the way.

- Knowledge Management: Offer expertise on best ways to easily update and access information.

SILO SECRET #155: At-a-glance metrics make it easy to monitor goals. Ideally, the dashboard confirms all is on target with positive results, but it also serves as a visible alert if action is required. For those who prefer the walk-up progress updates, there could be central area bulletin boards for people to walk up and check on updates. For example, I'm on the Fish and Wildlife distribution list for a team of people throughout Florida who help monitor water for red tide. They have an awesome online display for marine enthusiasts to see water quality. If red tide is detected, they reroute manatees to save them. Members of the UN Sustainable Water team could ensure results and trends are posted at walk-up locations as well, especially if action is needed.

SILO SECRET #156: Lean uses a one-page form called the A3 format. It is an easy-to-view report that shows a problem, impact, proposed solution, and some other points to tell a story on one page. This model could be used to easily share proposed solutions to get faster buy-in on moving forward on a solution or at least moving forward on next steps. It could easily be reviewed and shared for approval.

SILO SECRET #157: There are numerous best practice strengths that apply to all areas but are only known within a select area or city. A key mission of the S.S. Interdependence crew will be taking existing, proven best practices with evidence-based results and sharing those solutions in a way that all countries can easily access and be a part of global solutions.

REFLECT:

Do you think that, together, we can improve one of the United Nations' goals?

_____

_____

Chapter 11 Summary: The United Nations already provides icons for the top 17 problems affecting our world. In addition, we have global organizations with members across the world trained in the best problem-solving and implementation tools. Imagine the possibilities if we combine our talents to help coordinate and make it easier for people to contribute small but significant pieces. With a tap of a phone screen, each of us could see how we are making a difference as we contribute our passion to soar in our shared world goals.

12. THE POWER OF ONE

"If you want to make a permanent change, stop focusing on the size of your problems and start focusing on the size of you!" – ***T. Harv Eker*** (Businessman and motivational speaker, known for his theories on wealth and motivation, #1 New York Times bestselling author of Secrets of the Millionaire Mind™.)

"Everyone enjoys being acknowledged and appreciated. Sometimes even the simplest act of gratitude can change someone's entire day. Take the time to recognize and value the people around you and appreciate those who make a difference in your lives." – ***Roy T. Bennett*** (Thought leader and author of *The Light in the Heart.*)

12.1 The Stranger Who Saved My Life

Things happened so fast; I went to travel school and got offered a job to work for an airline in Tampa at the exact job I wanted, close to the exact college I wanted to go to. My best friend said, "Come stay with me at the dorm for a couple weeks while you find a place." When I arrived, Penelope, with her vibrant megaphone-like voice, yelled, "Hey, Lisa!" from the second-floor window. Yes, she took out the screen to stick her head out the window to get my attention. Afterward, even the people who lived on the downtown streets knew my name and said hi to me each day.

Since my new job at the airline had training in the evening, I often returned late to the dorm. Being just 18 years old—naïve and excited—I felt safe because there always seemed to be a lot of people and activity on the streets when I returned each evening. I started noticing that the same people walked the same exact routes each night. I even wrote to my mom about how nice the homeless people were and how I thought it was interesting that they seemed to have schedules. Seriously, if there was one perk to being homeless, I thought it would be sleeping in and not having a schedule—so I found it intriguing that they walked the same route each night, down to predictable details.

In particular, I was fascinated by one homeless man. With my training, I had to carry three large binders plus heavy official airline guide books that were like those thick, heavy, old phone books so I was especially grateful to him as he opened the door for me each night. I would say, "Thank you very much," and he'd respond saying things like "You are quite welcome." When I asked how he was, he would answer, "Very well, thank you" or "Quite well, and you?" Despite his ragged exterior, I could tell he was very intelligent and kind. He seemed more like a butler in an exclusive hotel than a homeless person.

Perplexed that he seemed more like a PhD college professor than a homeless man living on the street, I curiously asked, "You are very well educated, aren't you?" He looked me in the eyes, smiled, and in a hearty, jolly, Santa-like tone, he replied, "Yes. I am very, VERY well educated." I felt like he must have been a captain of a ship, a chief officer, or some big position before landing in his current situation, sleeping in front of a door with his main purpose in life seeming to be opening the door for college students. As I looked back at him, I thought there must be a very sad story of how he'd gotten here. I was not ready to hear that story and not sure he was up to sharing, so we just paused for a moment and went on our way.

One night, I had to stay at work much later because we had to do a special training after the office closed that required full access to the computer systems. By the time I headed back to the dorm, the streets were totally deserted. Even though it was a short walk, I didn't feel good about walking alone. I considered going to a hotel, but I had a very bad experience when I was a kid when a gang tried to break into my family's hotel room. Plus, I'd seen way too many movies where the single lady walks alone through a parking garage and something bad happens. Plan B was sleeping in the car, but I pictured myself waking up to an angry police officer or worse yet—a mad stranger. As many times as I said I was going to stay up all night, I was always the first to fall asleep, so not sleeping was not really an option. No option really seemed good, and I had to be back to training in a few hours, so I decided the best of the bad options was to go to Penelope's dorm.

My crime watcher, "be-aware" mindset kicked in. One of the things I'd learned was to have your actions planned out so that if something does happen, you jump into action versus wasting valuable seconds trying to figure out what to do. Having a big pile of heavy books, my action plan was to immediately throw the books at the sign of any trouble. The only other option would be to run to my car, and I had seen way too many suspenseful horror films with the person jingling their keys and the predator right behind them. Throwing my books would pretty much be throwing away my perfect job, but that was my emergency plan. I figured it would distract them and slow them down as they would have to avoid tripping on the binders or slipping on the papers.

As I walked in my business suit with my pile of books in hand, my pump-shoe heels made a tap-dance type sound on the cement sidewalk with each step. It seemed like the sound echoed through each intensely quiet crevice of the downtown block, announcing my presence. As a precaution, I scanned the neighborhood just in case I needed to run. I looked across the street and closely examined alleys and inlets between the downtown buildings.

No cars, no people—I could almost hear my heart beating. Then I took a step forward and looked to the right. In between two buildings, I saw five men dressed in all dark clothing. As one of them uttered, "Get her," I saw five shiny silver objects flash as they flicked their knives open. At that moment, I threw my books to the right and ran as fast as I could. Most people run well in sneakers, but for whatever reason, I could book it in high heels.

I got to the first-floor dorm entrance, pulled open the door, and ran up the stairs. While I never looked back, I heard the door open and slam and then immediately open and slam again. I imagined at least one of the five men had gotten into the corridor, but I could not imagine why the door slammed hard two times close together. I kept running, got to the second-floor door, and went inside. I heard a rugged voice yell, "Leave her alone. Stay away from her!" The sounds of the door opening and shutting quickly and then quickly again made sense now. Whoever that man was, he must have stopped the gang of men from opening the bottom door—causing it to slam and then slam again. I stayed up most of the night wondering what had happened and who that man was, where he had come from, and whether he had literally taken on a gang of five men.

The next day, the homeless man seemed upset and said, "Why didn't you tell me you changed your schedule?" He acted like a protective father, upset at his daughter for staying out too late. I'd never had that experience because my father passed when I was very young, but at that moment, I suddenly felt like he was the caring, upset father—up all night, worried sick about his daughter. Confused as to why a homeless person would ask me such a question, I paused in silence. He then said, "We arranged our entire schedule to protect you—reserving a parking spot, having someone at various points. Why didn't you tell me you were going to get home so late?"

At that moment, he handed me the school and airline books I had thrown into the street. He must have stayed up for hours putting the papers back into the binders, in perfect order. When I went to work, I noticed that there would be one page that still had mud or a stain from a puddle and then the next page would be in perfect condition, showing that he'd taken the papers that had flown out and had put them back into the binders where each page belonged. You could even tell how he'd tried to clean off the dirt and mud stains as there were brush marks on the papers. It was then that I knew for sure that he was the mystery man who'd stopped the gang members from getting to me.

Later, I learned that the college had flyers sent out saying not to go out at night. My friend was fearless and super busy, so she ignored the flyers and didn't share the flyer until I mentioned the gang that chased after me. The flyer basically said that the campus police were escorting students, but then the escorts started getting beaten up, so the new instruction was not to go out at night.

The good news is this expedited my new apartment search. I moved into a new apartment that week. Weeks later, I came back to say hello to my friends and stopped by to talk with the wonderful homeless man who had saved my life. I asked someone if the homeless man by the door was around. The person responded, "It's safe now. They got rid of those homeless people." The irony is that, had it not been for that gang, I would have never known that the homeless people arranged their schedule to protect me. I hope that kind, well-educated gentleman realized how grateful I am to him. Many times in corporate life I have been advised to stop caring so much for the "little people." Those little people may just save your life someday.

SILO SECRET #158: *Seven habits of highly effective people*—but wait, there's one more. Stephen Covey's *The 8th Habit: From Effectiveness to Greatness* is an upgrade of *The 7 Habits of Highly Effective* People. The eighth habit is "Find your voice and inspire others to find theirs." (Covey, The 8th Habit: From Effectiveness to Greatness, 2006)

SILO SECRET #159: Be aware. Have actions in your mind worked out. You don't need a detailed project plan but have a basic plan. A.L.I.C.E., an acronym for Alert, Lockdown, Inform, Counter, and Evacuate, is a safety strategy emphasizing "alert" as the first key step. This is a new technique being taught in schools.

SILO SECRET #160: Be nice. I always thought it was kind of silly when I saw bumper stickers that said things like that, but the more I look at evidence-based success models, the more I see the foundation is basically being nice and considerate. For me, I think being nice may have saved my life.

REFLECT:

I was reluctant to tell the campus police that the homeless people might have had a good strategy to protect students. If you were in their position, would you value ideas from a homeless man?

_____

_____

"Failure is another stepping stone to greatness." – **Oprah Winfrey**

12.2 Growing Great Grown-Ups

A few years ago, I volunteered to be a mentor during my lunch breaks. When I went to the school, they said I had a choice between two students. There was a little girl who was passing school but really needed attention along with a little boy who lacked confidence. I asked, "What happens to the other student if I do not pick that student?" The school liaison explained that the child would basically not have a mentor because they were short on volunteers. Not wanting to see a kid be denied a mentor, I asked if I could do the two-for-one special. The liaison smiled and said, "We have not done that before, but we can split the time between the two kids."

With the little girl, it was easy to see why she needed a little attention. One time, she was naming off her brothers and sisters. She told me she had 10 siblings, but I thought I counted 11 so I asked, "Do you have 10 or 11 brothers and sisters?" She replied, "I really do not know. All I can tell you is there are way too many kids in my house." Her mom had a newborn, the eleventh or twelfth child, so little Diana was really craving attention now. We came up with ideas to help free up her mom's time so that her mom might have a little more time to spend with her. One idea was Diana reading to the baby. This had the added benefit, of course, of helping Diana improve her reading skills.

Diana was doing better and better, but Jay, the little boy that I was mentoring, was very sad. He had failed a grade and was about to fail again. He was great at sports and math, but as he would say, "I am not so good at reading." The principal told me that the best thing I could do for him was to help him build his confidence. She said, "He needs to believe the goal is possible." Everyone loved him. We would walk through the hallways to go to our spot in the library and every single person would enthusiastically say, "Hi, Jay." While he would reply, he almost never looked up.

He had blond hair and these long, straight eyelashes that almost looked like they were too heavy as he walked with his face looking down to the ground. One day, when he told me how he could not read, I said, "I know you will be a great reader."

For the first time, he looked up as if to study my response as he asked, "How are you so sure?"

I said, "Well, everyone knows you're great at math."

He stopped me and said, "But I'm not good at reading."

I replied with confidence, "Math is reading numbers, and reading numbers is way harder than reading letters; I know you will be good at reading because you are already great at reading numbers."

I came up with that on the fly, but Jay looked at me and said, "That actually makes sense." That was the first time I saw Jay's light blue eyes so clearly. You could almost see the glimmer of hope.

I knew he needed a lot of time and nurturing to catch up for all the years of reading that he'd missed. While Jay used to read with his mother, his reading had suddenly ceased with her passing. My limited time mentoring and tutoring him was simply not enough. He needed more. His father was able to help him with sports, but Jay explained that his father got upset when Jay asked him for academic help. I let Jay know that he was so lucky to have a dad to play ball with every day, as many kids would love to have that experience with their father.

Realizing that his dad might be upset because he did not have the skills to help Jay, I asked if Jay's brothers liked jokes, thinking that a joke book might be a fun thing they could read together. He said, "Yes, my brothers love jokes." We picked out a knock-knock joke book at the library and he and his brothers read that book every day. Jay memorized the text. The repetition helped him quickly learn key words. When he wore out that book, he eagerly searched for more joke books to share and rapidly grew his reading skills.

When I went back to mentor the next year, the volunteer coordinator said, "We'll need to get you a new student to mentor." She said, "Jay doesn't need a mentor this year. He's back on track." I was looking forward to seeing Jay, but I was happy that he was like a baby bird that had flown from the nest. As I walked into the class to greet my new student, the partition between the classrooms was half open and I got a glimpse of Jay in the class next door. He was in the front, reading a book to the class. I have never in my life seen anyone so excited to read. As he flipped the pages, he turned the book around and made sure that each and every student saw the picture on that page. He showed the book to each child in the class, one by one, and waited. It was as if he was looking each child in the eyes to ensure that each of them felt his excitement before he turned the page. When the last student returned the big smile, Jay enthusiastically read the next page.

A couple weeks later, I was in the library mentoring a little girl and I noticed Jay. I wondered if he remembered me. I figured that he wouldn't, but he looked up and saw me, and I saw him smile for the first time. As he walked across the room—he stopped suddenly and just stood there looking right at me with a radiant, contagious smile. I think I was so stunned that I just stood there at first. He kept that smile in place, as if he was going to hold that smile until I returned it, showing him that I felt the happiness that he now had inside of him. He stayed patiently still, standing in the middle of the library, until I smiled back—giving confirmation that he'd successfully passed his happiness over to me. It was just like in the classroom where he'd waited for each student to show him that they felt the happiness that the picture and words in the book gave him. Having him pass that happiness on to me was one of the happiest moments of my life. Jay then held his new library book up high to ensure that I saw it. With confidence, he swiftly turned around and headed back to class.

SILO SECRET #161: Many mentors have told me that they are uncertain if they make a difference. I was so fortunate to be able to see firsthand how the gift of mentoring helps a child grow into a great grown-up. Guardian ad litem, child advocates, mentors, tutors, teachers—you are making a difference! Thank you!

SILO SECRET #162: Laughter really is the best medicine. Knock knock, who's there? A simple joke book helped one boy learn to read, and that joy is going on to help so many others. A sense of humor and a smile go a long way. Jay is now inspiring others to thoroughly enjoy reading.

SILO SECRET #163: Finland, ranked number one for years in education, does not put high pressure on children to read early. Instead, they help children grow life skills such as persistence and confidence. After failing school for multiple years due to his lack of reading skills, confidence enabled Jay to go on to read and even be a mentor for other students.

SILO SECRET #164: When I was about to give up on Jay, thinking his challenges were way out of my league, the principal asked me to just help him believe he could do it. Once he had confidence, he achieved his goal. One of the reasons it took me a while to write this book is that I know the hardest part is getting people to believe that we can make a difference, that we can solve problems or fix clunky 30-year-old systems that have "always been that way." What gave me hope is seeing that there are success stories everywhere, and for many, "seeing is believing." We have 10-year-old kids and grandmas all over the world showing us the amazing possibilities.

REFLECT:

Think of a goal that you may have on hold. What can you do to help you realize the goal is possible?

"I have witnessed the softening of the hardest of hearts by a simple smile." – Goldie Hawn (Actress, producer, and singer. Earned Academy Award, Golden Globe Award, and People's Choice Award. Offers MindUP, the signature program of The Goldie Hawn Foundation, to help children develop the mental fitness necessary to thrive in school, work, and life.) (The Goldie Hawn MindUP Program, 2019)

12.3 What If We Each Do Something?

Each of us is born with a superpower to do that one thing—that is truly what interdependence is all about. Let's look at some seemingly small things that made a big difference.

1 phone call – On a phone call with her mother, a teacher mentioned that a young boy in her class was struggling to make friends. As the teacher explained how the boy sits alone folding small pieces of paper, her mother was inspired to buy a children's origami book to share with him. Soon, other children were lining up to learn how to make jumping frogs out of paper. Friendships grew as the children created new animals together.

1 smile – Jane went to Target to buy groceries. As she walked toward the building, a lady was wearing a T-shirt with a picture of Grumpy Cat.

(Grumpycats.com, 2019) It said, "This IS my happy face." Jane smiled, thinking the shirt was funny and somewhat appropriate. The person behind Grumpy Cat thought Jane was smiling at her so she smiled back. Of course, Jane kept her smile going. Now the gentleman behind that lady smiled and he added in a little wink. Of course, this made Jane hold onto that smile as she held in her laughter. Jane says whenever she is feeling down now, she thinks of Grumpy Cat and his contagious smile.

1 connection – Observing how children were petrified about surgery, the Delta Theta Chi Sorority donated a remote control hot rod car so the kids could cruise into the surgery room in style. Rather than fear the seemingly endless hallway trip to the surgery room, children now wish the hallway was longer with a few extra sharp turns. This solution has everyone smiling, including the nurses, doctors, and family members. (Kleib, 2018)

1 kid – When five-year-old Zack learned how bees, which contribute to one out of three bites of our food, are disappearing, he planted flower seeds. Zack's mom, Brittany, forgot all about the seeds until Zack came running in from the backyard, saying, "Momma, momma—look, we made some bees!"

1 adult – Officer Bobby White, a police officer, received a call about some kids making too much noise. He stopped by and asked the kids if they wanted to shoot some hoops. He played a game with them. The community loved the response and is now sending basketballs to the police department. (Basketball Cop Foundation, 2016)

1 animal – A horse named Rio greeted three-year-old Luke when he arrived at the Serenity Saviors Equine Rescue & Therapy Center. Luke did not speak and, with his level of autism, was diagnosed as having a high chance of being nonverbal his entire life. A horse named Rio inspired Luke to speak on his second visit. Now Luke's mom can't get him to stop talking about "that horse named Rio." (Bornscheuer, 2019)

SILO SECRET #165: Based on best practices of Lean, small incremental changes can make a significant difference. These small but significant acts make a difference to those involved but continue to inspire, as people share ARK (acts of random kindness) stories. (Oedekerk, 2007)

REFLECT:

List one seemingly small thing that you would enjoy doing. Perhaps it is more significant than you realize.

_____

_____

Chapter 12 Summary: *It all started with that homeless man who saved my life. He helped me realize that every single person truly does have value and capabilities way beyond what we may have imagined. Phrases like "believe it to achieve it" appear on posters. It seems like a fluffy slogan, but believing in the goal is key to moving forward to achieving the goal. If we each believe we can make a cumulative difference, we can each simply do our part and together create a better world.*

*"How much do you engage yourself in what's truly real and important in life? That's the individual question." – **Jane Goodall** (English primatologist and anthropologist, best known for her over 55-year study of social and family interactions of wild chimpanzees.)

13. STOP. THINK ABOUT IT. NEXT STEP IS UP TO YOU.

"Stop. Think about it. Now what are you going to do?" – **Blue's Clues**

13.1 Stop. Think About It. Now What?

Roaming the hospital hallways in his Superman onesie, five-year-old Alex was ready at all times to put his superpowers into action. While family members came from other states to look after him, panic abruptly set in when the surgeon shared the news that Alex's mom would need to stay at the hospital another week. Uncle Mark blurted out, "What are we going to do? We can't stay to watch Alex. We have to go back to work!" Sweet Aunt Julie added, "We have obligations at home." His aunts and uncles spared back and forth with objections, emphasizing the impossibility of this feat.

Repeatedly trying to interject, the doctor had no success in getting even one word in, but Alex managed to push his way into the center of the shouting circle of conflict. He looked up at his aunts and uncles and calmly stated, "Stop. Think about it. Now what are you going to do?" Apparently, he'd heard this phrase on a kid's show called *Blue's Clues*. ((TV), 2015) It worked; the adults stopped to think and then started working out solutions. They started having calm, solution-oriented discussions like "maybe we could work out a schedule where we can all chip in and be at the hospital a half day here, a half day there, to not impact our jobs." At first, the adults could not get past that wall of despair, but Super Alex came to the rescue. The adults all chipped in and gave a little here and there to be there for that brave little five-year-old boy while his mom recovered.

SILO SECRET #166: No next step is too small. Remember, incremental small changes add up to significant results. Take a moment to stop, think about it, and decide what to do next.

SILO SECRET #167: The phrase "Stop. Think about it. Now what are you going to do?" can be a fun way to help groups stop to relax and even laugh a little bit. The best frame of mind to solve problems is sleeping; the next best frame of mind for problem-solving is relaxing, so relax. If you have and need more time, try that good advice to "sleep on it."

REFLECT:

Take a moment to stop and think about it. What would you like to do next?

_____

_____

"Be patient with yourself. Self-growth is tender; it's holy ground. There's no greater investment." – **Stephen Covey** (Educator and speaker, best known for his book *The 7 Habits of Highly Effective People.*)

13.2 Be Selfish; Take Time to Invest in You!

In one of my workshops, one attendee shared how her day planner calendar is brightly color-coded to easily see time for children, chores, driving, and work. We joked about her sharing a new color at the next workshop by adding in some "green me time." Watching how she became more vibrant as she openly committed to herself and the class to start scheduling bright "green me time" inspired all of us. Let's take time out for us. Here are some steps to help make some time for you.

1. Feel overwhelmed? We all do. Relax and start with you. Just like on the airplane where they say to put the oxygen mask on yourself and then help others, remember to relax and start by focusing on you.

2. Find something that takes up a fair amount of your time. The goal here is to find an activity that you can streamline to free up time to relax or do something that you are excited about.

3. Think Lean to help free up some time for yourself. For example, Jerry realized that he made two trips a week to the same shopping center. He freed up 20 minutes of time for himself by combining the trips.

4. Explore and discover your passion. Once you have a little extra time, you can volunteer or explore and gravitate to your passion (e.g., helping animals, people, environment, technology, or yourself). For Jerry, he always wanted to get back into art. He used the extra 20 minutes he saved to create a company picnic flyer. The marketing team saw his creative work and asked if Jerry was interested in helping with some graphic design projects. Things worked out great. Now, Jerry gets paid to do his passion.

Look back, look forward – be mindful of the now

Use the time that you freed up to be mindful to relax and identify an opportunity to enhance your life.

Below are the eight dimensions of wellness: Like those simulation games that measure our health, we can rate areas of wellness in life. Ideally, we are proactive in staying mentally fit. SAMHSA, the Substance Abuse and Mental Health Services Administration branch of the U.S. Department of Health and Human Services, encourages each of us to incorporate the Eight Dimensions of Wellness into our lives. (SAMHSA, 2016)

1. **Emotional** – Coping effectively with life and creating satisfying relationships

2. **Environmental** – Maintaining good health by occupying pleasant, stimulating environments that support well-being

3. **Financial** – Finding satisfaction with current and future financial situations

4. **Intellectual** – Recognizing creative abilities and finding ways to expand knowledge and skills

5. **Occupational** – Finding personal satisfaction and enrichment from one's work

6. **Physical** – Recognizing the need for physical activity, healthy foods, and sleep

7. **Social** – Developing a sense of connection, belonging, and a well-developed support system

8. **Spiritual** – Expanding our sense of purpose and meaning in life

Note: Recently, I co-presented with a wonderful lady named Sherry. Her children inspired her to add a ninth wellness area of "Fun" to the list to make sure we have plenty of fun on our schedules. Great addition!

SILO SECRET #168: There are many books on the great feeling of reducing clutter that bogs us down. As you free up your time or piles, you'll have more time to be with the people you care about and do the things that matter most to you. It can be painting, volunteering, going back to school— the sky really is the limit.

SILO SECRET #169: By taking the above steps, one goal is to free up time to be able to continually grow. In Stephen Covey's *7 Habits of Highly Effective People* (Covey, The 7 Habits of Highly Effective People, 1989), the first three habits are focused on you (self-mastery).

1. Be proactive

2. Begin with the end in mind

3. Put first things first

One way to prioritize is to get a piece of paper and put a "me" circle in the middle that represents you. Then, draw eight lines coming out from the circle to represent different areas of your life. Next, write down wellness activities you are doing in that area or note a goal that you'd like to accomplish. Below is a sample, followed by a blank diagram that you can use to jot down your own strengths and goals.

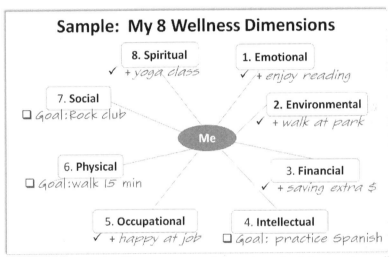

Figure 13.2a Sample of how you can update goals or check items going well.

REFLECT:

Below is a chart you can use like a checklist to easily reflect on your wellness. If there is an area that you would like to improve upon, you can jot down a brief goal for the respective area along with a checkbox to easily view areas you want to focus on. Feel free to add a ninth box just for fun.

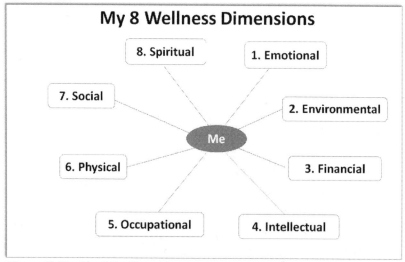

Figure 13.2b Blank Wellness Dimension Form to check off or update goals.

*"I can do things you cannot do. You can do things I cannot do. Together we can do great things." – **Mother Teresa*** (Awarded Nobel Peace Prize for her humanitarian work with the poor and known in the Catholic church as Saint Teresa of Calcutta, devoting her life to caring for the sick and poor.)

13.3 We Believe in You—4 Powerful Words

It was the final round of the Florida state robotics championship, the tournament that would determine the long awaited destiny of the middle and high school teams. With this being one particular team's first time competing, they were ecstatic to have made it this far. They'd worked day and night designing and building their robots for a chance to earn a spot at the World Robotics championship event with top-rated teams from over 40 countries. The gymnasium almost shook as people stomped their feet in unison and cheered for the first-place team and their robot. The onlookers leaped out of their seats with roars of excitement as the team won match over match.

Now, in the final stretch of the competition, it was time for this fierce team to pick a team to be their partner in the final match, the match that could possibly qualify them to earn the spot everyone wanted, which was a chance to be picked to represent Florida at the world competition. Suddenly, I had a flashback of my middle school basketball team member selection. One of my nicknames back then was "Shorty," leading me to naturally look around at the towering robots, wondering which would earn this incredible honor. However, the captain of the winning team looked past all of those super robots and pointed right at the novice team of underdogs who were just glad to be there and exclaimed, "We choose you!" Out of all the possibilities, the leading high school team chose the middle school team with the smallest, most unassuming robot to assist them in the final rounds of the tournament.

While the tiny but suddenly mighty robot team was thrilled, one of the team members had to ask, "What made you choose us?" The robot captain said, "We believe in you." He enthusiastically added, "While the crowd is focused on the giant robot arms thrusting large objects over the fence, I am watching all the value you add on the trenches pushing small to medium-sized objects under the fence." He explained that "together, we get all the pieces, big and small." With that mindset, they won the final match. In all the excitement, the nearly six-foot captain and co-captain of his team proudly picked up the captain of the push robot team, lifting him into the air to celebrate their victory. And the fans went wild!

As a spectator, I could not help but think of how perfectly that demonstrates interdependence, where we rely on one another. That feeling grew as I traveled to watch the big event with teens from over 40 countries come to one giant arena in Kentucky. The World Robotics event was one of the most inspirational events because you got to watch kids come up with solutions and approaches on their own. With no adults allowed in the thinking and building part, it was enlightening to watch how the teenagers solved what most adults would view as a barrier.

When other teams spoke another language, the youth just pulled out their translator app or showed a video of their robot features to communicate. Whether they were partnering or competing on the upcoming match, both teams eagerly grasped new ideas from each other to continually grow their skills.

When a robot lost a bolt or band, a team member from another country often came running to help with the part in hand. One day, it was raining and a boy from Korea had the driver of our comfortable bus pull over so he could get off the bus. We watched as he ran to offer an umbrella to help a competing team from another country protect their robot from the rain. Each night, the teams at the hotel convened in the conference room to test and refine their robots. A U.K. high school team came over to mentor the middle school teams and then stayed late to work on their robot. It is funny, but watching kids from different countries helping one another was just like a microcosm of what it could be like if we as adults could follow their lead. Even the speakers made comments about how they watched the news and sometimes felt down, and then they watched these kids and it helped them have a much better view of the world and the incredible possibilities.

SILO SECRET #170: Teams often had as little as 15 minutes to plan how to best combine their strengths for the next match. Often, they just had a notepad where they jotted down each other's strengths and weaknesses. The kids understood that all robots and all people have weaknesses so they openly shared as a way to partner to overcome their weaknesses and strategize to maximize their strengths.

SILO SECRET #171: When doing strategic planning, there is a SWOT model where you evaluate Strengths, Weaknesses, Opportunities, and Threats. This tool can help us objectively look at ourselves as 100% of us (people and organizations) have all four areas.

REFLECT:

I often hear of situations that get worse because people are not comfortable sharing a weakness. Do you think sharing a weaknesses can sometimes be a strength?

_____

_____

The first-place team selected a robot that was the opposite of their robot. Do you think being open-minded to partner with your opposite can sometimes turn out to be your strength?

_____

_____

Chapter 13 Summary: _The "Stop. Think about it. Now what are you gonna do?" came from a kids' TV show, but it inspired us to first take a moment to laugh and connect with each other. If you take a moment to relax, then you can think about what you would like to achieve and put the right activities at the top of your list. The eight areas of wellness can be a great checklist to identify how we want to grow. The young robotics teams remind us of how we can combine our strengths. Imagine what we can achieve together._

14. TIME TO WRAP IT UP

"No matter what your mission is, have some notion in your head. Forget the model, whether it's government or nonprofit or profit. Ask yourself the more important question: Is my mission improving the world? Are you sure about it? Seek to disconfirm that all the time. And if you can, change your mission." – **Jeff Bezos** (Technology entrepreneur, investor, and philanthropist well known as the founder, chairman, CEO, and president of Amazon.)

"Setting goals is the first step in turning the invisible into the visible." – **Tony Robbins** (#1 New York Times bestselling author, philanthropist, and the nation's #1 life and business strategist.)

14.1 Preventable Epidemics—Let's Change That!

In life, we continually add to our box of tools as we meet people and have experiences along the way. Ideally, this book has given you stories and tips to embrace your natural strengths and more easily solve the problems and achieve the goals that are most important to you. Ultimately, my mission is to help you improve your world, your way. Whether you want to improve the body you live in or some part of the community or world you live in is entirely up to you.

Jeff Bezos encourages us to make sure we are "improving the world." Seriously, you might be thinking that sounds a little far-fetched, but it really is much easier than it sounds. Imagine if you could contribute to preventing an epidemic by simply lightening your load or taking a break to go outside. Amazingly, there are three real preventable epidemics where doctors and researchers are stating that the solution is that easy.

To start, we have a growing epidemic estimated to impact half of the world in the next three decades. Some doctors believe the issue is that in our new world of cell phones, computers, and television, our eye muscles rarely get a workout looking at far away objects. The result is a rapid increase in nearsightedness, where we can see near but things further away are blurry. Recent research suggests that just going outside has incredible results. So, if someone tells you to "go for a walk," thank them and invite a friend. If it is late, too cold, or torrential rain outside, the alternative is to follow the 20-20-20 rule where you take a break after 20 minutes to look at something 20 feet away for 20 seconds. This is also great if you get caught daydreaming at work. "Really, boss, it is not what it looks like. I'm doing my part to prevent a world crisis and keep health care and vision care costs down."

If walking or looking away for 20 seconds sounds like way too much, then hey, take some weight off your shoulders. Yes, the heavy load in our backpacks is creating a second epidemic negatively impacting our health. The guideline is to carry a maximum of 10% to 15% of your weight in your backpack. So for a 100-pound middle schooler, they are lucky if they are just lugging around the equivalent of one or two bowling balls on their back. For the lightweight kids, one fast corner and they can easily tip over. What makes it worse is that we tend to lean forward, and a slight 15-degree lean causes the muscles to have to work twice as hard, adding up to 27 pounds of force (over three bowling balls). Going up stairs, leaning 30 degrees forward, effectively weighs 40 pounds, thus forcing little Johnny to now juggle the equivalent of five bowling balls as he charges up the stairs to get to class. (Hansraj, 2014)

This is actually a good segue to preventable epidemic number three. Just like little Johnny is juggling the equivalent of extra bowling balls, the same happens when you and I lean forward to check that text or email on our computers or cell phones. So, the next time you are at a party and your cell phone goes off, you can simply lift your cell phone screen to be level with your eyes, showing proper technique, and hopefully then turn it on silent to enjoy the party. Intrigued by your startling behavior to put your cell phone on vibrate, people will likely be curious and ask questions like "what did you do?" They will likely remember you when you say, "I'm doing my part to prevent an epidemic of text neck" or share your part-time hobby of "helping people retain their precious health and eyesight." If you just help one person, including yourself, you are contributing to solving the next world epidemic. (Impact Illustration, 2014)

SILO SECRET #172: Sites vary on the maximum percentage weight that is acceptable to carry in a backpack. Most recommend something in the range of 10% to 20% of your weight as a maximum to carry, noting that leaning forward is a sign of a problem. When one father joked that he could barely pick up his son's backpack, the doctor said his 100-pound son should at most be carrying 10 to 15 pounds in his backpack. It turned out other students complained of backaches so the school published some tips and policies to minimize the load.

SILO SECRET #173: There is an 80-20 rule of thumb based on the Pareto Principle, suggesting that we focus on 20% of the causes to improve 80% of the results. (Kruse, 2016) There are many opportunities where we could focus on one or two known solutions to prevent quite serious epidemics. Below are two examples:

- 80% of deaths from coronary artery disease can be attributed to preventable factors like eating healthy and being active according to the Centers for Disease Control and Prevention. (Willett, et al., 2002)

- 80% to 85% of all child abuse and neglect is preventable according to Child Abuse Prevention Council reports. (CAP Council Facts, 2019)

REFLECT:

Is there one tip you can share to help you or a loved one retain their health and/or eyesight?

_____

_____

*"To succeed in life, you need three things: a wishbone, a backbone, and a funny bone." – **Reba McEntire*** (American singer, songwriter, actress, and record producer; had her own television sitcom entitled *Reba*.)

14.2 Bouncing Back from Life's Falls

Someone recently asked me, "What is the hardest part about interdependence?" Each time, the answer is nearly always the same. The biggest challenge is simply believing—believing in yourself, believing in others, believing in best practices, and believing in the possibilities of what we can achieve together. The great thing is once you believe the idea is worth trying, all you have to do is convince one person to try it with you, and you'll be on your way to interdependence.

While believing is the hardest part, it is also the most rewarding part, especially when you watch a person believe that their part could be key to transforming the impossible to the possible. While it can be quite rewarding, it can be especially challenging when (1) you feel you have hit rock bottom or (2) all the experts are saying it's "time to move on." With that in mind, I thought it would be helpful to share a personal story of a seemingly impossible goal and highlight how the silo tips were applied along the way.

When I was 25 years old, I fearlessly climbed 2,425 feet to get to the top of one of the world's tallest waterfalls, Yosemite Falls in California. On the way down, there was a freak accident. The tour leader fell, and I went flying off the cliff of the mountain. Landing on a jagged, pointed rock somehow propelled me upward. While it prevented me from cascading down the mountain, my body snapped, leaving me with my back broken in two places and injuries from head to toe. It seemed appropriate that I landed in a rock formation that closely resembled a coffin. While I do not recommend this bumpy ride, I recall being so thankful that I had experience and training in problem-solving and solutions design. When doctors, nurses, and neurologists all stated, "Your system is broken, nothing we can do," my brain was trained to jump into crisis resolution mode.

When I eagerly inquired about starting therapy, the doctors reiterated that there was "no hope." One doctor showed me how the x-ray of my lower back was all gray and dark. There was a light-colored mark that looked like an eyelash. Not clear on how to read the x-ray, I asked, "Is that light-colored object the only thing that is wrong with me?" The doctor replied, "That miniscule mark is the only thing that is right with you." He emphasized, "You will never walk again, and therapy is pointless."

While I was willing to accept this outcome, the body that I live in is important to me, so I started out using the "5 Why" approach used in the Lean Six Sigma process improvement methodology to ensure a focus on fixing the problem versus treating the symptom. With this technique, you keep asking "why" until you get to the root issue. That evening, I asked one of the nurses, "Why do the hospital staff stop by, say hi, and touch my toe?" She explained that I had every symptom of a paralyzed person except that I could move my right toe. As I asked more "why" questions, she explained that if you can move your toe, it is a sign that there is a working connection between your brain and toe. So, I officially had the "toe of hope" and even though the wiggly toe rule was their rule, they still did not believe I would ever walk given all the other evidence. They had, in their words, "no hope."

So, now I applied the silo secrets in chapter 2 to ensure a clearly aligned vision. Using humor, joking about my mighty powerful toe, we openly discussed and addressed our concerns. Some feared that trying would just give me false hope, so I let them know, "I will be fine no matter what," but shared, "Imagine if we try and find that I can sit up on my own or maybe stand on my own?" I prompted them to envision success, asking, "Wouldn't it be great to tell your friends and family how you helped a 25-year-old walk after she was told she never would again?" Four nurses joined my team. We were a lot like the HAT (High Availability Team) highlighted in chapter 5. We now had a common vision and mission.

We now had **hope**, the foundation of a WRAP® (Wellness Recovery Action Plan®). Our hope was literally the size of a toe, but hey, we had hope that it just might be possible, along with the desire to try. With WRAP, the five key recovery concepts in order include (1) hope, (2) personal responsibility, (3) education, (4) self-advocacy, and (5) support network. So, it was time for concept 2—for me to take **personal responsibility** in using my skills to help my body recover as well as it could. (WRAP®, 2019) I reassured the nurses that I would be fine with any result, even if the outcome was less than desirable, and I empowered the nurses to use their expertise to maximize my recovery.

Next, I did concept 3 where I pursued **education**, learning about what the body needs to heal itself. I had to get to root causes and partner on solutions. A big barrier was that I passed out when I tried to sit up or lift my head, let alone tried to stand, so I went back to the 5 Whys—why do I pass out? One nurse explained, "You are not getting enough oxygen." Asking more whys, I said, "Why am I not getting enough oxygen?" She explained, "Your body only takes in the minimum oxygen required." At the risk of sounding like a toddler, I asked, "Why is my body only taking in a small amount of oxygen?" She explained that my body only took in enough oxygen to talk, so that was about all I could do without going unconscious.

With this important piece of education, I now went on to concept 4 **(self-advocacy)**, where I had to speak up to represent my views and interests. Since doctors didn't believe therapy would help, I was not given a therapist, so I decided to represent myself. I could not help but think it was kind of like being your own attorney, where you better be careful, but really the key was empowering the amazing nurses. I expressed that I was confident in letting them decide and do what is best.

The nurses made up my critical **support network**, concept 5 of WRAP. These four nurses came in on their own time to help me heal. Since I went in and out of consciousness during therapy, my roommate advised me that two nurses held my body up, one nurse held my head up, and the other nurse periodically put the oxygen mask on my face with the goal of getting my body to take in more oxygen to support standing.

Eventually, it worked. I was able to stand and take small steps. You would likely need a magnifying glass to see these steps, but it was progress. After a couple days, you could put down the magnifying glass and see some serious millimeter travel, but after a couple weeks, we were now ready for a night on the town. The nurses saved me a special mauve hospital gown to wear as a jacket to complement my periwinkle blue hospital gown. My roomie had been in bed in ICU (intensive care unit) for one year, but she was inspired to go out on the town with me. I told her, "If you fall, I do not have the strength to catch you." She said, "Well, I surely don't have the strength to catch you." But we did it!

Once out of the hospital, the journey continued. This time, I heard a new set of phrases like "this is as good as you will get," "you will always have pain," "you will never dance," and "you will never have a child." Again, I knew I had to find someone with the right skills who was receptive to embracing a common vision to simply try and continue to give my body the resources to recover as well as it could. A neighbor suggested that I consult a sport rehabilitation therapist. At first, the sport therapist started out with the same doom and gloom comments, but then I asked him to imagine his favorite sports hero came in with the same injury and asked for his help for an optimal recovery. The therapist quickly said,

"Well, insurance won't cover what I would recommend." I replied, "Remember, your sports hero is fine paying cash, so what would you recommend?" Removing the limits from his mind, he worked out a daily plan of exercises to do at home, and we used the scheduled visits as an opportunity for him to assess and tweak the plan as needed.

In recovery, I often had people ask if I was training for the Olympics. When I told them I was recovering from a broken back, they would often mention an injured friend or family member who "lost hope" in recovery. When they heard my story, they frequently introduced their friends to me so we could share tips to grow stronger and healthier. Without realizing it, we were doing peer support, which is evolving as a major movement in mental health where people share their stories to help others. I have met peer support specialists who have been through way worse than me, but they are grateful for their tragic backgrounds because it enables them to help others. I can relate to how they feel. My "toe of hope" has inspired people across the nation.

A core part of reaching a solution was that we engaged all **four sides of the solution** as described by the card analogy in chapter 1. The nurses were natural Caring Helpers and Change Agents. While some of the doctors were Problem Solvers by nature, they were trained in the medical silo of problem-solving methods. In my case, the medical books said if a patient can't move, lift their head, or sit up, it is like a classic textbook case of being paralyzed from a traumatic accident. They followed problem-solving models that they were trained in within the medical silo. My accident happened years ago, but I did fully recover. Today, an increasing number of hospitals are connecting with the engineering and quality management silos to learn how they can look at medical processes from a new view, further improving health care and creating life-changing approaches to recovery and medical care.

SILO SECRET #174: The best advice I got was that the body is the best healer. The follow-up advice was that we have to give our bodies the tools to heal.

SILO SECRET #175: In coaching organizations to achieve more challenging goals, the hardest step is almost always the very first step of believing the goal is possible. Mary Ellen Copeland, the founder of the WRAP® approach, studied people who were successful in overcoming a major mental health challenge and found that hope was consistently the first step.

SILO SECRET #176: Solutions are like tools where you can use different tools to achieve the same goal. While the WRAP® was initially designed for mental health recovery, we saw how it can be used for physical recovery as well. Today, it is used to help with wellness in the workplace and a variety of specific areas from finance to parenting. As you read the stories in this book, the goal is to have a solution mindset and be aware that there are many ways to come to solutions.

REFLECT:

Is there one of the key concepts of recovery that you can keep in mind to improve your life?

(Hope, Personal Responsibility, Education, Self-advocacy, or Support Network).

_____

_____

"Will we continue being able to take joint action or will we revert to our individual roles? I call on us to find joint positions and I hope we will do so. Let us work together to make the world a better place. It will then be a better place for each and every one of us." – **Dr. Angela Merkel** (Germany's Federal Chancellor. Advocate for cooperation and sustainable solutions for the European Union. Named "Person of the Year" by *TIME* magazine in 2015. Speech from 53rd Munich Security Conference, 2017.)

14.3 Cold Cuts on Lettuce or Interdependence?

For seven years now, I have been going to conferences and events where the speakers are over-the-top enthusiastic on the topic of connecting, collaborating, transforming, and a whole bunch of other motivational words ending with "-ing." Yet, when it is time to leave, even those of us wanting so much to connect tend to go on to do the same ol' thing. We get back to our desk or home, now at least a day behind, and a coworker, friend, or family member says, "While you were out, so-and-so called, and oh, did you realize you have a slight oil leak under your car" and then it happens. Actually, then it doesn't happen. All those grandiose ideas from the conference go into the "dream" file. So, how do we move them to the reality file? One of the mottos I love to live by is, "If you want change, you have to change your mind." To do the things that are important to us, work on the goals that are important to us, and be with the people who are important to us, requires a focused mindset. So, at the next conference, let's go with a goal in mind and turn that dream, no matter how big or small, into a reality.

Here is the science behind this goal mindset. As a manager, I had to approve people to go to training classes. The headquarters office told us that studies show that the best way to ensure effective training is to have employees attend the training with a goal in mind of what they want to achieve after the training. They said studies show having a goal in mind helps trainees learn and retain the information much better.

By accident, I tested this theory for about 10 years, and it worked every time. My employees would come back saying, "You are the only manager who tells their employees to come to the event with a goal in mind." Within a year, people from the other departments would ask if they could come and shadow employees in my department to learn the skills taught in the class. They were in the same class, but since they didn't apply the new skill or even mindset right away, the skills faded. The good news is we were always happy to help, and it actually facilitated interdependence because it brought our two different departments, our two different silos, together. Even though they viewed us as the trainer or mentor, it was always a two-way exchange of information.

SILO SECRET #177: The Learning Pyramid shows us that with participatory teaching methods, retention is much higher (Group Discussion: 50%, Practice by Doing: 75%, Teaching Others: 90%). If we have a goal in mind, it helps us think through applying the learning and gaining the benefits of participatory teaching methods versus passive teaching methods. Even if the class is more lecture (5% retention) or audio visual (20% retention), having a goal in mind fosters a more participatory style of learning and enables us to ask questions that relate to implementing the goal. (Kelly, 2012)

REFLECT:

Think of a time you went to a class or a home improvement store with a goal in mind. Did having an applicable goal or project in mind help you get more value out of your class or visit?

_____

_____

Imagine you leave your next meeting with a choice of (1) a full belly or (2) a full belly and a plan of a simple way you can partner to make a difference. Which feels better to you?

_____

_____

"Go for great. Own your game. Be kind. Get big things done." – **Robin S. Sharma** (Rated among the top five leadership experts in the world. Founded The Robin Sharma Foundation for Children.)

14.4 Game On! Interdependence Can Be Fun!

4-Card View is meant to be a light, fun interdependence game. While you often hide your hand with card games, the objective of 4-Card View is to gather and share all four personality views (all four cards) to reach better solutions.

Going from left to right, each player will have a chance to help fill in the blanks, prompting them to think from the viewpoint of each of the four personality strengths to achieve a more well-rounded solution.

Step 1 – Hearts card: Play the view of the Caring Helper to identify a PROBLEM or area to focus on improving. Come up with three contributing factors and then circle the one you would like to solve.

Step 2 – Spades card: Play the view of the Problem Solver to come up with three SOLUTION options and circle the selected solution to focus on.

Step 3 – Diamonds card: Play the view of the Solid Leader to ensure you have a PLAN to follow.

Step 4 – Clubs card: Play the view of the FUN Change Agent to make sure your solution is enjoyable.

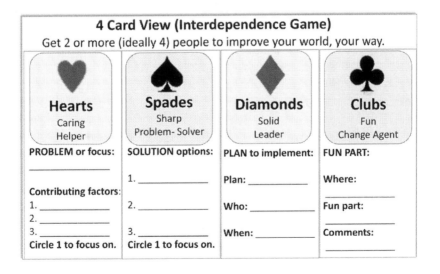

If you are missing a card, you can role-play and try to represent that view, or you can go fish for the missing card view. You can even call a friend. Have fun, have a sense of humor, and enjoy connecting to improve your world.

The game offers an easy way to practice networking by inviting others to share their ideas. Kids tend to like to jump in as you get to the FUN Clubs card. Let them share ideas for a more fun, lasting solution!

Some examples for reference are listed on the pages that follow.

4-Card View – Solitaire Version (one player):

Keeping it simple, you can start out playing on your own like the game of solitaire, only instead of lining up cards in order, you'll step through the four cards to get to your solution. The key is to ensure you put on the view of each of the four perspectives. If, for example, you consider yourself to be the fun, less responsible person in the room, you can picture a person you know who is very responsible and imagine what they would do.

Sample of Solitaire Goal:

James was fine with his messy desk until it was Friday night and he could not find the tickets to his favorite team's championship game. This motivated him to face the problem and note on the first card, the Hearts card, that his "desk is too cluttered." Looking at his desk, it was filled with bills, mail, and papers to review. He had reminders to pay bills so he put that aside and circled his choice to focus on the bothersome "papers to review."

Progressing to the second card, the Problem Solver Spades card, he listed three options but decided to use the 5 Why concept to dig deeper. His internal questioning went something like this, "1) Why so many papers? I plop papers on desk. 2) Why do I plop papers on desk? I feel overwhelmed. 3) Why do I feel overwhelmed? Nowhere to put papers. 4)

Why no place to put papers? I need a filing system. 5) Why do I not have a file system? I need to set up a file system.

With that 'aha' moment, James decided to set up a file system to "sort and file by topic." After James headed to the Dollar Store and got some colorful files, he moved to the Diamonds card where he came up with a plan to "Set aside 20 minutes to sort and file by topic." Knowing that he got bored easily, he was happy to move to the Clubs card to think of ways to make this activity a little more enjoyable. Loving upbeat music, he decided to set aside some 'me' time on Tuesday morning to relax to his favorite tunes while he did his filing. Now, he enjoys his clear desk and looks forward to Jammin' Tuesdays.

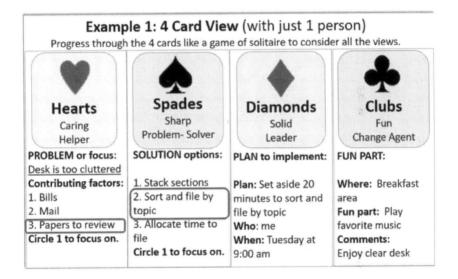

Example 1: 4 Card View (with just 1 person)
Progress through the 4 cards like a game of solitaire to consider all the views.

Hearts	Spades	Diamonds	Clubs
Caring Helper	Sharp Problem-Solver	Solid Leader	Fun Change Agent
PROBLEM or focus: Desk is too cluttered	SOLUTION options:	PLAN to implement:	FUN PART:
Contributing factors:	1. Stack sections	Plan: Set aside 20 minutes to sort and file by topic	Where: Breakfast area
1. Bills	2. Sort and file by topic		Fun part: Play favorite music
2. Mail		Who: me	Comments: Enjoy clear desk
3. Papers to review	3. Allocate time to file	When: Tuesday at 9:00 am	
Circle 1 to focus on.	Circle 1 to focus on.		

4-Card View – Two-Player Version:

Once you practice playing on your own, you can engage another person to work though solutions. Below is an example of how Mike used 4 Card View to reduce his emails. Asking 'why' helped Mike realize that he was cc'd (carbon copied) on a lot of emails and gets a good amount of junk email. By sorting his emails, he determined that 80% of his emails came from a couple people, Joe and Lee. Using the Problem Solver Spades card, he thought through alternatives to email, noting that he could "Meet on email topics" or have a "Phone call on email topics." While they could also write-up a summary of the emails, he felt he needed more interaction.

Of the three options, Mike decided on and circled "Meet on email topics." Viewing the solution from the responsible Solid Leader card view, he defined a plan to "Meet & summarize." Finally, he and Joe played the Clubs card to identify how they could add a little more fun to the meeting. Since both love Bagel Day, they decided to meet on Bagel Wednesday. Now, they have more fun and save about 5 hours in emails so both view the solution as sustainable. They also made a pact to find a new, fun place to meet if the powers that be somehow put an end to the bountiful bagel day.

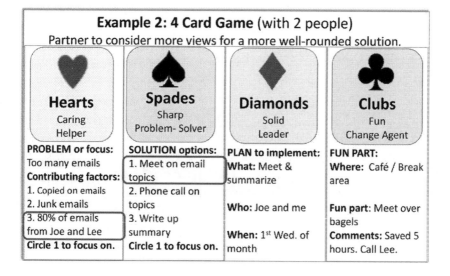

Example 2: 4 Card Game (with 2 people)

Partner to consider more views for a more well-rounded solution.

Hearts	Spades	Diamonds	Clubs
Caring Helper	Sharp Problem-Solver	Solid Leader	Fun Change Agent
PROBLEM or focus: Too many emails **Contributing factors:** 1. Copied on emails 2. Junk emails 3. 80% of emails from Joe and Lee **Circle 1 to focus on.**	**SOLUTION options:** 1. Meet on email topics 2. Phone call on topics 3. Write up summary **Circle 1 to focus on.**	**PLAN to implement:** **What:** Meet & summarize **Who:** Joe and me **When:** 1st Wed. of month	**FUN PART:** **Where:** Café / Break area **Fun part:** Meet over bagels **Comments:** Saved 5 hours. Call Lee.

4-Card View – Multiple-Player Version:

Of course, the ideal version of the 4-Card View interdependence game will include at least four players, representing all four personality views. At team meetings or conferences, you can engage in conversations and try this game approach to include more perspectives to reach more sustainable solutions. Eventually, it will be second nature as you'll be inspired to see how different views add to solutions.

4 Card View (Interdependence Game)
Get 2 or more (ideally 4) people to improve your world, your way.

Hearts	Spades	Diamonds	Clubs
Caring Helper	Sharp Problem- Solver	Solid Leader	Fun Change Agent
PROBLEM or focus:	**SOLUTION options:**	**PLAN to implement:**	**FUN PART:**
_____	1. _____	Plan: _____	Where: _____
Contributing factors:			
1. _____	2. _____	Who: _____	Fun part: _____
2. _____			
3. _____	3. _____	When: _____	Comments: _____
Circle 1 to focus on.	Circle 1 to focus on.		

Scoring: For each of the 4 cards, add 1 point if that personality view was considered in the solution.

(**2 or less** = Go Fish; **3** = Almost There; may want to call a friend; **4** = Excellent Interdependence)

Notes:

_____

_____

SILO SECRET #178: You can be innovative and create different versions of the interdependence 4-Card View game. You can even further simplify the game by folding a piece of paper into four sections to jot down the four views. Those of you who are more active can write the four views on a ball and then play catch with the ball. Wherever the catcher's thumb lands, that person has the challenge of coming up with an idea that represents that personality view. You can even play real Four Square, writing the four views in chalk on the squares. The key is to have fun and appreciate the four sides to a solution.

SILO SECRET #179: You can use the game as an opportunity to build a network of people who enjoy working on solutions. People attending the same conference or event as you likely have common goals or interests. Invite them to email or text you if they could use another "view" to help with a challenge they are having. You'll soon have a network of the four views to consult for better solutions.

SILO SECRET #180: For the last silo secret, try an experiment where you look for solutions. You will be amazed that whatever you are looking for, problems or solutions, you will find it. When my daughter was younger, she wanted to go on the playground and I said, "It is a little wet." She responded, "It is a little dry." I also saw a fun shirt that said the glass is always full because even if it has half liquid, it has half air. Solutions start with a mindset that solutions are all around us. Enjoy the fun of discovering them.

REFLECT:

Think of a family goal that you could work on using the game of interdependence. Better yet, try it.

_____

_____

Chapter 14 Summary: This last chapter was really about the foundational importance of believing. While it technically should have been the first chapter, it is sometimes hard to believe in the importance of believing so we saved it for last. Enjoy the game of interdependence. We tend to get busy with that to-do list and forget to have fun, but now fun is one of the four cards to check. Best wishes in achieving those goals that are most important for your world.

AFTERWORD

It is great that we each have different inspirations. Some want to save the whales. Some enjoy sorting food cans at a local food shelter. Others want to sing at a senior living home. We could come up with a million scenarios, and that is a wonderful thing. We each offer a different piece. It is also exciting to evolve in our contributions. Over the past few months, a few people have inspired me to do just that.

First, I was inspired by hearing a radio interview with Tara Richter of Richter Publishing. While there are many publishers, Tara stood out as she continually helps people just like you and me write our stories to help others. Through her, I have met numerous authors who have helped others by writing on topics such as how to get through adversity, get through breast cancer, help a child with autism, or even sail around the world after a major hardship. By sharing our experiences and strengths, we help each other.

Second, I was inspired as I recently reconnected with a wonderful speaker known as Absolutely Abby. About five years ago, I was so impressed by Abby's determination. After years in human resources, she was keenly aware of how job seekers are often just one or two tips away from achieving their career aspirations. Wanting to make a difference, she bravely did what no one else has done. She sold her house, bought an RV, and went on a nationwide tour with a mission to educate one million job seekers. When I let Abby know how she inspired me to work toward a mission to help one million people improve their world, their way; her response was, "Let me know how I can help." Thank you, Absolutely Abby! (Kohut, 2019)

Third, Admiral McRaven, ninth commander of the U.S. Special Operations Command, invites us to reflect on the power of each of us helping 10 of the nearly 10,000 people we will meet in our lifetime. He shared with the University of Texas class graduates how their one class of 2014, with each student helping 10 people who then go on to help 10 more people, could literally change the world population over six generations. With that being just one of the over 100,000 school graduations occurring each year, imagine the possibilities. (McRaven, 2014)

Last but not least, I was inspired by my dear friend Phyllis. For her twenty-first 29th birthday, she held an awesome party and invited about 100 guests. She is very popular so she could have racked up some serious gifts, but instead, she asked her guests to simply do one nice gesture for someone else as her gift. Since most of her friends invited a guest to the party, she got a two-for-one special, inspiring over 200 actions that made the world a little nicer. She far exceeded her quota of helping 10 people in her lifetime and continues to inspire positive thoughts and positive actions. It was fun to figure out and plan what nice thing to do on her behalf. I hope the stories in this book have inspired you in that same way.

Best wishes on your interdependence journey and thank you.

ABOUT THE AUTHOR

About the Author: Lisa Blackburn Ullven, with 25+ years of being a global problem solver for Fortune 500 companies that are in the Top 3 in the industry, has strong experience using the best problem-solving tools in the world. Her passion is sharing these tools to strengthen our communities. In college, a professor said, "If you want to help people, learn about systems," so she did just that.

Credentials: After earning her MBA with a bachelor's degree in Management Information Systems, Lisa earned globally recognized certifications: Certified PMP® Project Management Professional; Certified Wellness Recovery and Action Plan® Facilitator; Certified Wraparound Coach and Trainer; Certified Help Desk Director and Manager; Lean Six Sigma Black Belt and ITIL® Certificate; and Certified Recovery Peer Specialist for Families. She is a partner and founding board member of Peace4Tarpon (Peace4Communities) and CEO of Guided Results LLC.

Purpose for writing this book: When Lisa asked her then-five-year old daughter which children's audiobook she wanted to listen to and her daughter replied, "Please, Mom, no more world problems," it reinforced that we are leaving our children with plenty of problems. This book is intended to share some of the top globally recognized best practices to help children and adults design and implement solutions.

Value to reader: Many people feel overwhelmed by trying to do it all. This book will help you see that you are not supposed to do it all. The book will help you "find your piece" to "find your peace."

How readers feel after reading the book:
Readers walk away feeling empowered with the tools they need to lead or be a part of positive changes that align with their passion.

Lisa Blackburn Ullven
www.guidedresults.com

REFERENCES

45 Fire Safety Slogans. 2019. https://www.thefreshquotes.com/fire-safety-slogans/. Accessed June 18, 2019.

AirNow.gov. 2019. https://airnow.gov/index.cfm?action=resources.whatyoucando#trans. Accessed May 29, 2019.

—. 2019. *Current AQI.* May 28. https://airnow.gov/index.cfm?action=airnow.main. Accessed May 28, 2019.

—. 2019. *EPA Right Respirator.* May 28. https://airnow.gov/static/topics/images/epa-infographic-respirator.jpg. Accessed May 28, 2019.

—. *Wildfire Smoke Frequently Asked Questions.* 2019. https://airnow.gov/index.cfm?action=topics.smoke_wildfires_faqs. Accessed May 29, 2019.

Altshul, Sara. 2019. *How Mindfulness Provides Relief from Chronic Pain.* May 6. https://www.mindful.org/how-mindfulness-provides-relief-from-chronic-pain.

American Society for Quality. 2019. *The Global Voice of Quality.* June 17. http://asq.org/customer-service/contact-asq/index.html. Accessed June 17, 2019.

ASQ. 2019. *About Pareto Chart.* ASQ. May 20. https://asq.org/quality-resources/pareto. Accessed May 20, 2019.

Association of State and Territorial Health. 2019. *Health in All Policies.* May 28. http://www.astho.org/HiAP/Framework/. Accessed May 28, 2019.

Baker, Vicky. 2018. *Tourism pressures: Five places tackling too many visitors.* BBC News. April 16. https://www.bbc.com/news/world-43700833. Accessed May 28, 2019.

BBC News. 2005. *Net fuels Live 8 extravaganza.* July 5. http://news.bbc.co.uk/2/hi/technology/4648003.stm. Accessed May 29, 2019.

—. 2017. *London: Lambeth school to offer parents advice on pollution face masks.* March 31. https://www.bbc.com/news/uk-england-london-39443508. Accessed May 29, 2019.

Berguno, G. 2004. *The American International University of London.* The American International University of London. September 3. https://core.ac.uk/download/padf/51086961. Accessed May 28, 2019.

Berkeley Earth. 2019. *Air Quality Real-time Map.* http://berkeleyearth.org/air-quality-real-time-map/. Accessed June 2, 2019.

Bianca Rey and Cyd Oppenheimer, J.D. 2016. *Letting Kids Be Kids: Promoting Normalcy for Connecticut's Youth in Foster Care .* January. www.ctvoices.org/sites/default/files/Letting%20Kids%20Be%20Kids%20Complete.pdf. Accessed June 2, 2019.

Billboard. Chart History. *Logic.* © 2020 Billboard. All Rights Reserved. Billboard is a subsidiary of Prometheus Global Media, LLC. June 3. https://www.billboard.com/music/Logic/chart-history/billboard-200. Accessed June 3, 2019.

Blanch, Andrea, David Shern, Clare Reidy, and Leslie Lieberman 2019. *Building Stronger Networks.* May. http://marc.healthfederation.org/building-stronger-networks. Accessed May 30, 2019.

Bloom, S. L. 1994. *The Sanctuary Model: Developing Generic Inpatient*

Programs for the Treatment of Psychological Trauma. Handbook of Post-Traumatic Therapy, A Practical Guide to Intervention, Treatment, and Research. M. B. Williams and J. F. Sommer. Pages 474-491. Westport, Connecticut: Greenwood Publishing. Accessed June 1, 2019.

Bornscheuer, Allen. 2019. https://www.serenitysaviors.org/. Accessed June 8, 2019.

BrainyQuote. 2019. *BrainyQuote.* May 28. https://www.brainyquote.com. Accessed February 2, 2019.

Brown, Keith. 2019. *This is our Movement.* KEITH L. BROWN ©. May 28. http://keithlbrown.com/about-keith/. Accessed May 28, 2019.

Burke Harris, Dr. Nadine. 2019. *Together we can build a healthier future for children exposed to adversity.* May 30. https://centerforyouthwellness.org/. Accessed May 31, 2019.

Burton, Neel. 2015. *Hide and Seek.* Maslow. September 30. https://www.psychologytoday.com/us/blog/hide-and-seek/201509/philosophical-cure-anxiety?amp. Accessed August 5, 2019.

Caballero, Ivette. 2019. https://www.linkedin.com/pulse/why-you-succeed-when-your-vision-clear-ivette-k-caballero/. Accessed May 2019.

Cain, Tonier. 2019. *In her own words.* Tonier Cain International. https://www.toniercain.com/about/. Accessed May 20, 2019.

California Air Resources Control Board. 2019. *California Certified Air Cleaning Devices.* https://ww2.arb.ca.gov/our-work/programs/air-cleaners-ozone-products/california-certified-air-cleaning-devices. Accessed May 29, 2019.

Capra, Fritjof and Pauli, Gunter A. 1995. "Steering Business Toward Sustainability." Tokyo: United Nations University Press. P. 3.

CareerBuilder. *Press.* 2017. August 24.
http://press.careerbuilder.com/2017-08-24-Living-Paycheck-to-Paycheck-is-a-Way-of-Life-for-Majority-of-U-S-Workers-According-to-New-CareerBuilder-Survey. Accessed May 2019.

Carter, Megan. 2017. *Why Your Brain Can't Process The Word 'Don't'.*
June 6. Accessed May 29, 2019.
http://www.readunwritten.com/2017/06/06/brain-cant-process-word-dont/.

Casey Family Programs. 2019. *Casey Organization.*
https://www.casey.org/turnover-costs-and-retention-strategies/. Accessed June 1, 2019.

Census.gov. 2018. *U.S. Census Bureau Statistics.* August 1.
https://www.census.gov/newsroom/stories/2018/volunteer-week.html. Accessed May 1, 2019.

Chibanda, Dr. Dixon. 2017. *Why I trained grandmothers to treat depression.* TEDWomen 2017. November.
https://www.ted.com/talks/dixon_chibanda_why_i_train_gran dmothers_to_treat_depression. Accessed May 28, 2018.

Child Welfare Information Gateway. 2013. *Protective Factors Framework.* Youth and Families Administration for Children.
https://www.childwelfare.gov/topics/preventing/promoting/pr otectfactors/protective-factors/. Accessed June 3, 2019.

—. 2019. *Child Welfare Worker Turnover.* August 31.
https://www.childwelfare.gov/topics/management/workforce/r etention/turnover/. Accessed September 1, 2019.

Christenson, Peter, Silvia de Haan-Rietdijk, Donald F. Roberts, and Tom ter Bogt. 2018. *Psychology of Music.* January 23.
https://journals.sagepub.com/doi/full/10.1177/0305735617748 205. Accessed May 20, 2019.

City of Greensburg. 2008. *Rebuilding Stronger, Better, Greener.* May 20. http://www.greensburgks.org/. Accessed May 29, 2019.

Cole, Alex. 2019. Cole, Alex. 2019. *IREX.* May 19. https://www.irex.org/newsroom. Accessed May 27, 2019. The Community Solutions Program is sponsored by the U.S. Department of State with funding provided by the U.S. Government and supported in its implementation by IREX.

Covey, Stephen. 1989. *The 7 Habits of Highly Effective People.* New York: Free Press.

—. 2006. *The 8th Habit: From Effectiveness to Greatness.* Edited by Inc. Simon & Schuster. New York, NY: Free Press.

Dauncey, Guy. 2009. *The Climate Challenge: 101 Solutions to Global Warming.* Gabriola Island, British Columbia: New Society Publishers.

Denison, Sean. 2018. *WUFT News.* November 20. https://www.wuft.org/news/2018/11/20/opioid-recovery-care-pilot-program-sees-success-in-first-year/. Accessed May 28, 2019.

Doran, George, Arthur Miller, and James Cunningham. 1981. *S.M.A.R.T goals - the world's most popular way to set goals!* Management Review. November. https://www.smart-goals-guide.com/smart-goal.html. Accessed June 2, 2019.

Dosomething.org. 2019. *Do Something.* May 28. www.dosomething.org. Accessed May 28, 2019.

Doty, Dr. James. 2008. *Center for Compassion & Altruism Research & Education—CCARE.* https://charterforcompassion.org/science-and-research-partners/center-for-compassion-alturism-research-education-ccare. Accessed June 3, 2019.

Ebb, Fred, and John Kand. 1972. *Money Makes the World Go 'Round.* Performed by Liza Minnelli. Cabaret, New York.

Elzinga, BM, CG Schmahl, E Vermetten, R van Dyck, and JD Bremner. 2003. *Higher cortisol levels following exposure to traumatic reminders in abuse-related PTSD.* September 28. https://www.ncbi.nlm.nih.gov/pubmed/12838270. Accessed May 30, 2019.

Earth Day Network. 2019. *End Plastic Pollution.* https://www.earthday.org/2018/04/05/fact-sheet-plastics-in-the-ocean/. Accessed June 2, 2019.

Enos, Gary A. 2019. *Peer Specialists Beginning to Boost Florida's Service System.* May 13. https://www.addictionpro.com/article/peer-specialists-beginning-boost-floridas-service-system. Accessed June 6, 2019.

Erikson, Erik H. 1950. *Childhood and Society.* New York: Norton.

Evans Price, Deborah. 2017. *Country: Nashville Song Hall Honoree Tim Nichols Talks Co-Writing Tim McGraw's Hit 'Live Like You Were Dying'.* October 20. https://www.billboard.com/articles/columns/country/7998881/tim-nichols-interview-tim-mcgraw-live-like-you-were-dying-nashville-song-hall-honoree. Accessed June 2, 2019.

Fackler, Martin. 2017. *After the Tsunami, Japan's Sea Creatures Crossed an Ocean.* September 28. https://www.nytimes.com/2017/09/28/science/tsunami-japan-debris-ocean.html. Accessed June 2, 2019.

Family and Youth Services Bureau. 2019. *National Runaway Safeline.* May 30. https://www.1800runaway.org. Accessed May 30, 2019.

Felitti, Vincent, R. F. Anda, D. Nordenberg, D. F. Williamson, A. M. Spitz, V. Edwards, M. P. Koss, and J. S. Marks. 1998. *U.S. National Library of Medicine.* National Institutes of Health. May 14. https://www.ncbi.nlm.nih.gov/pubmed/9635069. Accessed May 20, 2019.

Felitti, Vincent, Robert Anda, Dale Nordenberg, David Williamson, Alison Spitz, Valerie Edwards, Mary Koss, and James Marks. 1998. *Relationship of Childhood Abuse and Household Dysfunction to Many of the Leading Causes of Death in Adults.* Vers. May 1998 Volume 14, Issue4, Pages 245–258. Elsevier Science Inc. May. https://www.ajpmonline.org/article/S0749-3797(98)00017-8/fulltext#Defining%20Childhood%20Exposures. Accessed May 12, 2019.

Finkel, Ed. 2014. *Trauma-informed judges take gentler approach, administer problem-solving justice to stop cycle of ACEs.* September 14. https://acestoohigh.com/2014/09/24/trauma-informed-judges-take-gentler-approach-administer-problem-solving-justice-to-stop-cycle-of-aces/. Accessed June 3, 2019.

Fiorella, Sam. 2016. *The Friendship Bench.* The Lucas Fiorella Friendship Bench. https://thefriendshipbench.org/the-lucas-fiorella-friendship-bench/. Accessed May 28, 2019.

Florida Department of Juvenile Justice. 2019. *CINS and FINS.* May 28. http://www.djj.state.fl.us/services/prevention/youthprograms. Accessed May 28, 2019.

Ford of Europe. 2019. *Ford Go Further 2019.* Ford. http://www.fordmedia.eu/project/ford-go-further-2019/. Accessed May 10, 2019.

Forster, Katie. 2015. *Secrets of the teenage brain.* January 25. https://www.theguardian.com/lifeandstyle/2015/jan/25/secrets-of-the-teenage-brain. Accessed May 30, 2019.

Gohara, Miriam. 2019. *A prison program in Connecticut seeks to find out what happens when prisoners are treated as victims.* March 7. http://theconversation.com/a-prison-program-in-connecticut-seeks-to-find-out-what-happens-when-prisoners-are-treated-as-victims-111809. Accessed May 20, 2019.

Google Science Fair. 2013. *Google Science Fair.*
https://www.googlesciencefair.com/competition/featured-
story/flashlight-canada. Accessed May 27, 2019.

Grandin, Megan. 2019. *Homeless Experiences of Parents Have a Lasting
Impact on Children.* July 31. www.samhsa.gov/homelessness-
programs-resources. Accessed August 19, 2019.

Greensburg, K. S. 2019. *Sustainability.* May 29. Accessed May 29, 2019.
http://www.greensburgks.org/sustainability/top-10-
sustainable-buildings.

Grassman, Deborah. 2019. *Opus Peace.* June 8.
https://opuspeace.org/Opus-Peace/Meet-the-Team.aspx.
Accessed June 8, 2019.

Grumpycats.com. 2019. *This is my Happy Face.* Grumpy Cats.

Guevara-Stone, Laurie. 2015. *How one Alaskan island went 100%
renewable.* July 27. https://www.greenbiz.com/article/how-
one-alaskan-island-went-100-renewable. Accessed June 6,
2019.

Gustin, Georgina. 2018. *More Than 100 Cities Worldwide Now Powered
Primarily by Renewable Energy.* InsideClimate. February 27.
https://insideclimatenews.org/news/27022018/renewable-
energy-cities-clean-power-technology-cdp-report-global-
warming-solutions. Accessed May 10, 2019.

Hansraj, Kenneth. 2014. *Assessment of stresses in the cervical spine
caused by posture and position of the head.* November 25.
www.ncbi.nlm.gov/pubmed/25493825. Accessed May 28, 2019.

Hardie, Daimen. 2015. *Community Forests International.* December 15.
www.forestsinternational.org/news/post/problem-focus-vs-
solution-focus. Accessed May 5, 2019.

—. 2015. *Problem-Focus vs Solution-focus.* December 15.
https://forestsinternational.org/news/post/problem-focus-vs-
solution-focus. Accessed June 19, 2019.

Haritos, Sergio. 2019. Tarpon Springs, January 5.

Heskett, James L., Jr., W. Earl Sasser, and Leonard A. Schlesinger. 1997.
The Service Profit Chain. New York: The Free Press.

Heskett, James L., Jr., Thomas O. Jones, Gary W. Loveman, W. Earl
Sasser Jr., and Leonard A. Schlesinger. 2008. *Harvard Business
Review.* July. https://store.hbr.org/product/putting-the-service-
profit-chain-to-work-hbr-classic/R0807L. Accessed May 30,
2019.

Hicks, Robin. 2018. *Eco-Business Special Report - Singapore's battle with
disposable plastic addiction.* July 17. https://www.eco-
business.com/news/singapores-battle-with-disposable-plastic-
addiction/. Accessed May 20, 2019.

Institute for Healthcare Improvement. 2016. *Shortening Waiting Times:
Six Principles for Improved Access.*
www.ihi.org/resources/Pages/ImprovementStories/Shortening
WaitingTimesSixPrinciplesforImprovedAccess.aspx. Accessed
May 20, 2019.

iSixSigma-Editorial. 2019. *Determine the Root Cause: 5 Whys.* June 2.
https://www.isixsigma.com/tools-templates/cause-
effect/determine-root-cause-5-whys/. Accessed June 2, 2019.

Israel, Shel. 2013. *Marc Benioff to Write Age of Content Foreword.*
March 18.
https://www.forbes.com/sites/shelisrael/2013/03/18/marc-
benioff-to-write-age-of-context-foreword/#5dbda30e4a10.
Accessed March 31, 2019.

Jensen, Frances E. 2014. *The Teenage Brain.* New York City:
HarperCollins Publishers.

Jr. Ocean Guardians. 2018. *About us.*
https://www.jroceanguardians.org/about. Accessed May 1,
2019.

Kabat-Zinn, Jon. 2017. *Jon Kabat-Zinn: Defining Mindfulness.* Mindful.
January 11. https://www.mindful.org/jon-kabat-zinn-defining-
mindfulness/. Accessed May 28, 2019.

Kanti, Anurit. 2017. *5 Global Success Stories On Battling Air Pollution
Can Delhi Learn From Them.* November 13.
http://www.businessworld.in/article/5-Global-Success-Stories-
On-Battling-Air-Pollution-Can-Delhi-Learn-From-Them-/13-11-
2017-131422/. Accessed June 8, 2019.

Katrina Destruction. 2005. September 30. www.katrinadestruction.com.
Accessed September 30, 2005.

Kelland, Kate. 2016. *By 2050, six million people will die per year due to
air pollution.* Edited by Andrew Heavens. Reuters. September
16. https://www.reuters.com/article/us-health-air-
pollution/air-pollution-could-kill-6-6-million-people-a-year-by-
2050-idUSKCN0RG2CO20150916. Accessed June 3, 2019.

Kelly, James. 2012. *Learning Pyramid.* September.
http://thepeakperformancecenter.com/educational-
learning/learning/principles-of-learning/learning-pyramid/.
Accessed May 27, 2019.

King, Martin Luther, Jr. 1968. *I Have a Dream; the Quotations of Martin
Luther King, Jr.* New York: Grosset.

Kleib, Jesse. 2018. *Sorority Donates RC Power Wheels For Kids to Get
Around The Hospital.* April 20.
https://speedsociety.com/sorority-donates-rc-power-wheels-
for-kids-to-get-around-the-hospital/. Accessed March 19, 2019.

Klein, Christopher. 2018. *The Great Smog of 1952.* August 22.
https://www.history.com/news/the-killer-fog-that-blanketed-london-60-years-ago. Accessed June 3, 2019.

Knight, Rob, Jack Gilbert, and Sandra Blakeslee. 2017. *Dirt Is Good.* New York: St. Martin's Press.

Kohut, Abby. 2019. *Absolutely Abby's Job Search Success Tour 2019.* Absolutely Abby®. May 20.
https://abbyacrossamerica.com/#!/speaking/. Accessed May 20, 2019.

Kruger, Susan. 2018. "True Colors: The Personality of Education." *Study Skills by SOAR Learning.* SOAR Study Skills. April 29. Accessed May 27, 2019. studyskills.com/educators/true-colors-the-personality-of-education/.

Kruse, Kevin. 2016. *The 80/20 Rule And How It Can Change Your Life.* March 7.
https://www.forbes.com/sites/kevinkruse/2016/03/07/80-20-rule/#2e1dfefe3814. Accessed May 20, 2019.

Kubler, Annie. 2002. *Head, Shoulders, Knees and Toes.* April 1. Accessed May 28, 2019.

LACASA. 2019. *Child Abuse Prevention (CAP) Council.* May 20.
https://lacasacenter.org/child-abuse-prevention-council/. Accessed May 29, 2019.

Lasasso, Bill, and Steve Cleveland. 2019. *Community Outreach.* May 30.
http://floridadreamcenter.org/outreach/adopt-a-block. Accessed May 30, 2019.

Leggett, Theo. 2018. *BBC News.* BBC News. May 30.
https://www.bbc.com/news/business-43925712. Accessed May 28, 2019.

Levchenko, Mariia. 2018. *YGP.* YGP. September 21.
http://youthgp.org/partnering-for-stronger-communities/.
Accessed May 28, 2019.

Lewis, Carol. 2019. *University of Florida Health.* May 30.
https://ufhealth.org/carol-lewis. Accessed May 31, 2019.

Lifestrength Physical Therapy. 2014. *Life Strength - How Heavy is your head?* November 25.
http://lifestrengthpt.com/news/view/how-heavy-is-your-head/.
Accessed May 20, 2019.

Lowry, Don. 2019. *True Colors: Valuing Differences - Creating Unity.* May 28. Accessed May 28, 2019. https://truecolorsintl.com/.

—. 2019. *True Colors: Valuing Differences - Creating Unity.* Don Lowry.
May 20. Accessed May 27, 2019.
www.truecolorsintl/personality-assessment/.

Mansfield, Matt. 2018. *Cyber Security Statistics: Numbers Small Businesses Need to Know.* December 31.
https://smallbiztrends.com/2017/01/cyber-security-statistics-small-business.html. Accessed June 3, 2019.

Maslow, A. H. 1954. *Motivation and Personality.* New York: Harper.

Maxwell, Scott. 2014. *Florida's mental-health epidemic reaches crisis point.* December 20.
https://www.orlandosentinel.com/opinion/os-florida-mental-health-scott-maxwell-20141220-column.html. Accessed June 2, 2019.

McClinn, Kate, Mark Rains, and Jane Stevens. 2006. *Got Your ACE, Resilience Scores?* January 1.
https://www.acesconnection.com/blog/got-your-ace-resilience-scores. Accessed June 3, 2019.

McCraty, Rollin. 2019. *The Science of HeartMath.* HeartMath Institute Research. May 30.

https://www.heartmath.org/resources/videos/scientific-foundation-of-the-heartmath-system/. Accessed May 30, 2019.

McKinney, Paul. 2019. *Just in Time Inventory: Definition, Advantages & Examples.* Study.com. May 20. https://study.com/academy/lesson/just-in-time-inventory-definition-advantages-examples.html. Accessed May 20, 2019.

McRaven, Admiral William H. 2014. University of Texas at Austin 2014 Commencement Address. Licensed under CC BY 3.0. https://www.youtube.com/watch?v=pxBQLFLei70.

Mejia, Zameena. 2018. *Harvard's Longest Study of Adult Life Reveals How You Can Be Happier and More Successful.* Harvard University. March 20. www.cnbc.com/2018/03/20/this-harvard-study-reveals-how-you-can-be-happier-and-more-successful.html. Accessed May 28, 2019.

Mineo, Liz. 2017. *The Harvard Gazette.* Robert Waldinger. April 11. https://news.harvard.edu/gazette/story/2017/04/over-nearly-80-years-harvard-study-has-been-showing-how-to-live-a-healthy-and-happy-life/. Accessed May 28, 2019.

Miscisin, Mary. 2019. *Personality Systems Compared.* Personality Lingo. May 28. https://personalitylingo.com/personality-systems-compared/. Accessed February 20, 2019.

Morrison, Dan and Christopher Tyree. 2017. *Invisibles.* September 5. https://orbmedia.org/stories/Invisibles_plastics/text. Accessed May 20, 2019.

Morrison, Dan and Christopher Tyree. 2018. *Microplastics Found In Global Bottled Water.* March 15. https://orbmedia.org/stories/plus-plastic/text. Accessed May 20, 2019.

NBC. 2007. *Saturday Night Live.* January 23.
https://www.nbc.com/saturday-night-live/video/don-novello-
monologue/n9170. Accessed May 30, 2019.

NOAA. 2019. *Hazard Mapping System Fire and Smoke Product.* National
Oceanic and Atmospheric Administration. August 30.
https://www.ospo.noaa.gov/Products/land/hms.html. Accessed
May 30, 2019.

Oedekerk, Steve. 2007. *Evan Almighty.* Film. Directed by Thomas
Shadyac. https://www.quotes.net/mquote/113014.

Olweus, D. 1993. *Bullying at School: What We Know and What We Can
Do.* Cambridge, MA: Blackwell Publishers, Inc. Accessed June 3,
2019.

O'Rourke, Tracy. 2019. *8 Wastes.* May 27.
https://goleansixsigma.com/8-wastes/. Accessed May 29, 2019.

Pattillo-Beals, Melba. 2019. *Melba Pattillo Beals.* May 28.
http://melbapattillobeals.com/about-melba/. Accessed May 28,
2019.

Peace4Tarpon. 2019. https://www.peace4tarpon.org/. Accessed May
29, 2019.

Pinellas County. 2019. http://pinellascounty.org/justice/JJCA.htm.
Accessed May 28, 2019.

Plafke, James. 2013. *Extreme Tech.* LLC. Ziff Davis. June 29.
www.extremetech.com/extreme/160003-15-year-old-girl-
invents-flashlight-powered-by-the-heat-of-your-hand. Accessed
May 15, 2019.

Plays, Rob. 2018. *Why Are There No Mosquitos at Disney World?* June
18. https://www.neatorama.com/2018/06/18/Why-Are-There-
No-Mosquitoes-at-Disney-World/.

Powers, Madison. 2019. *Losing Ground: Re-thinking soil as a renewal resource.* May 1. https://www.fewresources.org/soil-science-and-society-were-running-out-of-dirt.html. Accessed June 8, 2019.

Radlauer-Doerfler, Julie and Shari Thomas. 2015. *What is Wraparound?* September 14. https://www.childandfamilyfocus.org/services/high-fidelity-wraparound-hifi/. Accessed May 30, 2019.

Ramsey, Dave. 2019. *Getting out of Debt: Tired of Keeping Up With the Joneses?* Ramsey Solutions. May 28. https://www.daveramsey.com/blog/tired-of-keeping-up-with-the-joneses. Accessed May 28, 2019.

Redford, James. 2019. *About KPJR.* June 6. https://kpjrfilms.co. Accessed June 6, 2019.

Reneau, Annie. 2019. "This Teacher's Viral 'Check-in' Board Is a Beautiful Example of Mental Health Support." *Upworthy.* Cloud Tiger Media Inc. April 1. www.upworthy.com/this-teacher-s-viral-check-in-board-is-a-beautiful-example-of-mental-health-support?c=upw1. Accessed April 20, 2019.

Rhaiti, Adam. 2016. *'It Takes a Whole Village to Raise a Child' – An African Saying.* July 7. https://rightforeducation.org/2016/07/it-takes-a-whole-village/. Accessed June 6, 2019.

Rich, Jennifer L. 2017. *People Experience Homelessness, They Aren't Defined By It.* June 28. https://www.usich.gov/news/people-experience-homelessness-they-arent-defined-by-it/. Accessed May 30, 2019.

Ries, Eric. 2011. *The Lean Startup.* New York: Crown Publishing Group, a division of Random House, Inc.

Rosenberg, Linda. 2019. *Trauma-Informed Care.* August 24.
www.thenationalcounil.org/topics/trauma-informed-care.
Accessed August 24, 2019.

Rotary. 2019. *Peace Fellowships.* Rotary International. May 28.
https://www.rotary.org/en/our-programs. Accessed March 10,
2019.

Saenger, Robin. 2019. *Peace4Tarpon.* June 3.
https://www.peace4tarpon.org/. Accessed June 3, 2019.

Safe Place. 2019. June 3. https://www.nationalsafeplace.org/. Accessed
June 3, 2019.

Safi, Michael. 2017. *Delhi's deadly dust: how construction sites are
choking the city .* February 15.
https://www.theguardian.com/cities/2017/feb/15/delhi-
deadly-dust-how-construction-sites-choking-city. Accessed June
9, 2019.

Sandford, Kathryn. 2019. *7 Keys to Having a Courageous Conversation
With Anyone.* May 20.
https://www.lifehack.org/articles/productivity/7-keys-having-
courageous-conversation-with-anyone.html. Accessed May 30,
2019.

Santich, Kate, and Kunerth, 2019. *Florida's mental-health epidemic
reaches crisis point.* Accessed May 28, 2019.
http://interactie.orlandosentinel.com/mental-illness/intro.html.

Seppala, Dr. Emma. 2013. *The Best Kept Secret to Longevity: Love.* April
28. http://ccare.stanford.edu/psychology-today/the-best-kept-
secret-to-longevity-love/. Accessed June 2, 2019.

Shankar, Sri Sri Ravi. 2019. *Art of Living.* The Art of Living Foundation.
May 28. www.artofliving.org.

Sierra Club. 2019. *100% Commitments in Cities, Counties, & States* https://www.sierraclub.org/ready-for-100/commitments. Accessed May 20, 2019.

Sierra-Vargas, Martha Patricia, and Luis M. Teran. 2012. *National Institutes of Health.* Wang W, Kan H, Xu X, Chen B Li Y. September 21. https://www.ncbi.nlm.nih.gov/pmc/articles/PMC3532603/. Accessed June 8, 2019.

Six Sigma Material. 2019. *Six Sigma Performance.* June 17. http://www.six-sigma-material.com/Six-Sigma.html. Accessed June 17, 2019.

Smith, Jen. 2017. *14 Times Drake Was Basically Telling You: "You Can Do This!".* September 17. https://www.modernfrugality.com/drake-quotes-about-life-and-money/. Accessed June 3, 2019.

Smith, Patricia. 2019. *Compassion Fatigue Awareness Project.* May 15. http://www.compassionfatigue.org/. Accessed May 15, 2019.

Sparks, Nicholas, and Todd Kessler, Traci Paige Johnson. With Steve Burns, Traci Paige Johnson, Seth O'Hickory, Aleisha Allen Angela Santomero. 2015. *Blue's Clues.* Children's Television Show. Directed by Playrific. Produced by Nickelodeon Network (1996-2006) (USA) (TV). Performed by Donovan Patton, Duarte Gomes Steve Burns. http://www.playrific.com/m/164/blues-clues-official-website.

Stevens, Jane. 2017. *Join the movement to prevent ACEs, heal trauma & build resilience.* January 1. https://www.acesconnection.com/blog/got-your-ace-resilience-scores. Accessed May 20, 2019.

Stewart, Chris. 2016. *High staff turnover and burnout puts child welfare system in crisis.* December 9. https://www.daytondailynews.com/news/local/high-staff-

turnover-burnout-puts-child-welfare-system-
crisis/lDxydAqvyWqr3lNdDikMWM/. Accessed May 17, 2019.

Substance Abuse and Mental Health Services Administration. 2016.
April. https://store.samhsa.gov/product/Learn-the-Eight-
Dimensions-of-Wellness-Poster-/SMA16-4953. Accessed May
29, 2019.

Sullivan, Judge Irene. 2019. *Raised by the Courts.* New York: Kaplan
Publishing.

Sweem, Debby, interview by Lisa Ullven. 2019. *Dixie County Anti-Drug
Coalition* (May 30).

Sweeney, Angela, Beth Filson, Angela Kennedy, Lucie Collinson, and
Steve Gillard. 2018. *BJPsych Advances.* September 24.
https://www.ncbi.nlm.nih.gov/pmc/articles/PMC6088388/.
Accessed May 20, 2019.

Tapping.com. 2019. *The Science of Tapping.* May 28. Accessed May 28,
2019. http://www.tapping.com/videos/the-science-of-
tapping.html.

The Annie E. Casey Foundation. 2012. "Kids Count Data Center." January
1. https://datacenter.kidscount.org/publications. Accessed
August 24, 2019.

The Goldie Hawn Foundation, 2019. *Empowering children through
mindful practice based in neuroscience.* Accessed May 29, 2019.

The Workforce Institute at Kronos Incorporated and Future
Workplace. 2018. *"The Case for a 4-Day Workweek?"*
September 4. https://workforceinstitute.org/the-case-for-a-
4-day-workweek-nearly-half-of-employees-worldwide-could-
do-their-jobs-in-5-hours-or-less-each-day/. Accessed May
29, 2019.

Thompson, Derek. 2012. *2.6 Trillion Pounds of Garbage: Where Does the
World's Trash Go?* June 7.

https://www.theatlantic.com/business/archive/2012/06/26-trillion-pounds-of-garbage-where-does-the-worlds-trash-go/258234/. Accessed May 1, 2019

Torgovnick May, Kate. 2018. *How the bail system in the US became such a mess — and how it can be fixed.* LLC TED Conferences. August 31. https://ideas.ted.com/how-the-bail-system-in-the-us-became-such-a-mess-and-how-it-can-be-fixed/. Accessed May 20, 2019.

Tracy, Brian. 1998. *The Gift of Self-Confidence.* p.19. India: Jaico Publishing House.

Tuckman, Bruce. 1965. Tuckman, Bruce W. 1996. *Theories and Applications of Educational Psychology.* New York: McGraw Hill. Third edition with D. Moneth published 2001.

Ulvee, and Philip. 2018. *Department of Health.* Healthy Beginnings, Florida Prevention Research Center at USF, Dr Kerry Littlewood DOH-Pinellas. July. pinellas.floridahealth.gov/programs-and-services/community-health-planning-and-statistics/data-and-reports/_documents/exec-summary-2018-pinellas-co-community-health-assess.pdf. Accessed September 1, 2019.

Undark.org. 2019. *IQ Air: AirVisual Earth.* June. https://undark.org/breathtaking/.

—. 2019. *The Weight of Numbers: Air Pollution and PM2.5.* June 8. https://undark.org/breathtaking/. Accessed June 8, 2019.

United Nations. May 29. © 2019 United Nations. Reprinted with the permission of the United Nations. http://www.un.org/en/sections/issuesdepth/global-issues-overview/.

Unknown. 1950. *Head, Shoulders, Knees and Toes.* May 28. https://allnurseryrhymes.com/head-shoulders-knees-and-toes/. Accessed May 28, 2019.

U.S. Green Building Council. 2019. *LEED Certification.* May 20. https://www.usgbc.org/help/what-leed. Accessed May 20, 2019.

Vartan, Starre. 2018. *Earth Matters: Dutch inventor launches ocean cleanup mission.* MNN. October 29. Accessed May 12, 2019. https://www.mnn.com/earth-matters/wilderness-resources/blogs/remember-kid-who-invented-way-clean-ocean-plastic-hes-back-and-its-happening.

Weather.gov. 2007. *The Rebuilding of Greensburg – one year later.* The National Weather Service and FEMA. https://www.weather.gov/media/ddc/Greensburg_1year_later.pdf. Accessed May 29, 2019.

Weisburg, Jeff, and Heart Phoenix. 2019. *RPCP.* May 28. https://www.centerforpeacebuilding.org/about. Accessed May 28, 2019.

Wheatley, Margaret J. 2019. *The community of Warriors expands and deepens.* https://margaretwheatley.com/the-community-of-warriors-expands-and-deepens/. Accessed June 8, 2019.

Wideman, Austin, and Sam Ayers. 2014. *Under the Surface.* Everyone Matters. February 7. http://www.youtube.com/watch?v=AZ-pU7ozt3q. Accessed May 31, 2019.

Willett, Walter C., Jeffrey P. Koplan, Rachel Nugent, Courtenay Dusenbury, Pekka Puska, and Thomas A. Gaziano. 2002. *Bookshelf: Chapter 44 Prevention of Chronic Disease by Means of Diet and Lifestyle Changes.* Edited by The International Bank for Reconstruction and Development/The World Bank Group. National Center for Biotechnology Information. Accessed May 20, 2019. https://www.ncbi.nlm.nih.gov/books/NBK11795/.

Worldbank.org. *World Development Indicators.* 2017. http://datatopics.worldbank.org/world-development-indicators/themes/environment.html. Accessed February 1, 2019.

World Health Organization. 2019. *World Health News* https://www.who.int/airpollution/en/. Accessed May 28, 2019.

—. 2019. *World Health Organization Health Topics.* https://www.who.int/airpollution/en/. Accessed June 8, 2019.

WRAP® and Wellness Recovery Action Plan® are trademarks of Advocates for Human Potential, Inc. WRAP® and Wellness Recovery Action Plan® are copyrighted by Advocates for Human Potential, Inc. Visit WRAPandRecoveryBooks.com/permissions for more information.

Yesmagazine.org. 2018. *Journalism for People Building a Better World.* April 6. http://www.yesmagazine.org/happiness/call-for-submissions-the-mental-health-issue. Accessed May 31, 2019.

Yuko, Elizabeth. 2018. *Disney World Has No Mosquitoes, Proving It Truly Is the Happiest Place on Earth.* June 20. https://www.sheknows.com/health-and-wellness/articles/1140025/disney-world-no-mosquitoes/. Accessed May 20, 2019.

Zeller, Tom, Jasmina Mironski, and Larry Price. 2019. *Special Projects / Breathtaking: The Weigth of Numbers: Air Pollution and PM2.5.* Undark Magazine & The Pulitzer Center on Crisis Reporting. June 8. https://undark.org/breathtaking/. Accessed June 8, 2019.

Made in the USA
Columbia, SC
03 February 2023

a8ec6c17-93a5-4fbd-9707-81d75bbeb647R02